KU-250-998

LEARNING to pass

ECDL

Angela Bessant

Heinemann Educational Publishers,
Halley Court, Jordan Hill, Oxford OX2 8EJ
Part of Harcourt Education

Heinemann is the registered trademark of
Harcourt Education Limited

© Angela Bessant 2001

First published 2001
New Edition 2002
2005 2004 2003
10 9 8 7 6 5 4 3 2

BARNET LIBRARIES		
Cypher	20.08.04	
004.16	£15.99	
	.	

A catalogue record is available from the British Library on request.

ISBN 0 435 45577 X

All rights reserved.

Apart from any fair dealing for the purposes of research or private study, or criticism or review as permitted under the terms of the UK Copyright, Designs and Patents Act, 1988, this publication may not be reproduced, stored or transmitted, in any form or by any means, without the prior permission in writing of the publishers, or in the case of reprographic reproduction only in accordance with the terms of the licences issued by the Copyright Licensing Agency in the UK, or in accordance with the terms of licences issued by the appropriate Reproduction Rights Organisation outside the UK. Enquiries concerning reproduction outside the terms stated here should be sent to the publishers at the United Kingdom address printed on this page.

Cover design by Sarah Garbett

Pages designed by Paul Davies and Associates

Typeset by TechType, Abingdon, Oxon

Printed and bound in UK by Thomson Litho Ltd

Acknowledgements
I would like to thank all those who helped in the preparation of this book, particular, Rosalyn Bass, Margaret Berriman, Gillian Burrell and Pen Gresford at Heinemann Educational. I would like to thank all past and present students and colleagues who have been uncomplaining when I have tries out course materials on them. Special thanks must go to my family; my mother and Conrad for their constant encouragement, Gemma for trialling and proofreading and Mike for his untiring support and patience.

Dedicated to my father.

Screen shots reprinted with permission from Microsoft Corporation, Yahoo! Inc. AltaVista and the Natural History Museum, London.

Limited of liability/disclaimer of warranty
The opinions stated herein are not guaranteed or warranted to produce any particular results, and the advice and strategies contained herein may not be suitable for every individual.

Tel: 01865 888058 www.heinemann.co.uk

Contents

Heinemann is an independent entity from the European Computer Driving Licence Limited, not affiliated with the European Computer Driving Licence Foundation Limited in any manner. This book may be used in assisting students to prepare for the European Computer Driving Licence. Neither the European Computer Driving Licence Foundation Limited ('ECDL-F') nor Heinemann warrants that the use of this book will ensure passing the relevant Examination. Use of the EDCL-F approved Courseware Logo on this product signifies that it has been independently reviewed and approved in complying with the following standards:

- ECDL-F does not review courseware material for technical accuracy and does not guarantee that the end user will pass the associated ECDL Examinations. Any and all assessment tests and/or performance based exercise contained in this book relate solely to this book and do not constitute, or imply, certification by the European Driving Licence Foundation in respect of any ECDL Examination. For details on sitting ECDL Examinations in your country please contact the local ECDL Licensee or visit the European Computer Driving Licence Foundation Limited web site at http://www.ecdl.com.

- ECDL Candidates using this courseware material should have a valid ECDL/ICDL Skills Card/Log book. Without such as a skills card/Log book no ECDL/ICDL tests can be taken and no ECDL/ICDL certificate, nor any other form of recognition can be given to the candidate.

- ECDL/ICDL Skills Cards may be obtained from any accredited ECDL/ICDL Test Centre or from your country's National ECDL/ICDL designated Licensee.

- References to the European Computer Driving Licence (ECDL) include the International Computer Driving Licence (ICDL). The ECDL Syllabus is published as the official syllabus for use within the European Computer Driving Licence (ECDL) and International Computer Driving Licence (ICDL) certification programme.

Introduction

In order to become proficient in using a computer, it is necessary to practise. This book, with its step-by-step approach and ample practice material, enables you to do that. In this way you will consolidate your understanding and so build up your confidence. Sample answers to exercises (where appropriate) are provided. Other useful information appears in the Appendix and Glossary.

This book assumes no prior computer knowledge. It covers all seven modules (listed below) for Version 3 of the European Computer Driving Licence (ECDL) syllabus. However, it is so packed with information and advice it would be equally suitable for anyone wanting to learn or brush up on their computer skills. The hardware and software you use in the ECDL examinations will depend on your chosen test centre. Examples used in this book are based on PCs running Microsoft software (Windows 95, Office 97, Internet Explorer 4). It should be relatively easy to apply any procedures to your own system. However, you will need to have access to software manuals for your applications and be prepared to make good use of online help menus.

There are many ways of performing tasks in Windows 95 and Office applications (for example, via the keyboard, using the mouse or using the menus). For simplicity, the practical exercises demonstrated usually show one method. There are, however, instructions given for other methods at the end of the chapters or in the Appendix. You will then be able to decide which is the best method for you.

ECDL Modules

Module 1   Basic Concepts of Information Technology

Module 2   Using the Computer and Managing Files

Module 3   Word Processing

Module 4   Spreadsheets

Module 5   Database

Module 6   Presentation

Module 7   Information and Communication

If you want to find out more about the ECDL syllabus, ECDL tests and test centres, the web address is:

http://www.ecdl.co.uk

Contact:
ECDL
The British Computer Society
1 Sandford Street
Swindon
Wiltshire SN1 1HJ

Module 1

Basic Concepts of Information Technology

Section 1 Getting started

1.1 Information technology and computers

Information technology

Information technology (IT) is the term commonly used to cover the range of computer and telecommunications technologies involved in the transfer and processing of information.

There has always been a need for accurate up-to-date information, even before the advent of computer technologies, but it used to be a time-consuming process to gather and process relevant information. The advent of very large *mainframe* computers, relying on specialised staff to operate them, brought a change in the ways big business handled information. Increasingly over the past decades, as the cost and size of computers have decreased, many tasks are now undertaken by powerful, inexpensive desktop PCs on a vast scale. Linking these computers together via the *Internet* has resulted in an explosion in the amount of data being manipulated every day. Today, almost all aspects of everyday life rely on information technology and this has generated an ever-increasing demand for IT skills.

The computer system – overview

A computer is a machine that processes data following a set of instructions. The computer system consists of *hardware* and *software*. Computer equipment you can touch and handle is called hardware. It is the name given to all the physical devices that make up the computer system. These devices include the input devices (how we get the information into the computer), such as a keyboard or mouse. It also includes the *central processing unit* – the 'brain' of the system that carries out all the instructions received from the operator or the program, and the memory devices that store information. Finally, it includes the output devices (how we get the information out of the computer), such as monitors and printers. Input and output devices are known as *peripherals*.

Software is the name given to the programs, each made up of a series of instructions that tell the computer what to do, allowing the hardware to do a useful job. Without software, hardware is useless. Applications packages such as word processing, spreadsheet, database and drawing programs are all examples of software. Microsoft Office and WordPerfect Office are software.

Types of computer

Computers vary in size and cost. They range from something that can fit in your pocket costing a few hundred pounds to those that fill a room and cost millions of pounds. They all have the common characteristics that they can store information and carry out stored instructions of tasks (programs) automatically using a *digital* data processor to make information meaningful. In contrast to humans, they can do this repeatedly, accurately and with great speed.

The main types of computers are classed to differentiate between them, as follows.

Mainframe

A mainframe (now often referred to as a 'large server') offers the ultimate in processing power and storage capabilities. A mainframe is any powerful general-purpose expensive computer system. It typically has many *dumb* terminals connected to it although these are increasingly being replaced by PCs. Dumb terminals consist of a keyboard and display unit *only*, usually with no disk drives or their own processor so they cannot work when not connected to the mainframe. Mainframes are used by large commercial organisations such as banks and insurance companies. Mainframes used to fill whole rooms and required specialised staff and air-conditioned clean environments but these days are more robust and take up much less space. They have vast storage capacity (hundreds of megabytes of main memory and terabytes (trillions of bytes of disk storage). It is interesting to note that the computing power of an average home computer now exceeds that of the typical 1970s' mainframe.

Minicomputer

With advances in technology a family of smaller and cheaper computers called minicomputers were introduced. The term 'minicomputer' is not used very often nowadays and they have evolved into 'mid-range servers' that are part of a network. Originally they were typically installed in smaller businesses and research establishments. The processing and storage capacity of the minicomputer is midway between the mainframe and the PC.

Network computer

Computer systems can be standalone (not connected to any other computer), or they can be connected together to form a network for data transfer, communications and backups. When computers are connected together, they are known as networked computers. Networked computers do not have to be in the same building. Using telecommunications, a computer can be linked to another computer anywhere in the world. PCs can be connected to a network for the processes of sharing information but they also operate when not connected to the network. There are advantages and savings in that they can share peripherals such as printers. They can be used as *intelligent* terminals. Networked computers are used in medium to large-sized organisations including schools.

Personal computer

This is a computer that is small enough to fit on a desktop and inexpensive enough to be bought by an individual for personal use. There are two commonly used personal computers. The most widespread out of the two is the computer based on the original IBM PC, and all clones of this machine are referred to as PCs. The PC is predominant in business and industry. The other common computer is the Apple Macintosh, known as the Mac, which is predominant in creative fields such as publishing and design. Personal computers vary in price, performance and storage capacity and can be chosen to suit requirements. Typically they range from £500 to several thousands of pounds. The price reflects the performance and storage capacity.

Laptop computer

The laptop computer is a small-sized PC that can use battery power and be carried around. It is used by people on the move (eg sales representatives and business travellers). As with the 'desktop' PC, it can be chosen to suit your personal requirements. Laptops are more expensive than desktop PCs with the same specification due to their components needing to be light, small and operating on low power consumption. They have flat screen displays.

1.2 Hardware

Central processing unit (CPU)

The *Central Processing Unit* (CPU) or processor is the processing part of the computer. It carries out all arithmetical and logical operations. It is made up of the *Arithmetic Logic Unit* (ALU) that carries out high-speed data manipulation – calculating and comparing. It also contains the *control unit* that controls the passage of data to and from the ALU by locating, analysing and carrying out instructions and sending information to be temporarily stored in high-speed memory. In a PC the CPU is a single microchip that looks like a thin wafer with legs. In a minicomputer, the CPU is usually contained on a printed circuit board. A mainframe CPU may take up several circuit boards. The speed of the CPU is called the clock speed or clock rate and is measured in megahertz (MHz). It is one of the crucial factors when determining a computer's overall performance. Currently a typical clock speed for a PC is 500 MHz.

Input devices

There are many ways of feeding information into the computer and this is done using input devices. There are many different input devices.

Keyboard
A keyboard consists of input keys. In the UK computer keyboards are based on the standard typewriter layout *QWERTY*. They have additional keys, such as function keys programmed to perform frequently used tasks, arrow keys, the Control (Ctrl) key used in conjunction with other keys to perform specific tasks, and often keys used for power saving.

Mouse
The mouse is a pointing device that enables you to interact with (eg select and move) items on the screen. The mouse's movements are tracked by a rotating ball and sensors in its base. When you move the mouse on your desk, the mouse pointer moves on the screen in the same direction. The mouse pointer changes depending on where it is and what it is doing. Mice have buttons that can be used to select and choose options.

Trackball
A trackball operates in a similar way to a mouse but is a stationary unit. Unlike a mouse, it has the rotating ball on top instead of underneath and is manipulated with the fingers or palm of the hand. Trackballs are commonly integrated on laptop computers since they are easier to operate in limited spaces.

Touchpad
A touchpad is another alternative to a mouse in that it is a device for interacting with a computer screen. A touchpad is also common on laptop computers for the same reasons as the trackball. It is a flat pad that works by sensing finger movements and downward pressure.

Scanner
A scanner can convert physical printed text or images into electrical signals the computer can understand. Scanners can be *flatbed* (which can scan a whole page of text or images at a time), or *handheld*.

Light pen

This is a light-sensitive detector in the shape of a pen. It enables the user to draw and change pictures by moving the pen across the screen. It is normally used in specialised application only.

Joystick

A joystick is able to interact with a computer program (eg control the movement of a shape on the screen). It has a stick that moves to effect corresponding movement on screen. Joysticks are usually used with games.

Output devices

There are many ways of getting information out of the computer. Some common output devices include the following.

Monitor

A monitor is the name given to any device that displays information on a screen (soft copy) and is normally separate from other parts of the computer. Laptop computers do not have separate monitors because the display is integrated into one unit. Monitors can be monochrome or colour. A VGA monitor can display up to 256 colours at one time and has a maximum definition of 640 x 480 pixels (a pixel is an abbreviation for *picture element*, the tiny dots on-screen that form an image). A super VGA (SVGA) monitor is higher definition with 800 x 600 pixels. Performance is improving at a rapid rate. Desktop monitors tend to have cathode ray tube (CRT as used in TVs) technology. Laptops generally have LCDs (liquid crystal displays) because they are lighter, use less power and less space. However, LCD displays are more expensive.

Visual display unit (VDU)

This is another device that displays computer output on a screen. It is very similar to a monitor except that it is usually associated with a keyboard and is often used as a terminal to a mainframe computer.

Screen

A screen is the display area of a monitor.

Printers

A printer provides printed (hard copy) output. There are three commonly used types of printer: *dot matrix*, *inkjet* and *laser*.

The *dot matrix* printer is a low cost printer but it is being superseded by newer technologies. It is an impact printer and produces its characters from patterns of individual dots striking the paper via a ribbon (usually) a line at a time. Dot matrix printers are noisy in operation and the print quality is not particularly good but they are cheap to run.

Both *inkjets* and *lasers* are quiet in operation and print to a higher quality. They are both non-impact printers. The inkjet sprays ink on to the paper from an ink cartridge. Laser printers use laser beams reflected from a mirror to attract ink (called toner) to selected paper areas as the paper is fed over a drum. Laser printers are generally quicker and produce the highest quality output. All types have models available to print in black and white and/or colour. Printers come with a recommendation for types of paper, since the quality of paper used has an effect on the quality of output produced. The resolution (clarity) of the printout is usually measured in dots per inch (dpi). The Epson laser printer (EPL-5800) has a resolution of 1,200 dpi and a speed of 10 pages per minute. Printers range greatly in price depending on the quality of output required and speed of print. Most printers have a local memory in order to speed up the print process.

Plotter

A plotter uses pens to produce drawings. The computer gives the instructions so the plotter knows which pen to use and where to draw. Plotters are normally used in engineering applications.

Speakers

Speakers produce output in audio format. They are used in music, games and speech.

Speech synthesisers

Speech synthesisers turn text into spoken words and vice versa. They can be used by the visually impaired.

1.3 Storage

Types of memory

Computer memory is the place where instructions and data are stored. A computer has two types of memory, *RAM* (**R**andom **A**ccess **M**emory) and *ROM* (**R**ead **O**nly **M**emory). RAM is the computer's fast short-term memory. It needs electricity to retain information and anything stored in RAM will be lost when the power is turned off. When the computer is running, the greater capacity it has to temporarily store instructions and data, the quicker larger programs will function. ROM permanently stores instructions and data. Its contents are stored when the computer is made and cannot be altered. RAM is faster than ROM and both are faster than disk. Access time to RAM is usually measured in nanoseconds (billionths of a second) whereas access time to a hard disk (see below for information on hard disks) or CD-ROM is usually measured in milliseconds (thousandths of a second).

Measuring memory

The binary system is the principle behind digital computers. Binary means 'two' and data is represented by the two digits 0 and 1 (0 is the off state and 1 the on state of the computer's memory cells). Eight *bits* make up one byte. A bit is short for **b**inary dig**it**. It is the smallest element of computer storage. Computer memory is measured in *bytes*. A byte holds the equivalent of a single character (eg the letter A or a full stop). Because a byte is such a small unit of storage, computer memory is more commonly measured in terms of thousands of bytes, *kilobyte* or KB (actually 1,024 bytes) or millions of bytes, *megabyte* or MB (1024KB), and even thousands of millions of bytes, *gigabyte* or GB. A word processor *file* (a document is called a file when it is saved) of 1,000 words will use approximately 15KB. A full-screen colour picture will take up approximately 300KB. A *field* is a unit of data that is more than one byte in size. A collection of fields make up a *record* (eg a person's name, address etc on a mailing list makes up one record; each individual part is a field).

Memory storage devices

If you want to store information so you can reuse it at a later date or just keep it safe, you would need to store it on one of the following non-volatile storage devices.

Hard disk

Most computers have hard disks installed. A hard disk is a fixed disk consisting of magnetic storage plates encased in a drive unit positioned inside the computer. A hard disk is used as the main permanent store of programs that have been loaded on to the computer so they are always available. If connected to a network, the computer is sometimes able to access other hard disks on other computers. External hard disks are also available. Hard disks provide fast retrieval of information compared with floppy disks. Because hard disk capacity is large, it is measured in MB or GB.

Floppy disk (diskette)

A floppy disk is a removable medium store used in Drive A or B. The $3^1/_2$" floppy disk has become the norm. It provides a cheap way of backing up small amounts of data. It has a hard plastic case (protecting its floppy interior) with a metal cover which slides back when the disk is placed in the disk drive. The amount that can be stored on a floppy disk depends on whether it is single or double sided and whether it is single, double or high density. A double-density floppy disk stores approximately 720KB, and a high-density disk approximately 1.44MB. Some disks come ready formatted, but if not, the first time you use a new floppy disk, you must *format* it so it is configured for your particular system.

Floppy disks have a notch, called the write-protect notch, which will stop you deleting or altering a disk's contents. On $3^1/_2$" disks there is a small tab in one corner that slides across to write-protect it.

Care of floppy disks
1 Always store disks carefully.

2 Keep the disks away from anything magnetic.

3 Keep the disks away from direct heat, (eg radiators or sunlight).

4 Do not touch the exposed recording surface.

Zip disk

A zip disk is a removable disk similar to a floppy disk but can store 100MB or 250MB of information and is much faster. As with other disk drives, zip drives can be internal or external. It is useful for storing unusually large files or putting your system on to another computer (eg a laptop).

CD-ROM

A CD-ROM (**C**ompact **D**isc **R**ead-**O**nly **M**emory) disk is a round and flat optical device. It uses a narrow laser beam to read the data, which has been etched on to its surface to form minute patterns. It is usually used in Drive D. It can hold in excess of 600MB, equivalent to about 250,000 pages of text or 500 floppy disks. It has fast data retrieval. As the size of software has increased, it is now usually distributed on CD-ROMs instead of floppy disks. A *CD-R* is a recordable CD that can be recorded on once only. A *CD-RW* is recordable and can be used many times. A *WORM* (**W**rite-**O**nce, **R**ead-**M**any) is an optical disk that allows the user to write data on to it once only.

Data cartridges

Data cartridges use magnetic tape technology and are often used for backing up data in large organisations. They are slower and cheaper than other storage devices because they have sequential access (scanning information starting at the beginning and working through until it finds the required information) rather than random access (accessing information without having to read everything that comes before it).

Computer performance

Computer performance can be determined by the following factors.

Speed of the CPU

There are different types of processor (eg Pentium, PowerPC). The speed at which they perform is measured in (MHz). The greater the number of MHz, the better the performance.

Amount of RAM

Most desktop and notebook computers sold today include at least 32MB of RAM, and can normally be upgraded to 128MB. The more RAM you have, the less frequently the computer has to access instructions and data from the more slowly accessed hard disk.

Hard disk speed and capacity

Hard disk speeds vary. It is always a good idea to buy a large hard disk so you will not run out of storage space and have to rely on using slower floppy disks or have to delete items stored on the hard disk to make room.

1.4 Software

Types of software

There are two main categories of software, *systems* software and *applications* software. System software includes the control programs, such as the operating system. Application software is any program that processes information for the user (eg word processor, spreadsheet, payroll).

Operating system software

The operating system (OS) is the software that controls the hardware and runs the programs. It is the first program run when the computer is turned on. Common operating systems include MS-DOS, Windows, Linux, Mac OS and UNIX. Windows is an example of a *Graphical User Interface* (GUI) because it uses icons (small pictures), menus and a mouse. These make the software more user-friendly since it is intuitive and you don't have to remember complicated commands. The Apple Macintosh also has a graphical user interface.

Applications software

Common applications software includes the following:

- *Word processing.* A word processing program allows you to enter and manipulate text on screen. The text can be saved as a file and then printed. It is the most commonly used application. Once the basics have been learnt, it is easy to produce professional-looking documents. These documents can be stored on disk so they can be recalled and altered at a later date. Microsoft Word is a word processing program.

- *Spreadsheet.* This program has some aspects of a filing system and some of a calculator. It consists of a large area, or grid, in which you enter data and text and work out sums. The program will do the calculations as instructed by you. When changes are made, the spreadsheet automatically recalculates new values. It is very fast, accurate and flexible. You can save the spreadsheets to disk and print them. It is used in accounting to produce budgets, balance sheets, payrolls and in scientific modelling and 'what if' analyses. Microsoft Excel is a spreadsheet

- *Database.* This is a program that allows you to store data in an organised record format. It is sometimes known as an 'electronic filing system'. It is structured so it can be used to retrieve, sort and search for data quickly and in many different ways. Databases can be saved to disk and can be printed. It is much faster than using a paper database, where filing cards are stored on a manual card index system, and has a much greater storage capacity. Databases are extensively used in all types of business and commerce. Microsoft Access is a database program.

- *Payroll.* There are many specialised programs available for payroll tasks. Spreadsheet packages are capable enough to carry out payroll tasks for small companies.

- *Presentation.* Presentation software allows you to create, organise and design effective presentations. These can produce overhead transparencies, 35 mm slides or automated presentations on the computer. Microsoft PowerPoint is a presentation program.

- *Desktop publishing.* Desktop publishing (DTP) software allows you to create professional-looking manuals and brochures. Microsoft Publisher is a DTP program.

- *Multimedia.* There are many programs available to use with multimedia (ie combining graphics, text, sound, video and user interaction). Paintshop Pro (image manipulation) and programs for music generation are popular.

Systems development

Computer systems development employs a number of specialised staff (eg systems analysts, programmers), who work together at different stages. It has a life cycle as shown below.

Research, analysis and design
This includes a feasibility study, the overall general design, prototyping, the detail design and the functionality requirement specifications.

Programming
This includes the design and coding of the system.

Testing
The system then needs to be tested to ensure it will perform correctly.

Implementation
This includes training of staff, converting from the old system and installation of the new one.

User acceptance
The user will accept the system once it has been fully implemented and tested.

Section 2 Information networks

2.1 Network systems

LAN and WAN

There are two distinct types of information networks:

1 *LAN* (Local Area Network) This is a network that connects computers within a local confined geographical area (eg a single office, building or across a site).

2 *WAN* (Wide Area Network). This connects computers over a wide area and across countries.

There are many advantages in working on a network. It is easy to share files and resources and to group-work on specific tasks because of this. It is easy to communicate via e-mail. Software programs can be installed centrally from one powerful server computer. Resources such as printers and scanners can be shared, thus keeping equipment costs down.

The telephone network in computing

LANs usually have cables that connect the computers on the network. However, WANs often use the national and international telephone systems that rely on the Public Switched Data Network (PSDN), the Integrated Service Digital Network (ISDN) and satellite communications. The purpose of these is to ensure people and computers can communicate over standardised connection facilities using common protocols.

When a computer wants to send information to another computer using the telephone system it must have a means of converting the digital signals (that have two distinct states) from the computer into analogue signals (not absolute values but ones that constantly change, eg audio tones) used by the phone line, and vice versa, for incoming information. (It must **mo**dulate and **dem**odulate.) The hardware that enables this is called a *modem*. The rate of signal changes when transmitting/receiving data is known as the *baud*. At very low speeds the baud rate is equal to bits per second (bps) (eg 300 baud is the same as 300 bps). Beyond this, one baud can be made to represent more than one bit. Currently the maximum rate over the public telephone network is 56 Kbaud.

Fax and telex machines also use the phone system. Fax machines communicate a printed page between remote locations. A standalone fax machine is made up of a scanner, printer and modem with fax signalling, but electronic fax/modems are available that can be attached to a computer either internally or externally. Telex machines were the first worldwide real-time data communications service to use terminals for transmitting and receiving messages. Telex messaging is now in decline.

Electronic mail

Electronic mail (e-mail) is a method of sending messages from one computer to another. You can send and receive the electronic equivalent of letters, faxes, pictures and sound. Some organisations have their own internal e-mail systems. Others are connected to the *Internet* in order to send and receive e-mail locally and internationally. It is a quick and efficient means of communication. It has the advantage that you can send and receive your messages when you choose (unlike telephone communication) and is cheaper because calls are charged at local rates (and sometimes even free!). In addition, you will usually be informed if your message has failed to reach its destination. E-mail messages (and any files transmitted with them) can be saved and edited by the recipient, whether text or graphics.

In order to send/receive e-mail over the Internet you will need the following:

- A telephone system to connect to, either dial-up (temporary) or a leased line (permanent) connection.

- A modem.

- Communications software.

- An account with an Internet service provider (ISP) who will register your unique e-mail address.

The Internet

The Internet is made up of interconnected networks all over the world that send, receive and store information. Originally developed by the military, it became widely used for research work in academia and commerce. It is now widely used by all walks of life for work and leisure pursuits. Access is provided (for individuals) through Internet service providers. The World Wide Web (WWW) is a part of this network. It contains millions of pages of words, pictures, sounds and graphics, stored on computers connected to the Internet. It has been called an 'information superhighway'. It provides information on almost every subject. Each document on the WWW is written in HTML (**H**yper**t**ext **M**arkup **L**anguage). This commonality of language makes it easy for a *web browser* (software that lets you select and view web pages) to display web pages. The two common browsers are *Internet Explorer* and *Netscape Navigator*. The web uses the **H**ypertext **T**ransfer **P**rotocol (HTTP) to download web pages to the browser and TCP/IP (**T**ransmission **C**ontrol **P**rotocol/**I**nternet **P**rotocol) allowing information to travel between networks. Web pages can contain hyperlinks (addresses, known as URLs (**u**niform **r**esource **l**ocators)) to other web pages so users can plot their own routes through the web pages depending on their area of interest.

When looking for specific information on the web, if you do not know an address where you can find it, you can use a search engine. A search engine will look through its database of sites that contain the 'key word(s)' you are looking for and will return a list of possible suitable sites. There are also search directories that sets out information in subject categories.

Section 3 Computers in everyday life

3.1 The use of computers

With the advent of microchip technology, computers have become smaller, faster, more reliable, easier to use and cheaper. Since the late 1970s when personal computers first became available, there has been an ever-increasing growth in their popularity that shows no signs of slowing down.

Computers in the home

An increasing number of households now have a computer, many with Internet access. It is used for various activities by all family members, including the following:

- Working from home (teleworking).

- Sending e-mails.

- Accessing the Internet to find information for various activities (eg homework, projects, hobbies).

- Keeping household accounts and income tax submissions.

- Shopping, banking, booking tickets.

- Playing games.

Computers at work or in education

Business, industry, government and educational establishments have a great need for computers since they have a great deal of data that needs calculating and analysing. They may have special systems known as IMS (**i**nformation **m**anagement **s**ystems) or DMS (**d**atabase **m**anagement **s**ystems). Even the smallest office has now come to rely on computers. However, in some situations, person skills cannot be replaced (such as in the caring professions, eg nursing and counselling, and anywhere where innovation, thinking and communication are vital). Typical computer uses include the following:

- Keeping databases of names and addresses (database applications) e.g. for mailshots, employee information and in government offices, large scale databases are required for tasks such as registering births, marriages and deaths, tax and census data.

- Account information (spreadsheet and database applications).

- Stock control and sales analysis (spreadsheet and database applications).

- Marketing, including advertising and selling via their web sites (using e-mail and the Internet and web browser software).

- Payroll (using spreadsheets or customised software) and electronic funds transfer (EFT), ie moving money from one account to another (eg wages).

- Student grades and project work (using database and spreadsheet applications and other specialised software for projects, (eg drawing software for art and design, language software).

- Producing all paperwork; letters, memos; brochures etc using word processing (word processing, DTP and integrated office suites).

- Designing products (computer-aided design (CAD) software).

- Automating industrial processes (specialised software), robotics.

- Traffic lights, which have sensors to detect traffic and which send messages to a controlling computer, that maintains regulated traffic flow.
- Computer-based training (CBT). Many specialised software packages are now available to assist with all types of training and for all age groups. People can work at their own pace and at a time that suits them.

Computers in daily life

In fact, computers are everywhere. Some common places they are used include the following:

- Supermarkets where bar codes are scanned and product and (sometimes) customer information is stored. This is known as electronic point of sale (EPOS). Using such methods stock levels can be managed. Bank cards are swiped and payment is taken directly for goods. This is termed electronic funds transfer at point of sale (EFTPOS).
- libraries where books are kept track of using database facilities and books are scanned when taken out and returned.
- Doctors' surgeries, where patient records are computerised
- Bank/building society cash machines (known as automated teller machines or ATMs) where cards are used to identify the customer by reading the magnetic strip and checking the user's PIN (personal identification number).

3.2 IT and society

A changing world

Information society

The society we live in today relies on computers to enable us to gather and disseminate information quickly and easily. Because of this it has become known as the Information Society. Some people feel unease about so much reliance on computers and wonder where it is leading us. Some people feel threatened by it, others feel empowered by it. You will have your own views. In situations where you see computers being used it is worth asking: 'Is this a job for a computer or would a human interface be better?' Sometimes there are no clear-cut answers and much depends upon your general values.

Information superhighway

This is another name given to the Internet – the telecommunications infrastructure that allows access to a never-ending source of information across the world. It is changing the way we live and work at an ever-increasing rate. Only our imagination can limit its usefulness.

Year 2000 issue

This issue affected computers that only used '00' and not '1900' in the year field, so 1988 was 88 and 1996 96 and so on. With memory being in short supply with some of the earlier computers, it had seemed prudent to try to save two bytes (the first two digits of the year). There were fears that the computer would understand year '00' as being '1900' and not 2000. Programmers needed to work on systems before the year 2000 arrived so that computers were not affected. Although the year 2000 bug created few problems there were predictions that it could have been much worse.

Electronic commerce

Electronic commerce (e-commerce) means doing business on-line. If you advertise a service or product, order a book, your groceries or arrange your holiday using the Internet, you are participating in e-commerce.

A good workspace

When you are using a computer it is important you make yourself comfortable, otherwise you may become easily fatigued, ill or injured. **Repetitive strain injury** (RSI), an injury arising from making awkward movements or the prolonged use of particular muscles, is a recognised condition. It can affect the hands, neck, back and eyes due to incorrect computer use. Be aware of the following.

Positioning of the screen

All screens should be adjustable so you can set them up for your requirements and so you avoid muscle strain in the neck and shoulders. The screen should be directly in front of you, roughly at arm's length. The top of the screen display should be just above eye level.

Positioning of documents

To prevent visual fatigue and muscle tension and to minimise re-focusing and twisting the neck, these should be near to the screen, at the same height and distance.

Positioning of the keyboard

If your keyboard is not comfortable (ie it is placed too near the edge of the desk so there is nowhere to rest your wrists), you could put unnecessary strain on the wrists causing RSI.

Type of chair

An adjustable chair is essential. Your back should be straight and your feet should rest on the floor. Your forearms should be roughly horizontal when using the keyboard.

Lighting

Screen glare should be avoided by adjusting background lighting and using window blinds or positioning the screen so it is unaffected. Anti-glare filters are available.

Ventilation

Adequately ventilated working areas should be provided.

Frequent breaks

It is important to take frequent breaks and to rest your eyes by focusing them in the distance and walking around.

Health and safety

There is legislation, administered by the Health and Safety Executive, covering computing environments. Some of the issues have been covered in the preceding paragraph. It is also important to ensure that equipment is safe. Power cables should be secured so they cannot be tripped over and power sockets should not be overloaded.

Section 4 Security, copyright and the law

4.1 Security

For security reasons it is always a good idea to produce a backup (exact copies) of your data (data is the information you put into the computer) on a regular basis. Then if anything goes wrong with your computer or the data becomes corrupted (damaged), you will be able to revert to the safely stored version. Various backup programs are available utilising removable disks or tapes. It is best to store the backups in a safe and separate place away from your computer.

If there is a power cut when you are using your computer, the documents and information you have not saved to disk will be lost. It is important you save your work regularly so you will minimise the amount of effort required to redo the work in such situations. Sometimes the computer may just crash (ie cease to function) either because there is a program error or a more serious system problem. If it is a program problem, restart the program. If it is a system problem, restart the computer by pressing the keys **Ctrl**, **Alt** and **Delete** at the same time. If this doesn't have any effect, turn the computer off and then restart it.

Computers can be password protected so that the user only can access the data on them. In some organisations several passwords are needed to access strictly confidential data, giving added extra security. Document files can also be password protected. It is always good practice to use a password that is not easy for anyone to guess and it must not be divulged to anyone. Data can also be encrypted (ie turned into a special sort of code). A key to this code is required to make the data readable again.

4.2 Computer viruses

A computer virus is a destructive program buried within an existing program. People with programming skills intending to cause disruption and damage to computer systems write them. Once the infected program is run, the virus coding is activated and attaches copies of itself to other programs. Infected programs copy the virus to other programs. In this way it can quickly spread causing severe damage to computers and networks. A virus cannot attach itself to data. To protect against viruses, always know the source of your software. When downloading software from the Internet always save it and virus check it before running it. Also be wary when opening e-mails. The *Iloveyou* virus affected 10% of business computer systems in the UK alone and many more throughout the world in May 2000, costing millions of pounds. It was spread via e-mail. The reason the virus spread so quickly was because when you clicked on the e-mail attachment, it opened your address book and was then e-mailed to everyone in the address book. Anti-virus utilities are available and are a good 'insurance' investment. If you are unfortunate enough to have a virus on your computer – close down the computer and restart it using a write-protected floppy boot disk and then run a virus utility.

4.3 Copyright

When you buy a software package (eg MS Office), you have an agreement (a user licence) with the manufacturer you will use it only for personal use (ie you will not duplicate it or lend it for someone else to use). Copying licensed software can be quite easy to do but it is illegal. It is a good way of allowing viruses to enter your system since shared resources like floppy disks and e-mail files could be infected. You should only purchase software from reputable sources so you know your software is not 'pirated'.

Freeware

Freeware is software you can use free of charge. Often it is given away with computer magazines or it can be downloaded from the Internet.

Shareware

Shareware software can also be downloaded from the Internet and is distributed with computer magazines. The idea is that, if you try it and would like to keep using it, you should register and pay for it.

4.4 Data Protection Act

The Data Protection Act in the UK was passed in 1984 and was updated on 1 March 2000. It sets rules for processing personal information on computers (and on some paper records). It gives individuals the right to know about the information held on them (exceptions being police and sometimes medical records). All organisations that hold computerised data on individuals must register with the Data Protection Registrar as a data user. Personal data is kept for many reasons (eg by tax offices, personnel departments, banks, hospitals). There are eight principles to ensure information is handled properly. The data must be:

- fairly and lawfully processed

- processed for limited purposes

- adequate, relevant and not excessive

- accurate

- not kept for longer than necessary

- processed in line with your rights

- secure

- not transferred to countries without adequate protection.

Module 1 practice tasks

1   List the main items that make up a computer.

2   Explain the differences between RAM and ROM.

3   What are the main factors affecting a computer's performance?

4   What is the CPU?

5   What unit is the CPU speed measured in?

6   What is an operating system?

7   What is hardware?

8   Name three output devices and three input devices.

9   Explain the terms bit, byte and megabyte.

10   What is a graphical user interface? Give some examples of its main advantages.

11   What is needed to send and receive e-mail? Name three advantages of e-mail compared with other methods of communication.

12   What is the Internet?

13   Explain the terms LAN and WAN. What are the advantages of group working?

14   How do you search for information on the World Wide Web?

15   Give three examples of computers in everyday life.

16   Explain the terms 'Information Society' and 'Information Superhighway'.

17   What is RSI? What can you do to prevent it?

18   Why do you need to backup computer files?

19   What precautions should you take to ensure unauthorised people do not have access to your computer files?

20   What is a computer virus? What effective measures can you take to minimise the risk of infection?

21   Describe the terms of the Data Protection Act. Give three uses of personal data.

Note: All answers to these questions can be found in the preceding text.

Note: This is only a practice test. Successful completion does not imply certification of the module by the ECDL Foundation.

Module 2

Using the Computer and Managing Files

Section 1 Getting started

In this section you will practise and learn how to:

* Start the computer.

* Use the mouse.

* Recognise parts of the desktop and parts of an application window.

* Use Help functions.

* Reduce/enlarge, resize, rescale and close a desktop/application window.

* Move windows on a desktop.

* Shut down the computer.

1.1 Windows 95

Windows 95 is an operating system that ensures all parts of the computer system work together. It controls the hardware and starts and operates software. It provides ways to manage files stored on the computer.

1.2 Starting the computer

 Method

1 Ensure the computer is plugged into the electricity socket.

2 Press the button on the computer base unit (and on the monitor, if it has a separate button) to switch the power on.

3 The computer will perform its start-up checks and load Windows 95 and accessories. You will see the Windows 95 desktop displayed. The items that appear on this screen depend on how your computer is set up. It will look something like Figure 2.1.

Note: The small pictures Windows 95 uses to represent programs, files etc are called *icons*.

i Info

If you are using a network or password protected computer, you will need to find out what the procedure is to log in to Windows 95.

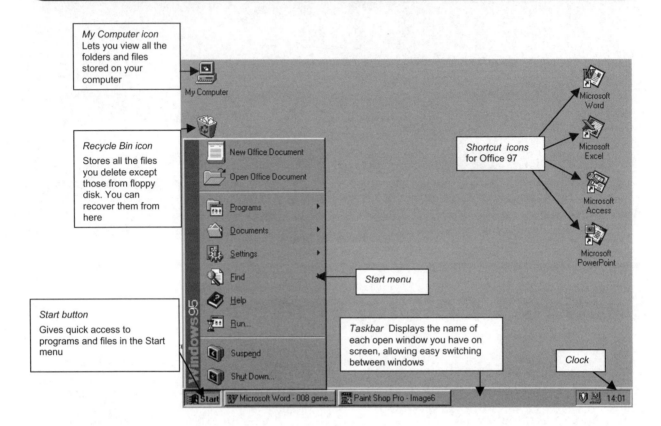

Figure 2.1 Windows 95 desktop

1.3 The Mouse

The mouse lets you select and move items on the screen. When you move the mouse on your desk, the mouse pointer ⤷ moves on the screen in the same direction. You will notice the mouse pointer changes depending on where it is and what it is doing. The mouse has a left and a right button. These can both be used to select and choose options. In Windows 95, the right mouse button is usually used to access alternative context-sensitive pop-up menus.

Mouse terms

Click Press and release the mouse button.

Double-click Quickly press and release the mouse button twice.

Drag and drop When the mouse pointer is over an object on your screen, press and hold down the left mouse button. Still holding down the button, move to where you want to replace the object. Release the mouse button.

Hover Place the mouse pointer over an object for a few seconds so something happens (eg another menu appears or a ToolTip).

Practice

An excellent way of practising mouse skills is to play the game of Solitaire that comes with Windows 95.

Using the Start button

To start Solitaire follow the directions given in Figure 2.2.

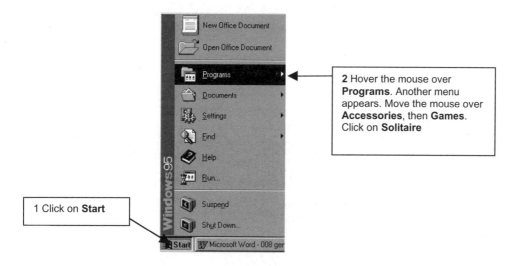

Figure 2.2 Starting Solitaire

i Info

If you do not have Solitaire on your computer, load any other Accessories program and practise some of the skills shown below.

The Solitaire window appears (Figure 2.3). Notice that the taskbar, at the bottom of your screen, now displays a button for Solitaire.

1.4 Parts of a window

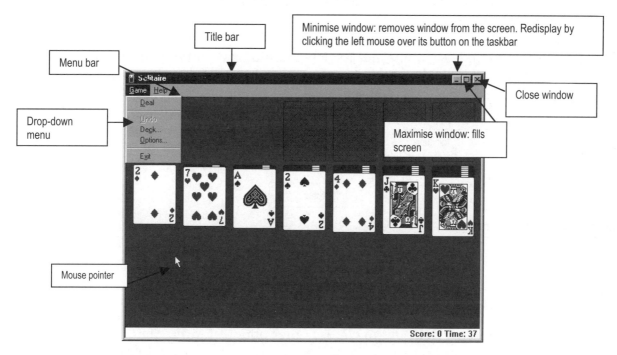

Figure 2.3 Parts of a window

Info

Windows can also contain toolbars. A toolbar is a strip of clickable shortcut buttons usually along the top of a window (directly below the Menu bar). See Module 3, Section 1.

Play Solitaire

Method

1 On the Menu bar, click on **Help**; a menu appears.
2 Click on **Help Topics**; the Help Topics: Solitaire Help window appears (Figure 2.4).
3 Click on the **Contents** tab, if not already selected (on top of **Index** and **Find** tabs).
4 Click on **How to Play Solitaire**. Then click on **Display**.

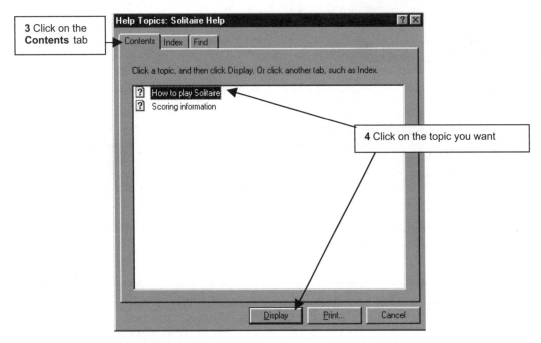

Figure 2.4 Solitaire Help window

5 The rules of the game are displayed. To view more of the contents of this window, click on the **Maximise** (middle) button at the top right of the window.

6 When you have read the rules, click on the **Close** button (Figure 2.5).

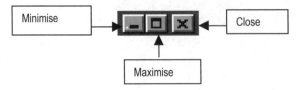

Figure 2.5 The Close button

You are now ready to play Solitaire!

Practise:

• The mouse actions whilst playing the game.

• Using the menus to get Help and to choose other options for the game.

• Moving the window by pointing to the Title bar and dragging and dropping.

• Resizing the window by moving the mouse pointer over the edge of the window until a double arrow appears. Press and hold down the left mouse and drag to the required shape. Release the mouse.

Note: To keep the same proportions of the window, drag from a corner.

When you have had enough practising, from the **Game** menu, click on **Exit** or click on the **Close** button.

1.5 Getting Help

You can get Windows 95 Help by clicking on **Start**, then on **Help**. The Help Topics: Windows Help window appears (Figure 2.6).

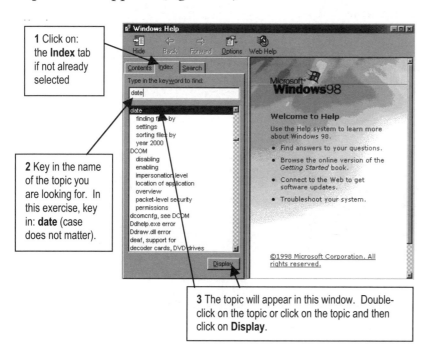

1 Click on: the **Index** tab if not already selected

2 Key in the name of the topic you are looking for. In this exercise, key in: **date** (case does not matter).

3 The topic will appear in this window. Double-click on the topic or click on the topic and then click on **Display**.

Figure 2.6 Windows Help

Windows Help appears (Figure 2.7). Click on the grey buttons to find out more about Windows Explorer and other Windows 95 topics. Return to the Help Index by clicking on the **Help Topics** button. Close the windows by clicking on the **Close** button.

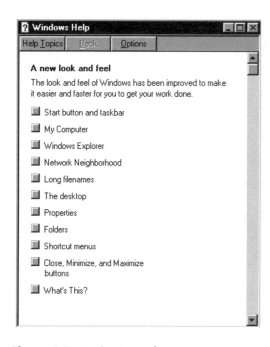

Figure 2.7 Topics Found

Scroll bars

When a window is not big enough to display all the information in it, scroll bars appear, vertically and/or horizontally (Figure 2.8). In the Help window there is a vertical scroll bar.

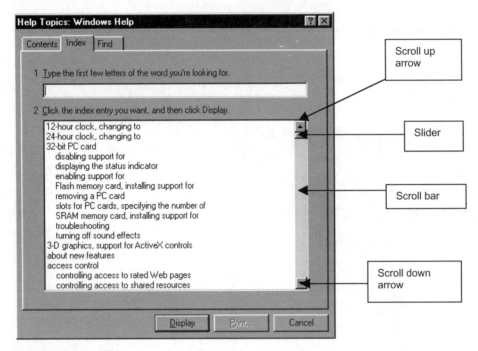

Figure 2.8 Scroll bar

Practise:

- Clicking on the scroll bar arrows to move through the index entries.

- Dragging the slider along the scroll bar to move more quickly through the entries.

- Searching for other Help topics.

When you have finished searching for Help topics, close the help window by clicking on the **Close** button.

1.6 Shutting down the computer

From the **Start** menu, click on **Shut Down.** The Shut Down Windows dialogue box appears (Figure 2.9).

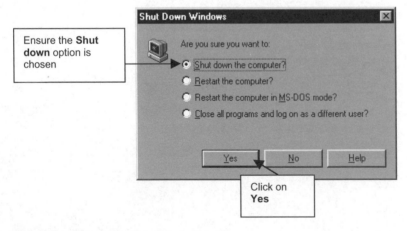

Figure 2.9 Shutting down windows

A message 'It's now safe to turn off your computer' is displayed. You can now switch off.

Info

It is important you close down Windows correctly when you have finished your work. Sometimes a program will tell you to restart your computer. When this happens you can use the **Restart the computer** option.

Section 1 CHECKLIST

Are you familiar with the following?

Starting the computer	
Using the mouse	
Recognising parts of the desktop and parts of an application window	
Using Help functions	
Reducing/enlarging a desktop/application window	
Resizing, rescaling and closing a window	
Moving windows on a desktop	
Shutting down the computer	

Section 2 Working with icons

In this section you will practise and learn how to:

* Restart the computer.

* Recognise icons.

* View the computer's basic system information (eg operating system, processor type, installed RAM etc).

* View the computer's desktop configuration: date and time, volume settings, desktop display options (eg background options, screen settings, screen saver etc).

* Select and move desktop icons.

* Create a desktop shortcut icon.

2.1 Recognising icons

1 Restart the computer as in section 1.2.

2 Double-click on the ![My Computer icon] **My Computer** icon. The My Computer window appears.

3 Maximise the window, if not already maximised, by clicking on the 🗖 Maximise button. The window will look similar to Figure 2.10.

> **ⓘ Info**
>
> Notice the floppy disk drive icon (Drive A:), the hard disk drive icon (Drive C:) and the compact disk drive icon (Drive D:). Right-clicking on any of these icons will display a pop-up menu; select **Properties** for more information (eg free disk space). Try this now by selecting the hard disk drive. In Figure 2.10 notice there are 'special' folder icons including Printers and Control Panel. The Status bar is at the bottom of the window and will change to reflect current operations.

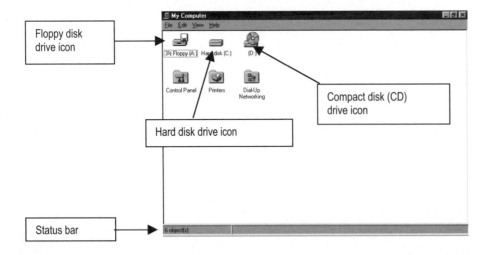

Figure 2.10 My Computer window

2.2 Viewing the computer's basic system information

> **ⓘ Info**
>
> You can use Control Panel to view and alter numerous settings on your computer.

1 Double-click on the **Control Panel** folder. The Control Panel window and contents are displayed.
2 Double-click on the 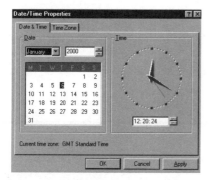 **System** icon.
3 The System Properties window is displayed. With the **General** tab selected, you can view the operating system, processor type and installed RAM.
4 Close the System Properties window by clicking on **Cancel**.

2.3 Viewing and customising the computer's desktop configuration

Date and time

1 Double-click on the 🖳 **Date/Time** icon. The Date/Time Properties dialogue box appears (Figure 2.11).
2 Click in the relevant boxes to change date and time as necessary.
3 Click on **Apply**.
4 Click on **OK**.

Figure 2.11 Date/Time Properties dialogue box

Display options

Double-click on the 🖥 **Display** icon. The Display Properties dialogue box appears (Figure 2.12).

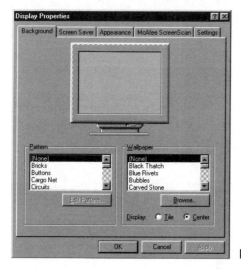

Figure 2.12 Display Properties dialogue box

Background

With the **Background** tab selected, you can change the wallpaper (desktop background). To do this:

1 Make a selection from the **Wallpaper** list. A preview will display on the screen graphic above. Click on **Browse** to select a file you want to use as wallpaper or click on **Pattern** to select a pattern.

2 In the Display section, select the type of display you want.

3 Click on **Apply**.

Screen saver

Select the **Screen Saver** tab to apply/change the screen saver. (A screen saver is displayed when you have not interacted with your computer for a while.) Set the time delay before the screen saver is activated. Click on **Apply**.

By selecting other tabs you can change other desktop settings. Experiment with this now, then close Display Properties (click on **OK** to save settings) when you have finished. Click on the **Close** button to close Control Panel.

Sound settings

1 You can adjust your computer's volume by either:

Double-clicking the **Volume** icon on the taskbar

or

From the **Start** menu, select: **Programs, Accessories, Multimedia, Volume Control**.

2 The Volume Control window appears. In the **Volume Control** section adjust as required using the sliders.

3 Click on **OK**.

2.4 Creating a desktop shortcut

> **i Info**
>
> It is a good idea to create desktop shortcuts for applications you use often. You can also create shortcuts for folders and files in the same way. This saves having to go through the Start menu. In this example we will create a shortcut for Notepad. This is one of the Accessories applications that is part of Windows 95. It is a simple 'no frills' word processor application.

1 From the **Start** menu, select: **Programs, Windows Explorer**.

2 The Exploring window appears.

3 Click on the **Restore** button so that part of the desktop is visible.

Note: A Restore button is displayed instead of the Maximise button when a window is already maximised.

4 Select the location of the application you want to make a shortcut for. In this case, in the **All Folders** section, double-click on the **Windows** folder.

5 In the right-hand section, select **Notepad** (Figure 2.13).

6 Hold down the right mouse button and drag Notepad on to the desktop. Release the mouse.

7 A shortcut icon appears on the desktop that looks like .

8 Close the Exploring – Windows window.

Figure 2.13 The Exploring window

i Info

You can rename a shortcut by right-clicking on it and selecting **Rename**. Key in a new name and press: **Enter**.

Note: Notepad has not been moved from its original location within the Windows folder. You have only created a shortcut to access it in its original location.

2.5 Recognising more desktop icons

The main types of icons you see on a normal desktop and that we will be working with are as follows:

- Application/Program shortcut icons such as Notepad, Word, Excel, Access and PowerPoint, shown below:

- File icons, shown below:

A Word file   An Access file   An Excel File   A PowerPoint file

- Folder icons that look like

i Info

There is more about files and folders in Section 3.

2.6 Arranging desktop icons

You can arrange desktop icons by dragging them to the required position on the desktop. If you right-click on the desktop, a pop-up menu appears (Figure 2.14).

Selecting **AutoArrange** automatically lines up your icons.

Figure 2.14 Arranging icons on the desktop

Section 2 CHECKLIST

Are you familiar with the following?

Restarting the computer	
Recognising icons	
Viewing the computer's basic system information (eg operating system, processor type, installed RAM etc)	
Viewing the computer's desktop configuration: date and time, volume settings, desktop display options (eg background options, screen settings, screen saver etc)	
Selecting and moving desktop icons	
Creating a desktop shortcut icon	

Section 3 Working with folders and files

In this section you will practise and learn how to:

* Use Windows Explorer.
* Understand basic directory and folder structure.
* Examine folders/files.
* View folder/file attributes.
* Recognise most widely used file types.
* Create a folder and subfolders.
* Rename folders/files.
* Delete folders/files.
* Use the Recycle Bin.
* Copy/move folders/files.
* Select an individual file, adjacent files and non-adjacent files.
* Make backups on to a floppy disk.
* Format a disk.
* Use Find to locate folders/files.

3.1 Windows Explorer

Windows Explorer is a program that allows you to view all the folders and files on your computer. It can be used for disk and file management.

Starting Explorer

 Method 1

From the **Start** menu, select: **Programs**, then **Windows Explorer**.

 Method 2

1 Right-click on **Start**.
2 Select: **Explore** from the pop-up menu.

The Explorer window appears. In this example (Figure 2.15), $3^1/_2$ Floppy (A:) drive is selected in the left pane and the contents of the disk in drive A are displayed in the pane on the right.

 Info

Your display may be set to show large icons. To change this from the **View** menu, select: **Small Icons**.

Spreadsheets

This is an example of a *folder*. It stores related information. It can contain files and other folders (which can also contain files). Sometimes folders are referred to as *directories*.

Gem news

This is an example of a *file*. When you save your work onto a computer disk, it becomes a file. The icon above the filename identifies its type (this is a Word file).

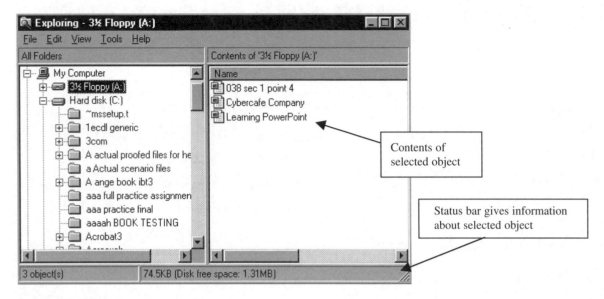

Figure 2.15 Windows Explorer

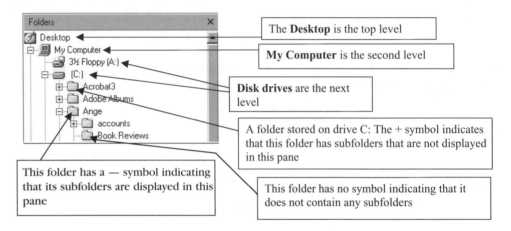

Figure 2.16 Structure of computer storage

Displaying the contents of a folder

Double-click on the folder.

> **ⓘ Info**
>
> It is better to double-click the icon rather than the text, as sometimes you will not get the action you expect (if you have not double-clicked properly). Instead, a box may appear round the text, waiting for your input. If this happens, press: **Esc** and try again.

Navigating

> **ⓘ Info**
>
> At some stages you may get lost. From the **View** menu, click next to **Toolbar** so a tick appears. Use the drop-down list and the **Up One Level** button to navigate.

3.2 Examining folders and files

To obtain more information about folders/files:

1 Right-click on the folder/file. A pop-up menu appears (Figure 2.16).

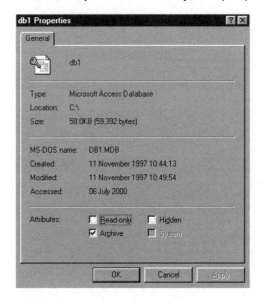

Figure 2.17 Right-click to display pop-up menu

2 Select: **Properties**. The object's properties are displayed (see Figure 2.17).

Figure 2.18 Displaying properties

3.3 Recognising file types

There are many different types of file and it is useful to be able to recognise those that are most common. Right-clicking on the **Gem news** file and selecting **Properties** displays the properties shown in Figure 2.18.

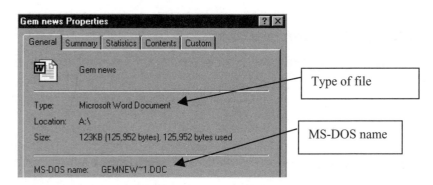

Figure 2.19 File properties

Info

When you save a file, the computer automatically gives it an extension ie **Gem news** becomes **Gem news.doc**. The .doc extension denotes it is a Word file. Other common file extensions are:

.xls   Excel

.mdb   Access

.ppt   PowerPoint

.bmp   Paint

.rtf   Rich Text Format – this is readable by most of the common word processor applications

.txt   Notepad

.htm   HTML files used on the World Wide Web.

Info

You can also use the toolbar buttons in Explorer to view file properties. Select the folder/file, then click on the **Properties** button. To see details of all visible folders/files from the **View** menu, click on **Details** so there is a dot next to it. File details are displayed as below:

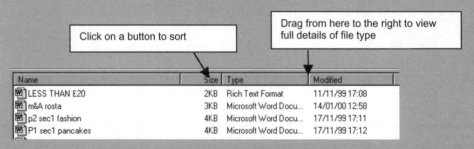

Click on a button to sort

Drag from here to the right to view full details of file type

Name	Size	Type	Modified
LESS THAN £20	2KB	Rich Text Format	11/11/99 17:08
m&A rosta	3KB	Microsoft Word Docu...	14/01/00 12:58
p2 sec1 fashion	4KB	Microsoft Word Docu...	17/11/99 17:11
P1 sec1 pancakes	4KB	Microsoft Word Docu...	17/11/99 17:12

Clicking on the button at the top of each section will sort the details. You can sort by name, file size, file type or date. In the above example the files are sorted into ascending order of size. If the information is not displayed in full (eg **Type** in the above example), drag the border as shown.

3.4 Creating a new folder and subfolders

You can create new folders in which to store related documents. This is always good practice as it makes for easier location at a later date.

Example

To create a new folder on the disk in Drive A:

1   In the left-hand pane of the Windows Explorer window, click on **3¹/₂ Floppy (A:)**.

2   The contents of the floppy disk in Drive A are displayed in the right-hand pane.

3   Right-click in the white space of this section. A menu appears.

4   Select: **New** and then **Folder**.

5   Key in the name for the new folder and press: **Enter**.

To create a subfolder within the newly created folder:

1   Double-click on the newly created folder.

2   Carry out steps 3–5 above.

3.5 Renaming a file/folder

 Method

1 Right-click on the file/folder.
2. Select: **Rename** from the pop-up menu.
3 Key in the new name and press: **Enter**.

3.6 Deleting a folder/file

 Method

1 Select the file/folder you want to delete by clicking on it.
2 Press: **Delete**.
3 You will be asked to confirm file delete.
4 Click on **Yes**.

Note: When you delete a folder, its contents are also deleted.

3.7 The recycle bin

You can restore a deleted file *(not one deleted from a floppy disk)* from the **Recycle Bin**.

 Method

1 Click on the **Recycle Bin.**
2 Select the file you want to restore
3 Select: **Restore** from the **File** menu.

Emptying the Recycle Bin
It is a good idea to remove files from the Recycle Bin from time to time. To do this:

1 Click on the **Recycle Bin** to select it.
2 From the **File** menu, select: **Empty Recycle Bin**.

3.8 Copying folders/files

Example
Copy the file **Gem news** so there is a copy in the folder **Word files**.

There are three main ways to copy a file:

 Method 1

Select the file **Gem news**, hold down the left mouse button and, at the same time, hold down the **Ctrl** key. Drag the file to the folder **Word files**. Release the **Ctrl** key and the mouse button.

 Method 2

1 Select the file **Gem news**.
2 Hold down the *right* mouse button and drag the file to the folder **Word files** (it will become highlighted).

3 Release the mouse – a menu appears.
4 Click on **Copy Here**.

 ## Method 3

1 Right-click on the file **Gem news** – a menu appears.
2 Select: **Copy.**
3 Right-click on the folder **Word files**. Select: **Paste.**

Info

The third method is sometimes easier when you have numerous files and folders, as they may scroll out of view when you are trying to drag them. Check the quick reference for keyboard shortcuts and toolbar button methods.

You can check the file **Gem news** is in the **Word files** folder by clicking on it to reveal its contents.

Note: Folders can be copied in the same way.

3.9 Moving folders/files

Files/folders can be moved following methods 1–3 above, except:

 ## Method 1

Do not hold down the **Ctrl** key when moving files/folders.

 ## Method 2

Select: **Move Here** instead of **Copy Here**.

 ## Method 3

Select: **Cut** instead of **Copy**.

3.10 Selecting adjacent folders/files

You can select more than one file to delete, copy or move.

 ## Method

1 Select: the first folder/file in the group.
2 Hold down the **Shift** key on the keyboard and select: the last file you want.

3.11 Selecting non-adjacent folders/files

 ## Method

1 Select: the first folder/file.
2 Hold down the **Ctrl** key on the keyboard and select: each file in the group.

3.12 Backing up a floppy disk

Backing up a disk means producing an exact copy of the contents of a disk. This is done as a security measure in case anything happens to the original disk.

Produce a backup of a floppy disk

 Method

1 Select: **3½ Floppy (A:).**
2 Right-click: a menu appears.
3 Click on **Copy Disk.**
4 Follow the instructions on screen.

Info

You can back up selected files only by copying them to floppy disks (as in 3.8).

3.13 Formatting a floppy disk

Most new floppy disks are already formatted for use on your computer. If not, you will need to format them before use. Formatting prepares the disk so it is recognised by your computer, and can quickly and easily store and access information on it. A floppy disk needs to be formatted only once. Formatting a disk will erase any information stored on that disk.

Formatting a disk in Drive A

 Method

1 Select: **3½ Floppy (A:).**
2 Right-click: a menu appears (Figure 2.19).

Figure 2.20 Formatting a disk

3 Click: **Format**. The Format dialogue box appears (Figure 2.20).
4 Check the capacity of your disk:

High density – 1.44 Mb
Double density – 720 Kb
Choose accordingly.

Note: High-density disks have two holes at the bottom.

5 Click on the **Full** button.
6 Click on **Start**.

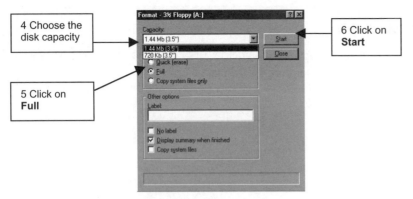

4 Choose the disk capacity

5 Click on **Full**

6 Click on **Start**

Figure 2.21 The Format dialogue box

Info

You can also carry out file maintenance within an application such as Word. See the Appendix for details.

3.14 Finding files

To find a folder/file use the following method:

1   In Windows Explorer, from the Tools menu select: **Find, Files or Folders** *or* from the **Start** button menu, select: **Find**, then **Files or Folders**.
2   The Find: All Files dialogue box appears (Figure 2.21).

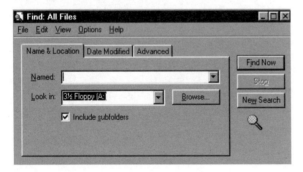

Figure 2.22 Finding files/folders

3   With the **Name & Location** tab selected, key in the name of the file you want to find and possible location.
4   Ensure **Include subfolders** is ticked if appropriate for your search.

Info

If you do not know exactly what the filename is, key in just a part of the name (eg phone will find telephone, phone list, headphones etc). Use the wildcard * (eg *.xls) to find all Excel files.

5   Use the **Date Modified** tab to refine your search to an approximate date.
6   Use the **Advanced** tab to refine your search to a specific file type and size and specific text it contains.
7   Click on **Find Now**.

Info

In this section we have used Windows Explorer. Windows Explorer gives a bird's-eye view of the system. However, it is possible to carry out most of the tasks using My Computer.

Double-click on the **My Computer** icon on the Windows desktop. Practise the exercises again using My Computer, choosing your own file/folder names.

Section 4 Using and printing from a text editing application

In this section you will practise and learn how to:

* Launch a word processing program and create a file.

* Save the file.

* Close an editing application.

* Print from an installed printer.

* Change default printer.

* View a print job's progress from a desktop print manager.

* Move between open windows.

4.1 Creating a folder for your file

Exercise 1

Create a folder named **Examples** on Floppy Drive A using the methods in section 3.

4.2 Creating a word processed file

Info

For the following exercises we will be using the program **Notepad**.

Exercise 2

Open Notepad and key in the following text:

This is an example of creating and saving a file.

Method

1   From the **Start** menu, select: **Programs, Accessories, Notepad** or double-click on its shortcut icon.
2   The Notepad window appears.
3   Key in the text.

4.3 Saving the file

Exercise 3

Save the file.

Method

1   From the **File** menu, select: **Save As**.
2   The Save As dialogue box appears (Figure 2.22).

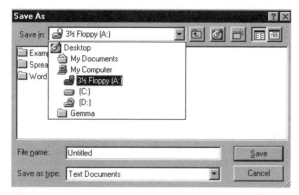

Figure 2.23 Saving the file

3 In the **Save in** box, select: **Floppy (A:)** by clicking on the down arrow and selecting it from the list.
4 Open the **Examples** folder by double-clicking on it.
5 In the **File name** box key in the filename (precede the name with your initials, in my case ajb) **ajb testing**.
6 Click on **Save**.

4.4 Printing the file

 Exercise 4

Print the file saved in 4.3.

 Method

1 Ensure the printer is loaded with paper.
2 From the **File** menu, select: **Print**.

4.5 Changing the default printer

Sometimes you may need to change from the default printer (eg to print in better quality). You can usually change from the default printer within the program you are using.

 Method (In Notepad)

1 From the **File** menu, select: **Page Setup**.
2 Click on **Printer**.
3 In the **Name** section, click on the down arrow and select another printer from the list. Click on **OK**.

Info

You can also change from the default printer for your computer using the following methods:

Using the Start menu
1 From the **Start** menu, select: **Settings**, then **Printers**.
2 The Printers box appears. Right-click on: the printer you want to be the default.
3 Click on **Set As Default**.

Using My Computer
1 Double-click on the **My Computer** icon.
2 Double-click on the **Printers** folder.
3 Right-click on the printer you want to use. Click on **Set as Default**.

4.6 Viewing a print job's progress

You can view how your print job is progressing by carrying out step 1 in the Info box above. At step 2 double-click on the printer.

4.7 Moving between open windows

When you are working you may find you have more than one window open. The open windows will appear (minimised) on the taskbar (Figure 2.23). In this case the Notebook file **ajb testing** is visible on screen (the button appears pushed in).

Figure 2.24 Open windows appear on the taskbar

It is easy to switch between windows. Just click on the button for the window you want displayed *or* select it from the **Window** menu.

4.8 Closing a program

To close Notepad, from the **File** menu, select: **Exit**.

Using the computer and managing files quick reference guide

Action	Keyboard	Mouse	Right-mouse menu	Menu
Back up a floppy disk			**Copy disk**	
Copy file/folder	Select the file/folder			
	Ctrl + C	Click: the 📋 **Copy** button	**C**opy	**E**dit, **C**opy
	Click where you want to copy the file/folder			
	Ctrl + V	Click: the 📋 **Paste** button	**P**aste	**E**dit, **P**aste
Create a new folder	Select where you want the new folder to be			
			New, **F**older	**F**ile, **N**ew, **F**older
Create a subfolder	Select the folder in which you want the subfolder to be and follow the steps for creating a new folder			
Delete a file/folder	Select the file/folder			
	Delete		**D**elete	**F**ile, **D**elete
Display contents of folder		Double-click: the folder		
Exit Windows Explorer		Click: the ☒ **Close** button		**F**ile, **C**lose
Find files/folders	**Start, Find, Files or Folders**			
Format a floppy disk	Select drive			
			Form**at**	
Load Windows Explorer	In Windows 95 desktop			
		Double-click: the **Windows Explorer** shortcut icon		**Start, Programs, Windows Explorer**
Move file/folder	Select the file			
	Ctrl + X	Click: the **Cut** button	**Cu**t	**E**dit, **Cu**t
	Click where you want to move the file/folder to			
	Ctrl + V	Click: the **Paste** button	**P**aste	**E**dit, **P**aste
Notepad, open		Double-click: the **Notepad** shortcut icon		**Start, Programs, Accessories, Notepad**
Notepad, close		Click: the ☒ **Close** button		**F**ile, **E**xit
Notepad, saving a document				**F**ile, **S**ave or **Save As**
Notepad, print				**F**ile, **P**rint
Notepad, change default printer				**F**ile, **Page Set**u**p**, **P**rinter

Action	Keyboard	Mouse	Right-mouse menu	Menu
Printer, change default, view print job's progress				**Start**, **Settings**, **Printers**
Recycle Bin, restore files	Double-click on the **Recycle Bin** icon Select the file you want to restore			
			Restore	**File**, **Restore**
Recycle Bin, empty			**Empty Recycle Bin**	
Rename file/ folder			**Rename**	**File**, **Rename**
Select files *adjacent* *non-adjacent*	Click: the first file Holding down: **Shift**, click: the last file Click: the first file Holding down: **Ctrl**, click: each file in turn			
Shortcut, creating	In Windows Explorer			
		Drag object to desktop	**Create Shortcut**	**File**, **Create Shortcut**
Shut down the computer	**Start, Shut Down**			
View all file/ folder attributes		Click: the **Details** button		
View individual file/folder attributes	Select file/folder			
		Click: the 📋 **Properties** button	**Properties**	**File**, **Properties**

Module 2 practice tasks

For this module you will need to have some folders and files already set up. Ask your supervisor or tutor to prepare them for you.

Preparation

1 Create a folder **ECDL Practice** within the **C:/** drive or on a floppy disk.

2 Create some files in the **ECDL Practice** folder with **Tea** as part of the filename (eg **Teabag, Green Tea, Teapot** etc).

3 Create 8 subfolders in the **ECDL Practice** folder. Name them **Sub1, Sub2, Sub3** etc.

4 Create two subfolders in each **Sub** folder. Folder names do not matter.

5 Put a selection of files (eg types, dates, sizes) into all the folders.

Practice tasks

1 Within the **ECDL Practice** folder, create a folder named **Test** and two subfolders named **Test One** and **Test Two**.

2 Open a text editor program (Notepad). Create an 'Answer' file by keying in your name, the date and the text **ECDL Module 2 Practice test**. The file will be referred to as **Answer** file

3 Find all files with the extension **.xls** in the **ECDL Practice** folder (include all subfolders) and key in the total number found on the next line of the **Answer** file.

4 How many files are there in the folder (include all subfolders) with '**Tea**' in the filename? Key in the number found on the next line of the **Answer** file.

5 How many files in total are there in the **Sub3** folder (include subfolders)? Key in the answer on the next line of the **Answer** file.

6 Copy all the files with the extension **.doc** from ECDL Practice**Sub1** to ECDL Practice**Sub5**.

7 Move the three smallest files from ECDL Practice**Sub2** to ECDL Practice\Test**Test One**.

8 Copy the two oldest files from ECDL Practice**Sub1** to ECDL Practice\Test**Test Two**.

9 Rename files starting with **Tea** so they start with **One** (eg **Teapot** becomes **Onepot**).

10 Delete all files in the ECDL Practice**Sub8** folder with the extension **.ppt**.

11 Answer the following questions in the **Answer** file:

What is the procedure for shutting down the computer?
How do you create a desktop shortcut icon?
How can you view the computer's processor type and installed RAM?
How do you change from the default printer in an application?

12 Save and print the **Answer** file.

13 Empty the Recycle Bin.

Note: This is only a practice test. Successful completion does not imply certification of the module by the ECDL Foundation.

Module 3

Word Processing

Section 1 Basics – getting started

In this section you will practise and learn how to:

* Load Word.

* Understand the parts of the document window.

* Understand and use the functions available, including Help functions.

* Modify the toolbar display.

* Create a document: enter text, insert text, delete text.

* Save a document.

* Exit Word.

1.1 Loading Word

 Exercise 1

Load Word.

 Method

1 Switch on your computer and log in until the Windows 95 desktop screen appears.
2 Move the mouse pointer over the **Start** button and click the left button – a menu appears.
3 Select: **Programs** by hovering the mouse over it – another menu appears.
4 Select: **Microsoft Word** and click the left button (Figure 3.1).

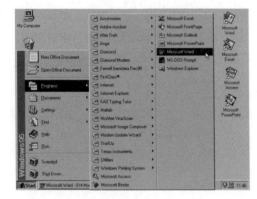

Figure 3.1 Loading Word

i **Info**

INFO If you have a shortcut icon to Word on your desktop, you can load Word by double-clicking on the 🖾 Word icon.

The Word Document window will be displayed on screen looking similar to Figure 3.2 showing a blank document with default values, (ie preprogrammed settings such as line spacing, width of margins, font type). These will remain unchanged until you alter them.

i **Info**

If there is no Document window, click on: the ⬜ **New** button on the top left of the toolbar *or*

From the **File** menu, select: **New**. The New dialogue box appears. Click on: the **General** tab, **Blank Document** and **OK**.

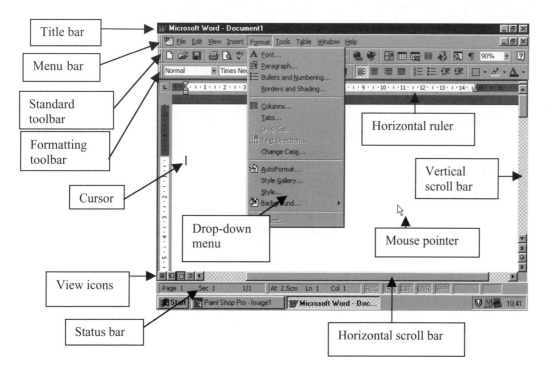

Figure 3.2 The Word Document window

1.2 Parts of the Document Window – an overview

Title bar. This shows the name of the application being used, Microsoft Word, and the current document name, **Document 1** (this is the default name).

Menu bar. This has menu names, which can be selected using the mouse/keyboard. A *drop-down menu* then gives you options within that menu.

Standard toolbar. This contains shortcut buttons for actions used frequently. For example, to open an existing file, click on the button shown in Figure 3.3.

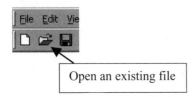

Open an existing file

Figure 3.3 Standard toolbar Open button

To quickly find out what each button on the toolbar does, point the mouse over the button and wait for a few seconds. A *ToolTip* will appear giving a brief explanation of the button. Try this now.

Formatting toolbar. This allows shortcuts to formatting your document, such as underlining text and centring text.

---

i Info

Modifying the toolbar display

There are many toolbars available in Word. The content of your work will dictate which ones are useful to you.

To display other toolbars
From the **View** menu, select **Toolbars,** then click on the toolbar name so a tick appears.

To hide toolbars
Click on the toolbar name to remove the tick.

To customise toolbars:
1 From the **View** menu, select **Toolbars,** then **Customise**.
2 Click on the **Options** tab to set preferences.
3 Click on **Close**.

Cursor. The cursor shows where your text will appear.

Horizontal ruler. This shows the position of text and can be displayed in centimetres or inches. (See the Appendix to change the default.)

Mouse pointer. This will move when you move the mouse – use to select items in the window.

Scroll bars. You can quickly scroll through your document using the scroll bars.

Status bar. This provides information about the position of the cursor and the text displayed on your screen.

View icons. There are different ways of viewing your text. (See section 3 for more information on types of view.)

1.3 Getting help

Note: Throughout this book, the Office Assistant facility has been hidden so as not to distract from the main objectives. More details of the Office Assistant are found in the Appendix. From the **Help** menu, select: **Contents and Index**. The Microsoft Word Help window is displayed (Figure 3.4).

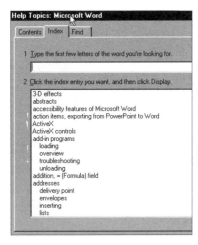

Figure 3.4 Microsoft Word Help

You can select:

- The **Contents** tab for a list of help topics. By clicking on a topic, a display of that topic will appear.

- The **Index** tab. This allows you to key in key words and click on **Display**. Again, the topic will be highlighted and displayed as above.

ScreenTips

From the **Help** menu, select: **What's This?** Then click on the item you want to know about. A short description appears. Press: **Esc** to remove the ScreenTip.

For context-sensitive help, press: **F1**.

1.4 Entering text

Info

Before you begin entering text you need to be aware of the following:

- You do not need to press **Enter** at the end of each line as, if the text is too long to fit within the space available, it will automatically be carried over to the next line. This is known as *word wrap*.
- You should be consistent with spaces after commas and full stops. One space after a comma and one/two space(s) after a full stop is acceptable, looks neat and is easy to read. You can check that you have been consistent by clicking on the ¶ **Show/Hide** button. This displays spaces as dots. Therefore a space appears as one dot. Look to see what other hidden characters are displayed as. To turn Show/Hide off, click on the **Show/Hide** button again.
- You should leave a blank line after headings and between paragraphs. To do this press: **Enter** twice.
- To join two paragraphs together, position the cursor before the first word of the second paragraph and press: ← **Del** (**Backspace**) twice.
- To key in capital letters, hold down: **Shift** at the same time as the key for the letter you want to key in.
- If you are keying in a block of capital letters, press: **Caps Lock** to start keying in capitals and press: **Caps Lock** again to stop. (See **Change case** in the quick reference at the end of this module.)
- Don't worry if you make mistakes, you can correct them later.
- You may notice you have wavy lines under some of your keyed in text. The reason for this is explained in section 2, so you can ignore it for now.

(For more information on layout, see the Appendix).

Exercise 2

With the new Word Document window on your screen, key in the following text (see Figure 3.5).

Picnics can be enjoyed in the early summer when the weather is warm and dry.

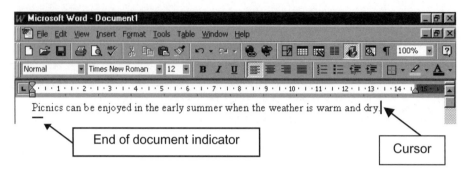

Figure 3.5 The keyed-in text will look similar to this

1.5 Moving around your text

Here we will learn three methods to move around the text:

1   Using the arrow keys.
2   Using the mouse.
3   Using two keys together, **Ctrl + Home**, and **Ctrl + End**.

1 Moving around your text using the arrow keys

The arrow keys →↑ ←↓ (located at the bottom right of the main keyboard) allow you to move the cursor (a flashing black vertical line) in the direction of the arrows.

You can move one space forwards or backwards at a time, or you can move up or down one line at a time. If you keep an arrow key pressed down, the cursor will move quickly through the document. Remember to release the arrow key when you reach the required place.

2 Moving around your text using the mouse

As you move the mouse around the screen, you will notice the I-beam moves with you. Move it until you have reached the required position, click the left mouse button once and the cursor will appear where you clicked.

3 Using Ctrl + Home and Ctrl + End

Hold down: **Ctrl** key at the same time as the **Home** key to move to the top of your text.

Hold down: **Ctrl** key at the same time as the **End** key to move to the bottom of your text.

Info

There are other ways to move around the document and these are included in the quick reference at the end of this module.

1.6 Inserting text

Exercise 3

Insert the word **usually** between the words **is** and **warm**.

 Method

Position the cursor at the point where you want to insert text (in this case after the space after the word **is**), and then key in **usually** and a space (Figure 3.6).

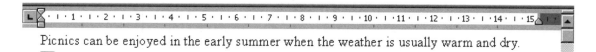

Figure 3.6 Inserting text

Notice how the text to the right of the cursor moves to make room for the new text.

 Info

If your text does not move across but overwrites text already there, check that **OVR** is not displayed on the Status Bar. If it is, press: **Insert** to remove overwrite.

1.7 Deleting text

Exercise 4

Delete the word **early**.

 Method

Either:

Position the cursor to the left of the first character you want to delete, (ie the **e** of **early**) and press: **Delete** until all the letters of **early** (and the space) have been deleted

or:

Position the cursor to the right of the last character you want to delete and press: ← Del (Backspace) key (top right of main keyboard) until all the letters of **early** (and the space) have been deleted.

Exercise 5

Now try keying in a longer piece of text.

 Method

Click on: the ☐ **New** button.

Key in the following **LANDMARKS IN LONDON** text. (This should not be in bold lettering and the line endings will not necessarily be in the same place.)

LANDMARKS IN LONDON

St Paul's Cathedral

St Paul's Cathedral is one of London's landmarks and is renowned throughout the world. It is the largest church in the city and was built on the same site and to replace a Norman church that was destroyed by the Great Fire of 1666.

The Whispering Gallery

This famous Renaissance building was designed by Sir Christopher Wren and has many interesting features. One of its most intriguing is the Whispering Gallery which runs round the inside of the great dome. If you speak in this gallery the sound waves of your voice are carried round the entire circumference of the gallery because the waves are prevented from going outwards by the stones lining the circular wall. These acoustic properties enable someone sitting far away on the opposite side of the gallery to hear your voice, even if you are whispering.

Famous people

Many famous people are buried at St Paul's and their tombs can be found either in the church or in the crypt beneath. They include Nelson, Wellington, Turner and Sir Christopher Wren.

1.8 Saving text

 **Exercise 6**

Save the text.

 Method

 Info

Note that the text will now be referred to as a file.

1   From the **File** menu, select: **Save As** (Figure 3.7).

Figure 3.7 Saving a file for the first time using Save As

2   The **Save As** dialogue box is displayed (Figure 3.8).

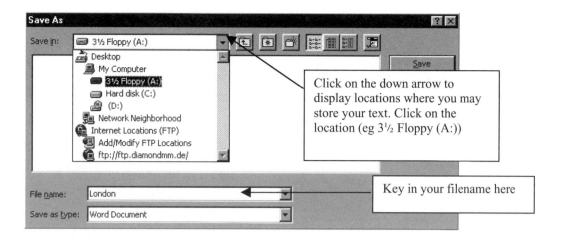

Figure 3.8 The Save As dialogue box

3   Click on the down arrow as shown in Figure 3.8 and click on the location where you want to save your text. (If you are saving to a floppy disk, remember to have your disk inserted in the drive.)

4   Click in the **File name** box at the beginning of the name that is already there and delete it by pressing: **Delete**.

5   Key in the filename **London** (case does not matter).

6   Click on **Save**.

---

i Info

Notice that the default filename (**Document1**) has been replaced with the new filename (**London**) on the Title bar.

1.9 Closing a file

 Exercise 7

Close the file **London**.

 Method

From the **File** menu, select: **Close**.

1.10 Exiting Word

 Exercise 8

Exit Word.

 Method

Click on the ☒ **Close** button in the top right-hand corner.

Info

You will be asked if you want to save the one-sentence practice file. Click on **Yes** and follow the method above using the filename **Picnic**.

Section 1 word processing practice

Practice 1

1 Load Word, open a new file and ender the following text:

THE WORLD WIDE WEB

Many commercial services are now offered on the WWW. You can order books, arrange a car rental anywhere in the world, and even purchase and download new software direct to your computer. If you live in the right area, you can even order a pizza via the WWW!

It was developed to help scientists share information and has rapidly become a general service for everyone. Using a suitably configured computer, users can access information on the WWW (known as web pages) from anywhere in the world. These pages can be created by anyone, from schoolchildren right up to the world's largest companies.

The ability to combine text, pictures, videos and sound makes the WWW ideal for entertainment pages. Most bands, films and computer games have their own official pages, and there are often many more set up by fans.

Be wary of what you find on the WWW. Always check the source of any information given. Remember that anyone can set up a website and the content authenticity will not always have been scrutinized.

2 Save the text with the filename **P1 sec1 www**.

3 Close the file and exit Word.

Practice 2

1 Load Word, open a new file and ender the following text:

Thank you for filling in our recent Holiday questionnaire.

We are constantly striving to improve our services for you and to offer the kind of holidays that you will enjoy. Your comments have been noted and we will do our best to exceed your expectations.

Our new brochure features more than 1,100 idyllic cottages, 160 luxury villas with pools (usually available in the summer months only), more than 2,000 hotels and over 40 apartments at holiday villages, with superb on-site facilities. We also offer deluxe camping and mobile homes at 20 wonderful 4-star sites and theme parks including Disneyland, Paris, Parc Asterix and Futuroscope.

We would like to reward you for helping us with our survey. We are delighted to offer you a 10% saving on your next holiday. If you would like to benefit from this offer, please quote code Q2000 when you call.

We look forward to hearing from you soon.

2 Save the text with the filename **P2 sec1 holiday**.

3 Close the file and exit Word.

Section 2 Basics – editing and printing

In this section you will practise and learn how to:

* Open an existing document.

* Spellcheck and make changes where necessary.

* Use grammar tool and make changes where necessary.

* Resave a previously saved file.

* Preview and print a document and print part of the document from an installed printer.

* Insert/delete text.

* Insert a new paragraph.

* Use the Undo command.

* Select character, word, sentence, paragraph or entire document.

* Replace words with other words.

* Use the Find command for a word or phrase within a document.

* Copy/move text within a document and to another document.

* Open several documents.

* Insert special characters/symbols.

* Modify document setup: page orientation, margins, page size etc.

2.1 Opening an existing document

 Exercise 1

Load Word and open the file **London** saved in Section 1.

 Method

Click on the 📂 **Open** button.

Carry out the instructions given in Figure 3.9 that shows the Open dialogue box.

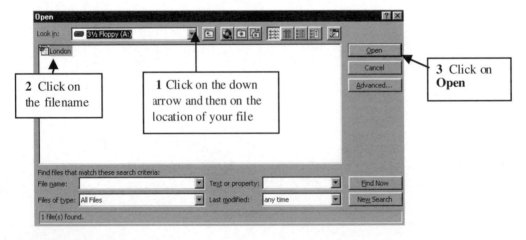

Figure 3.9 Opening a file

Info

Recently opened files appear listed at the bottom of the File menu. Click on the filename to open it.

2.2 Proofreading and correcting errors

It is important to proofread your work carefully against the hard copy. Correct any errors in the text using the methods described in section 1.

2.3 Spellchecking

 Info

It is always important to use the spellchecker before you print a document as it will pick up most misspelt words and provide you with the chance to correct them. Word provides an option to check spelling and grammar together. It also provides the option to check spelling and grammar as it is being keyed in. For a beginner this can be quite distracting since it places wavy red lines under misspelt words and wavy green lines under possible grammatical errors. Throughout this book I have chosen to turn the **Check spelling as you type** off. To do this from the **Tools** menu, select **Options**. Click on the **Spelling and Grammar** tab, then in the **Spelling** section, click in the box next to **Check spelling as you type** to remove the tick. Do the same in the **Grammar** section.

Note: There are limitations to the spellchecker's abilities and it may not pick up wrong usage of words, (eg where and were, stair and stare). Although these words are spelt correctly they may be used in the wrong context. Similarly, do not rely unquestionably on the grammar checker.

 Exercise 2

Run the spellchecker through the document.

 Method

1   Position the cursor at the start of the document by pressing **Ctrl + Home**.
2   Click on the **Spelling and Grammar** button (Figure 3.10).

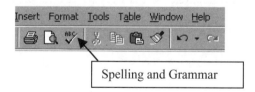

Figure 3.10 The Spelling and Grammar button

3   The Spelling and Grammar dialogue box appears (Figure 3.11).

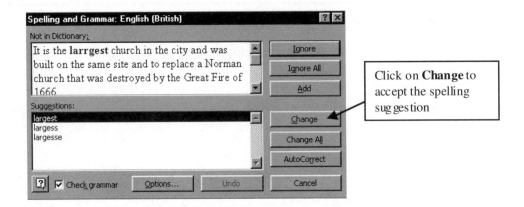

Figure 3.11 Spelling and Grammar dialogue box

The spellchecker will go through your text and match it with the words in its dictionary. It will highlight unrecognisable words and offer suggestions. (You may not have made any spelling errors!) In the example above, it has highlighted the word **larrgest** and it is offering its preferred replacement, **largest**, also highlighted in the lower box. In this case accept the suggestion by clicking on **Change**. If you do not want to accept a suggestion the spellchecker has made, click on **Ignore**. If you want to accept one of the other suggestions it may have made, click on it to select it and then click on **Change**. The spellchecker will repeat this process until it has finished checking all the text. It will then display a message telling you the spellcheck is complete.

2.4 Resaving a previously saved file

 Exercise 3

Resave the file **London**.

Info

As you have already saved the first draft of this document, you will now be able to do a quick save instead of using **Save As**. This will overwrite your original with the changes you have made, but still keep the same filename **London**.

 Method

Click on the **Save** button (Figure 3.12).

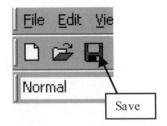

Figure 3.12 The Save button

2.5 Previewing a document

Exercise 4

Print Preview your document.

 Method

If you want to see how your document is going to look on the page before printing it, you can use Word's Print Preview facility.

1 Click on the **Print Preview** button. The Print Preview screen appears (Figure 3.13).

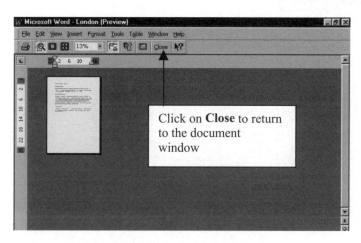

Click on **Close** to return to the document window

Figure 3.13 The Print Preview screen

> **Info**
>
> The cursor, when placed over the document, appears in the shape of a magnifying glass. You can zoom in to any part of the document by clicking over it with the left mouse button. To zoom out, click again. The **Multiple Pages** button is useful when your document has more than one page.

2 Press: **Esc** or click on **Close** to return to the document window.

2.6 Printing a document

Exercise 5

Print one copy of the document on A4 paper.

 Method

1 From the **File** menu, select: **Print** (Figure 3.14).

Figure 3.14 File menu, Print

2   The Print dialogue box appears (Figure 3.15)

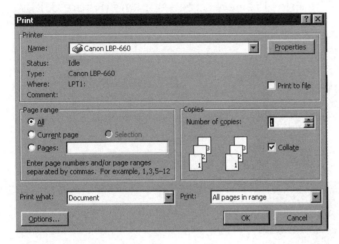

Figure 3.15 The Print dialogue box

3   Check the printer you are using. If it is not the one shown in the **Printer** section of the Print dialogue box, click on the down arrow and select the correct printer so it appears in the **Name** box. Check the printer is ready and loaded with paper.

4   There are several other default control options concerning printing (shown in the Print dialogue box (Figure 3.15) and in the Info box below). At this stage, you should not need to change any settings, so just click on **OK**.

---

i Info

Quick method to print
On the toolbar, click on the 🖨 **Print** button.

Use this if you know that you do not need to alter anything in the Print dialogue box.

Useful printing options
In the **Page range** section, choose which pages to print.

In the **Copies** section, select the number of copies to print.

In the **Print** section, you can select to print **Odd** or **Even** pages only.

2.7 Inserting text

Exercise 6

Using the instructions for inserting text in section 1.6 and below, insert the new paragraph (shown below) after the second paragraph ending **even if you are whispering.**

Sir Christopher Wren

Over the north door, Wren's epitaph is inscribed in Latin. It is – Si monumentum requiris, circumspice. This translated into English means – If you seek his memorial, look around you.

Method

1   Position the cursor at the beginning of the blank line in between the two paragraphs.
2   Press: **Enter**.
3   Key in the text.
4   Press: **Enter**.

Info

Remember when you insert or delete text, check the spacing between words, sentences and paragraphs is still consistent. Use the ¶ **Show/Hide** button to check this.

Exercise 7

In the second sentence of the last paragraph, insert the following after **include** and before **Nelson**:

Roberts, Jellicoe, Beatty,

Method

Follow the method given in section 1.

2.8 Deleting text

We have already learnt how to delete text using the **Delete** or ← **Del (backspace)** key. However, this is not the quickest method to delete whole sentences or longer portions of text. To do this we need to select the text to be deleted.

Exercise 8

In the second sentence of the first paragraph, delete the words: **on the same site and.**

Method

1   Move the cursor to the beginning of the text you want to delete – in this case the **o** of **on** (Figure 3.16).

St Paul's Cathedral

St Paul's Cathedral is one of London's landmarks and is renowned throughout the world. It is the largest church in the city and was built on the same site and to replace a Norman church that was destroyed by the Great Fire of 1666.

Figure 3.16 Positioning the cursor

2   Hold down the left mouse button and drag the I-beam pointer across the words to be deleted (Figure 3.17).

St Paul's Cathedral is one of London's landmarks and is renowned throughout the world. It is the largest church in the city and was built on the same site and to replace a Norman church that was destroyed by the Great Fire of 1666.

Figure 3.17 Selecting text

3   Release the mouse. The highlighting shows the text that is selected. If you need to cancel the selection, click anywhere on the screen or press any arrow key.
4   Press: **Delete**.
5   Check for consistency of spacing.

> **Info**
>
> If you want to undo the last action(s), click on the 🔄 **Undo** button on the toolbar. This button is very useful and can be used at any time. When you click on the arrow next to the **Undo** button, a list of your most recent actions is displayed so you can select exactly which action to undo.

> **Info**
>
> There are many ways to select text. These are given in the quick reference at the end of this chapter. There is no right or wrong way and if you experiment you will find your own preferred method.

2.9 Replacing text

> **Info**
>
> There is no need for you to scan through text manually to replace text because Word can automatically find and replace text.

> **Exercise 9**
>
> The word **church** appears three times in the text. Replace the word **church** with the word **cathedral** each time it appears.

 Method

1   Move your cursor to the top of the document (**Ctrl + Home**).
2   From the **Edit** menu, select: **Replace** (Figure 3.18).

Figure 3.18 Edit menu, Replace

3 The **Find and Replace** dialogue box appears (Figure 3.19).
4 Click on the **Replace** tab (if not already selected).
5 Click in the **Find what** box, key in the word **church.**

Note: **Do not press Enter yet.**

6 Click in the **Replace with** box, key in the word **cathedral** (lower case).
7 Click on **Replace All**.

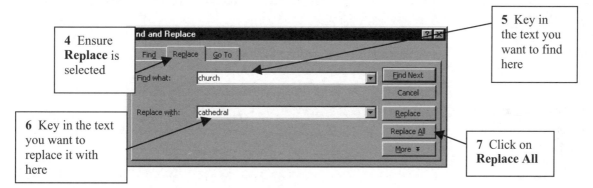

Figure 3.19 The Find and Replace dialogue box

8 A box appears telling you how many replacements have been made (Figure 3.20).

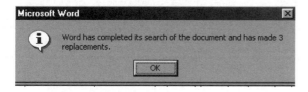

Figure 3.20 You are advised how many replacements have been made

9 Click on **OK**.
10 Click on **Close**.

---

i Info

There are options available within Find and Replace. The commonly used option is **Match Case**. Use this if you are replacing a word consisting of capital letters. If you do not use it, the replacement word will also have capital letters (it will not have matched the case you have keyed in). To set Match Case, in the **Find and Replace** dialogue box, click on: **More**, click on **Match Case** and proceed as before. Also be aware of options available by clicking on the **Special** button.

2.10 Searching for words or phrases

Info

When working with long documents, it is useful to be able to find words or phrases quickly. To do this:

1   From the **Edit** menu, select: **Find.**

2   Key in the word or phrase you want to find and click on **Find Next.**

2.11 Moving text

Exercise 10

Move the third paragraph and its heading: **Sir Christopher Wren . . .** so that it then becomes the second paragraph.

Method

1   Select the paragraph as in Section 2.8 (page 59).

2   Click on: the ✂ **Cut** button. The text will be saved on to the clipboard (you will not see or be told this).

3   Position the cursor where you want the text to reappear, then click on the 📋 **Paste** button.

Info

Remember to check spacing is still consistent.

Info

The Clipboard

The clipboard is a memory store. Whenever you cut or copy an object, the computer temporarily stores the copy on the clipboard. It can then quickly retrieve it when you want to paste it somewhere else, even into other Office applications such as Excel or PowerPoint. Items on the clipboard are removed when the computer is turned off.

2.12 Copying text

Exercise 11

Copy the heading **LANDMARKS IN LONDON** so it is repeated at the end of the text.

Follow the method shown in 2.11, except at step 2 click on the 📋 **Copy** button instead of the **Cut** button.

2.13 Saving and printing

 Exercise 12

Save your file with the filename, **London1**, (as shown in Section 1.8) and print one copy on A4 paper.

Info

By saving your file as **London1**, you will ensure the original file is not overwritten. When practising working through assignments you will then be able to go back and correct any errors should this be necessary.

Note: It is good practice to get into the habit of saving your work regularly. If you encounter a problem you can always revert back to the most recently saved version of your work.

2.14 Copy text to another document

 Exercise 13

Copy the first paragraph beginning **St Paul's Cathedral . . .** of the document currently open ie **London1** to a new Word document. Do not include the paragraph heading.

Method

1   Select the text to be copied so it is highlighted.
2   Click on the **Copy** button.
3   Open a new Word document by clicking on the **New Blank Document** button. A new document appears.
4   Click on the **Paste** button.

Info

You will notice the document **London1**, which you have copied from, is hidden from view. To return to the document **London1**, from the **Window** menu, select the document name.

 Exercise 14

Open the file saved as **Picnic** in section 1.10 and copy the same piece of text as in Exercise 13 so it becomes the second paragraph of the document.

Method

1   Open the file **Picnic** following the method shown in 2.1.
2   Position the cursor where you want the copied text to appear.
3   The text should already be on the clipboard so click on: the **Paste** button.

Note: You should now have three Word documents open ie **London1**, **Picnic** and **Document1** (which has not yet been given a filename).

Exercise 15

Save and print the documents **Picnic** and **Document1** choosing a suitable filename for **Document1**. Close all three documents.

 Method

Use the quick save method for documents **London1** and **Picnic** as in section 2.4. Save the file **Document1** using the method in section 1.8 so that you can give the document a filename.

Info

Always give your documents meaningful filenames so it will be easier to recognise them at a later date.

2.15 Inserting special characters

Exercise 16

Load the file **London1** saved in section 2.14 and insert the following text after and on the same line as **LANDMARKS OF LONDON** at the end of the document:

Walkabouts Company ©

 Method

    1 Open the file and position the cursor where you want to key in the text.
2   Key in **Walkabouts Company**.
3   The © symbol does not appear on the keyboard. To insert this special character, ensure that the cursor is positioned where you want the character to appear.
4   From the **Insert** menu, select: **Symbol** (Figure 3.21).

Figure 3.21 Inserting a special character/symbol

5   The Symbol dialogue box appears (Figure 3.22).

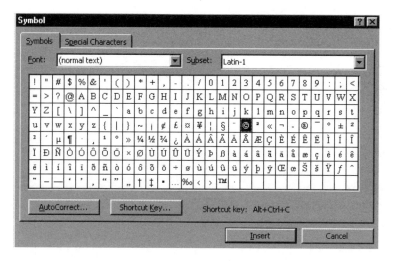

Figure 3.22 The Symbol dialogue box

6 With the **Symbols** tab selected, click on the special character to insert.
7 Click on **Insert** and then on **Close**.

Info

There are some commonly used special characters/symbols to choose from. It is worth taking time to acquaint yourself with some of them. There are other fonts (especially Wingdings and Symbol) that have some useful special characters. Select other fonts from the list in the **Font** box.

2.16 Modifying document setup

Exercise 17

Change the document layout to landscape display.

Info

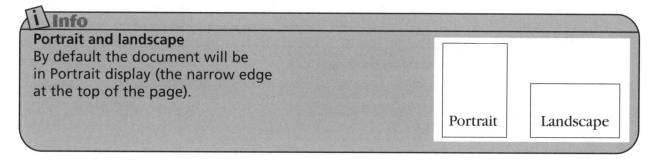

Portrait and landscape
By default the document will be in Portrait display (the narrow edge at the top of the page).

Portrait Landscape

Method

1 From the File menu, select: **Page Setup**.
2 The Page Setup dialogue box appears (Figure 3.23).

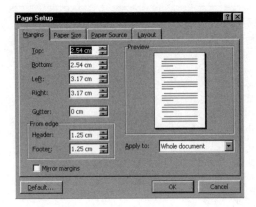

Figure 3.23 Page Setup dialogue box

3 Click on the **Paper Size** tab (Figure 3.24).

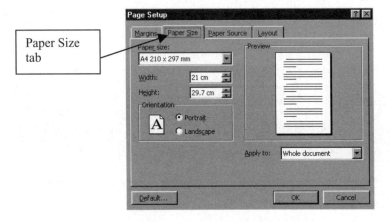

Paper Size tab

Figure 3.24 Selecting page orientation

4 In the Orientation section, click in the **Landscape** option button to select it.
5 Click on **OK**.

Note: You can check the new document orientation in Print Preview.

 Exercise 18

Set in both the left and right margins by 2 cm ($^1/_2$″).

Changing the margins

 Method

1 From the **File** menu, select: **Page Setup**: the Page Setup dialogue box appears (Figure 3.24).
2 Ensure the **Margins** tab is selected, the default landscape left and right margin width is 2.54 cm. Therefore to set in the margin by 2 cm we will need to add 2 cm to the default width of 2.54 cm. The result is 4.54 cm.
3 Delete 2.54 cm from the **Left** margin box and key in **4.54 cm**. Repeat in the **Right** margin box.
4 Click on **OK**.

Info

Note: The default left and right margins in portrait display are 3.17 cm. You will notice that the Page Setup dialogue box allows you to change many of the defaults. Take a look at these now.

2.17 Printing part of a document

 Exercise 19

Print only the end of the document from and including the heading **Famous people**.

 Method

1 Select the text to be printed so that it is highlighted (Figure 3.25).

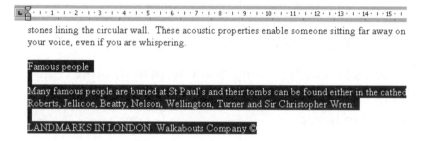

Figure 3.25 Section to be printed is selected

2 Follow the method in section 2.6 but at Step 4 in the **Page range** section of the Print dialogue box, click in the option button next to **Selection** so that a dot is shown (Figure 3.26).

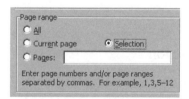

Figure 3.26 Printing part of a document

Info

If a document consists of more than one page, you can print selected pages only by clicking in the **Pages** option button (see Figure 3.26) and keying in the pages to print in the adjacent box.

2.18 Close the file, save changes and exit Word

Section 2 word processing practice

Practice 3

1 Load Word and reload the file **P1 sec1 www** saved in section 1.

2 Proofread and spellcheck the document, making corrections where necessary.

3 Quick save the document.

4 Print one copy.

5 Insert a new paragraph after the first one ending ... **you can even order a pizza via the WWW!**

   The possibilities are endless. User groups are growing daily. Who would have thought that people would be doing their weekly grocery shopping using the WWW?

6 In the third paragraph delete the sentence beginning **These pages can be created by anyone** ...

7 Replace **WWW** with the word **web** each time it appears.

8 In the first paragraph move the sentence beginning **You can order books** ... from being the second sentence so that it becomes the last sentence in the paragraph.

9 Change the page orientation to landscape.

10 Change the left and right margins so that they are both 5.54 cm

11 Save the document with the filename **P3 sec2 www** and print a copy.

12 Print only the last two paragraphs.

13 Close the file and exit Word.

Practice 4

1 Load Word and reload the file **P2 sec1 holiday** saved in section 1.

2 Proofread and spellcheck the document, making corrections where necessary.

3 Quick save the document.

4 Print one copy.

5 Insert the following sentence in the fourth paragraph after the sentence ending ... **saving on your next holiday.**

   However, you must act within 28 days.

6 In the second paragraph delete the sentence beginning **Your comments** ...

7 Replace the word **constantly** with the word **continually**.

8 Move the fourth paragraph so that it becomes the third paragraph.

9 Find the word **Asterix** and replace the **e** with an accented e ie é.

10 Set in the left and right margins by 2 cm.

11 Save the document with the filename **P4 sec2 holiday** and print one copy.

12 Close the file and exit Word.

Section 3 Basics – formatting

In this section you will practise and learn how to:

* Centre, embolden, italicise and underline text.
* Format superscript, subscript text.
* Apply different colours to text.
* Change line spacing.
* Control justification/alignment.
* Control hyphenation.
* Change font and font size.
* Copy the formatting from a selected piece of text.
* Indent text.
* Create a header and a footer, inserting date, author, page numbers etc.
* Apply basic text format in headers and footers.
* Change page display modes.
* Use the page view magnification tool/zoom tool.
* Use and change pagination.

3.1 Centring text

Exercise 1

Reload the file **London1**, saved in section 2 and ensure it is showing portrait display.

Centre the heading **LANDMARKS IN LONDON**

Info

When the display is changed back to portrait, the changes that were made to the left and right margins in landscape are now applied instead to the top and bottom margins. We do not need to be concerned with this for the following exercises but you will need to be aware for future reference.

Method

1   Select the text to be centred or position the cursor on the line where the text appears.
2   Click on the **Centre** button (Figure 3.27).

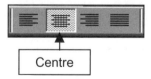

Figure 3.27 The Centre button

3.2 Emboldening text

Exercise 2

Embolden the heading: **LANDMARKS IN LONDON**.

Method

1   Select the text to be emboldened.

2   Click on: the **B** **Embolden** button.

3.3 Italicising text

 Exercise 3

Italicise the Latin text in the second sentence of the second paragraph that reads:

Si monumentum requiris, circumspice.

 Method

Follow the method shown in 3.2 except at step 2 click on the **I** **Italic** button.

3.4 Underlining text

 Exercise 4

At the bottom of the document underline the text **Walkabouts Company**. Do not underline the copyright symbol.

 Method

Follow the method shown in 3.2 except at step 2 click on the **U** **Underline** button.

> **i** **Info**
>
> Emboldening, italicising or underlining text is a way of giving emphasis to the text. There are also other ways to emphasise text. Practise using some different effects now:
>
> 1   Select the text to format.
>
> 2   From the **Format** menu, select: **Font**.
>
> 3   Choose from the **Effects** section.
>
> *Note*: Text can be made superscript (e.g. 3^2) and subscript (e.g. H_2O).

3.5 Applying different colours to text

 Exercise 5

Change the colour of the text: **Walkabouts Company** at the bottom of the document.

 Method

1   Select the text to be changed.

2   Click on the down arrow next to the **A** **Font Color** button to display colour choices (Figure 3.28).

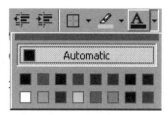

Figure 3.28 Changing text colour

3   Click on your selected colour.

Info

If you do not have a colour printer, the selected colours will display in grey shades.

3.6. Changing line spacing

Exercise 6

Change the whole document to double line spacing.

Info

Word lets you apply a variety of line space settings (the distance between individual lines of text). Examples are:

*   *Single line spacing* . . . this is the default.
*   *Double line spacing* . . . one blank line is left between the lines of text.

This is an example of single line spacing. The default setting is single line spacing where the gap between the lines of text is just over the type size. If the specification for a document is single line spacing, then usually you need do nothing.

This is an example of double line spacing. There is one blank line left between lines

of text. It is often used when a section needs extra emphasis.

Method

1   Select all the text using the quick method (Press: **Ctrl + A**).
2   From the **Format** menu, select: **Paragraph**. The Paragraph dialogue box is displayed (Figure 3.29).
3   Ensure the **Indents and Spacing** tab is selected.
4   In the **Spacing** section, **Line spacing** box, click on the down arrow and click on **Double**.
5   Click on **OK**.
6   Click in a white space to remove highlighting.

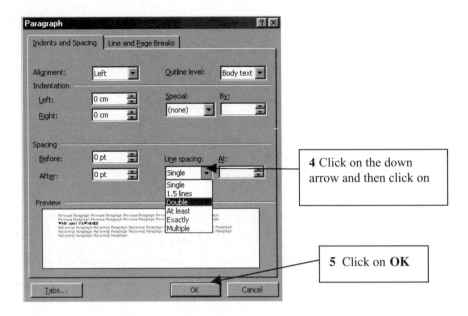

Figure 3.29 The Paragraph dialogue box – selecting double line spacing

Info

At Step 1, you can select a smaller portion of text if necessary and follow the same instructions.

Info

In double line spacing there are usually three lines between paragraphs. If you look on the Status bar you will notice your document now takes up two pages since 2/2 is displayed. When you scroll through your document you will see a dotted line across the page indicating Word has inserted a page break.

3.7 Control justification/alignment

Exercise 7

Justify the text at the right and left-hand margins (full justification).

Info

There are four types of alignment. They can be accessed via the Formatting toolbar:

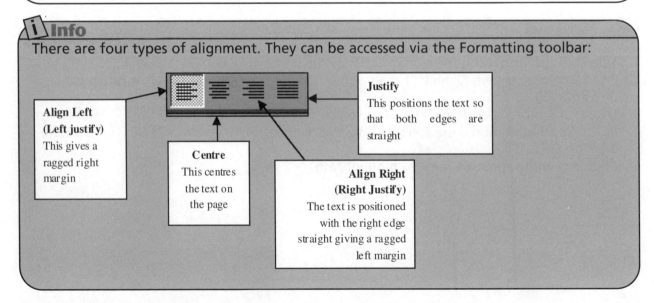

Method

1 Select all of the text (**Ctrl + A**).
2 Click on the **Justify** button (shown above).
3 Click anywhere to remove the selection.

You will notice that the centred heading **LANDMARKS IN LONDON** has also justified. Recentre it by following the instructions in 3.1.

 Info

You can select smaller portions of text (eg paragraphs) and change alignment and spacing.

 Info

When text is justified, the text is spaced out to sit flush with the margins. In such cases it can look better to hyphenate some words. You can hyphenate automatically or manually. To set hyphenation, from the **Tools** menu, select: **Language** and then **Hyphenation**. The Hyphenation dialogue box is displayed. Click in the box to **Automatically hyphenate document**. If you prefer to have more control over which words are hyphenated, deselect: **Automatically hyphenate document**. After keying in the text, select it and, from the **Tools** menu, select: **Language, Hyphenation** and click on **Manual**. Word will then ask before it hyphenates a word.

3.8 Save the file as **London2**.

3.9 Print one copy on A4 paper.

3.10 Changing font and font size

 Exercise 8

Change the font of the main heading to **Arial** and the size to **16 pt**.

Changing font type

 Method

 Info

Serif and sans serif fonts
The default font in Word is Times New Roman. This is a serif font. Serifs are small lines that stem from the upper and lower ends of characters. Serif fonts have such lines. Sans serif fonts do not have these lines. As a general rule, larger text in a sans serif font and body text in a serif font usually makes for easier reading. Examples:

Times New Roman is a serif font.

Arial is a sans serif font.

1 Select the heading **LANDMARKS IN LONDON** so that it is highlighted.
2 Click on the down arrow in the **Font** box (where Times New Roman is displayed, shown in Figure 3.30) to display fonts that are available on your computer.

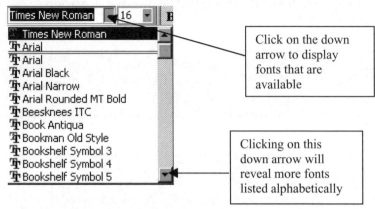

Figure 3.30 Fonts available in Word

3 Click on **Arial** to select it.

Changing font size

4 With the text still selected, click on the down arrow in the **Font Size** box (Figure 3.31).

5 Click on the size required.

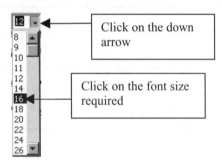

Figure 3.31 Changing font size

3.11 Copying the formatting from a selected piece of text

 Exercise 9

Change all other headings in the document to Arial, size 14 pt.

 Method

1 Follow the method shown in 3.10 to change the first heading ie **St Paul's Cathedral**.

2 With the changed heading still selected, double-click on the ✎ **Format Painter** button.
3 Select the other headings in turn. They will automatically reformat.

4 Press: **Esc** to turn the **Format Painter** off.

3.12 Indenting text

Info

Do not confuse indentation with page margins. An indent is the difference between the margin and the text.

Indenting on the left side

 Exercise 10

Indent the first paragraph on the left side only. Do not include the heading.

 Method

1 Select the text to be indented.
2 Click on the 🔲 Increase Indent button.

Info

The **Increase Indent** button moves the text in from the margin by 1.27 cm. Click on it again to increase the indentation further. To remove the indentation, use the 🔲 **Decrease Indent** button.

Indenting on the left and right side

 Exercise 11

Indent the second paragraph on both the left and the right by 2 cm.

Info

There are two ways to indent on the right-hand side. If you have good control of the mouse, using the ruler is a quick method.

📖 **Method 1**

(Indenting using the ruler)

1 Select the text to be indented.
2 Click and drag the Left Indent marker (the square block) on the ruler to the right as shown in Figure 3.32. The text will indent accordingly.

Drag the **Left Indent** (the square block) to the right

Drag the **Right Indent** to the left

Figure 3.32 Indenting using the ruler method

3 Drag the Right Indent marker to the left.
4 Click in a white space to turn the highlighting off.

Info

It is worth making a note of the measurements already showing on the ruler before altering them. Don't forget, you can use the **Undo** button if you make a mistake.

Method 2

(Indenting using the Format menu)

1 Select the text to be indented.
2 From the **Format** menu, select: **Paragraph**. The Paragraph dialogue box appears (Figure 3.33).

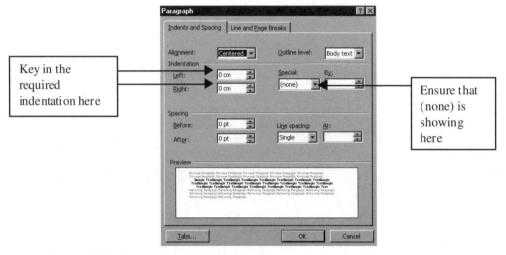

Key in the required indentation here

Ensure that (none) is showing here

Figure 3.33 Paragraph dialogue box

3 Ensure the **Indents and Spacing** tab is selected.
4 In the **Indentation** section, click in the **Left** box and key in the measurement you require.
5 Repeat in the **Right** box.
6 In the **Special** box, ensure **(none)** is displayed.
7 Click on **OK**.
8 Remove the highlight.

Info

This method can be used if you need a non-standard-sized indent. It can also be used to create special indents by selecting **First line** or **Hanging** in the **Special** box and keying in the size of the indent in the **By** box.

First line indents the first line of the selection only.

Hanging does not indent the first line but indents all the following lines.

Note: These special indents can also be achieved using the ruler (see Word Online Help for more detail).

3.13 Creating headers and footers

 Exercise 12

Create a footer in size 8 pt to display **London Information**, **today's date** and **your name**.

Method

1 Move the cursor to the start of the document (press: **Ctrl + Home**).
2 From the **View** menu, select: **Header and Footer**. The Header and Footer box appears (Figure 3.34).

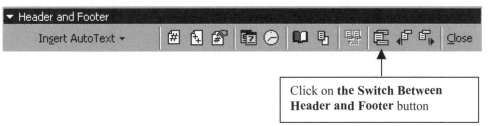

Click on **the Switch Between Header and Footer** button

Figure 3.34 Header and Footer box

3 Click on the **Switch Between Header and Footer** button. The Footer section appears (Figure 3.35).

Click on the down arrow and select options to automatically insert commonly used header and footer information

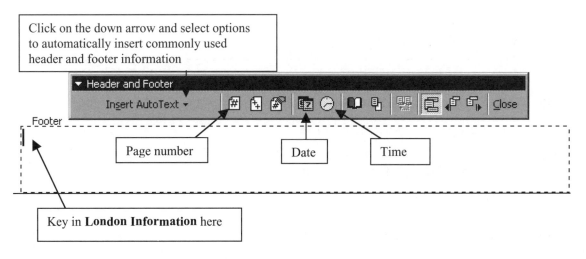

Page number   Date   Time

Key in **London Information** here

Figure 3.35 Footer section

4 Key in **London Information** directly into the Footer section.
5 Press: **Tab** (or the spacebar) several times to move the cursor across the page.
6 Click on the **Date** toolbar button (Figure 3.35) to insert today's date automatically.
7 Press: **Tab** (or the spacebar) again to move the cursor across and then key in your name.
8 It will look something like Figure 3.26.

| London Information | 27/01/00 | Angela Bessant |

Figure 3.36 Text inserted into footer

Info

Check the date is correct. The date may not be set up correctly on your computer. If it shows the wrong date, select the date only, then press: **Delete**. Key in the date manually or reset the computer's date.

Formatting the footer text

9   Select the footer text and change the size using the Formatting toolbar. You may now want to alter the spacing.

10 Click on **Close**.

Info

You will not be able to see the footer if you are in **Normal View** but it will show up on Print Preview. (See 3.14 for information on different types of view.)

 Exercise 13

Add page numbers to the top centre of each page.

Info

There are two ways of adding page numbers.

 Method 1

Using the View menu

1   Follow steps 1 and 2 in 3.13. The Header and Footer box appears.
2   Click on the **Centre** button so that the page numbers will appear in the centre.
3   Click on the 🔲 **Insert Page Number** button (Figure 3.37).

Info

You can click on **Insert Autotext**, then **-PAGE-** but you will need to realign it.

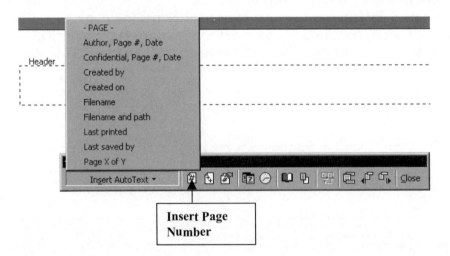

Figure 3.37 Inserting page numbers on a header

Method 2

Using the Insert menu

1 From the Insert menu, select: **Page Numbers**
2 The Page Numbers dialogue box appears (Figure 3.38).

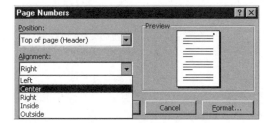

Figure 3.38 Page Numbers box

3 Use the down arrows next to **Position** and **Alignment** to select where you want the numbers to be.
4 Click on **OK**.

Should you need to adapt page numbers (eg start at a number other than 1), click on the
![icon] **Format Page Number** button in Method 1. For both methods, click on **Format** if you
need to amend further (ie select a different number format).

Info

Inserting document author's name on header/footer
*If you are not the regular user of a computer, it will not be set up to automatically display
your name as the author of the document. To display your name:*

1 With the document open, from the **File** menu, select: **Properties**.

2 With the **Summary** tab selected, key in your name in the **Author** box.

3 Click on: **OK**.

4 From the **View** menu, select: **Headers and Footers**.

5 Position the cursor where you want your name to display.

6 From the **Insert** menu, select: **Field**.

7 In the **Categories** box, select: **Document Information**.

8 In the **Field names** box, select: **Author**.

9 Click on: **OK**.

3.14 Changing page display modes

Info

There are four different types of view. The buttons for these are displayed at the bottom left of the Word window.

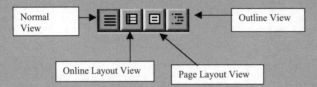

Normal View This is the default. It allows for quick and easy text editing.

Online Layout View This optimises the display for easier reading on screen.

Page Layout View This view allows you to see how objects will be positioned on the printed page. It shows margins, headers and footers and graphics.

Outline View This view allows you to see your document in an outline format.

 Exercise 14

Change to Page Layout View and use the Zoom button to magnify the footer text.

 Method

1   Click on the **Page Layout View** button shown above.
2   The header and footer will now be visible. The text, set at size 8 pt, will be small and, since header text is greyed out, it may be difficult to read. Use the **Zoom** box to enlarge the text on screen as follows.

Using the page method view magnification/zoom tool

3   Click on the down arrow in the **Zoom** toolbar box to reveal default zoom views (Figure 3.39).
4   Select a zoom greater than 100% (the default) to enlarge text.
5   To revert back, select zoom **100%**.

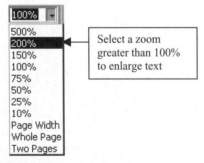

Figure 3.39 Using Zoom

3.15 Using and changing pagination

 Exercise 15

Insert a page break after the second paragraph ending **. . . look around you.**

Method

1 Position the cursor on the line in between the second paragraph and the third paragraph heading.
2 From the **Insert** menu, select: **Break**.
3 The **Break** dialogue box appears. Ensure the **Page break** option button is chosen and click on **OK** (Figure 3.40).

Figure 3.40 The Break dialogue box

---

i Info

It is important to set out the pages so they are easy to read. Check the default setting for **Widow/Orphan** control (**Format** menu, **Paragraph**, **Line and Page Breaks**) is ticked. This ensures paragraphs are not split so one stray line of text appears at the bottom or top of a page. Always check headings are not split from the text to which they refer.

There are soft and hard page breaks. As your text reaches the bottom margin of a page, a soft page break is automatically inserted by Word. This will reposition itself should you add or delete text from the document. A hard page break is inserted by you. Its position will always remain constant until you decide to alter it.

To delete a hard page break
1 Ensure you are in **Normal** View by selecting it from the bottom left corner of the document window.
2 Position the cursor on the page break (dotted line).
3 Press: **Delete**.

---

i Info

Instead of using the arrow keys to see the next/previous page, click on **Previous Page** or **Next Page** on the vertical scroll bar.

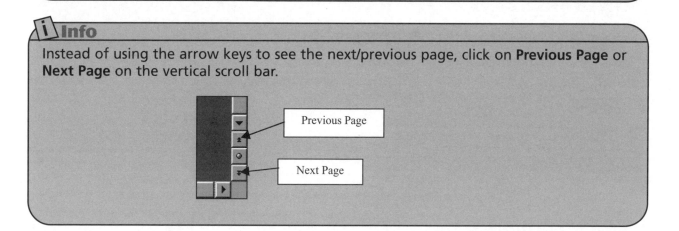

3.16 Save the document as **London3**

3.17 Print one copy on A4 paper

3.18 Close the file and exit Word

Section 3 word processing practice

Practice 5

1   Load Word and reload the file **P3 sec2 www** saved in section 2.

2   Centre and embolden the heading **THE WORLD WIDE WEB**.

3   Set in the whole document by 1.27 cm at the left margin.

4   Set the document in double line spacing.

5   Change the colour of all the text in the second and fourth paragraph to red.

6   Justify the first and second paragraphs only.

7   Change the font in the final paragraph to Arial 16 pt.

8   Add a header containing the text **World Wide Web** and **Your name**.

9   Format the header to 8 pt

10   Add page numbers at the bottom right, starting at 3.

11   Insert a page break after the second paragraph.

12   Save the document as **P5 sec3 www**.

13   Print one copy.

14   Close the file and exit Word.

Practice 6

1   Load Word and reload the file **P4 sec2 holiday** saved in section 2.

2   At the top of the document add a heading **Details of your reward** in Arial 16 pt.

3   Centre and underline the heading you just entered.

4   Except for the first and last paragraphs, give each paragraph a hanging paragraph by 1 cm.

5   Increase the font size of the fourth paragraph by 2 pt.

6   Save the document as **P6 sec3 holiday**.

7   Print one copy.

8   Close the file and exit Word.

Section 4 Basics – more formatting

In this section you will practise and learn how to:

* Use lists (bulleted and numbered).

* Use and set tabs.

* Add borders to a document.

* Save an existing document under another file format including saving a document for posting on the web.

* Apply existing styles to a document.

* Choose an appropriate document template for use in a specified task.

* Work within a template on a specified task.

4.1 Using lists (bulleted and numbered)

 Exercise 1

Open a new Word document and key in the following text. Perform a spellcheck and save the document with the filename **Volunteers**.

VOLUNTEERS REQUIRED

Do you meet the following criteria?

Age range 16 to 40
Computer literate
Available during the hours of 16.00 and 18.00

We are looking for volunteers to take part in a survey on computer usage. We are able to offer you a small payment and a cup of tea or coffee! If you think that you may be able to help us, we would like to hear from YOU.

We look forward to your call.

 Exercise 2

Make the section starting at **Age range . . .** and ending at **. . . 18.00** into a bulleted list.

 Method

1 Select the text to be bulleted.
2 Click on the ⁞≡ **Bullets** button.

Info

Bullets/numbering can be selected before keying in the text, if preferred.

Formatting bullets
Bullets can take many forms:

1   From the **Format** menu, select **Bullets and Numbering**.
2   Select your preferred option and click on **OK**.
3   Click on **Customize** if you require a different bullet type.

Numbered lists
Numbering lists is carried out following the same method but, at step 2, clicking on the
 Numbering button. This is useful if lists need to be in a specific order (eg a set of
instructions). You can format numbers:

1   Select the list.
2   From the **Format** menu, select: **Bullets and Numbering**.
3   The Bullets and Numbering dialogue box is displayed.
4   Click on **Customize**.
5   The Customize Numbered List dialogue box is displayed.
6   Select a format from the **Number style** list. Options include Roman numerals and A,
     B, C etc.

Turning bullets/numbering off
To turn Bullets and Numbering off, select the bulleted/numbered text, and click on: the
relevant **Bullets/Numbering** button.

4.2 Using and setting tabs

    Exercise 3

Using tabs, insert the following before the final sentence beginning **We look forward...**

Please contact one of the following: **Mike   ext 4448**
                                                Chris   ext 4462
                                                Jane   ext 4463

Info

Tabs are used to line up columns and Word offers several types of tab.

                          Left tab

             Right tab

                 Centre tab

             4567.890 Decimal tab

             Tab stop position

ℹ️ Info

By default, tabs are set every 1.27 cm (½") from the left margin. When a new tab is set, Word clears any default tabs set to the left of the new tab stop. The type of tab stop can be chosen by clicking on the tab button at the left hand edge of the ruler.

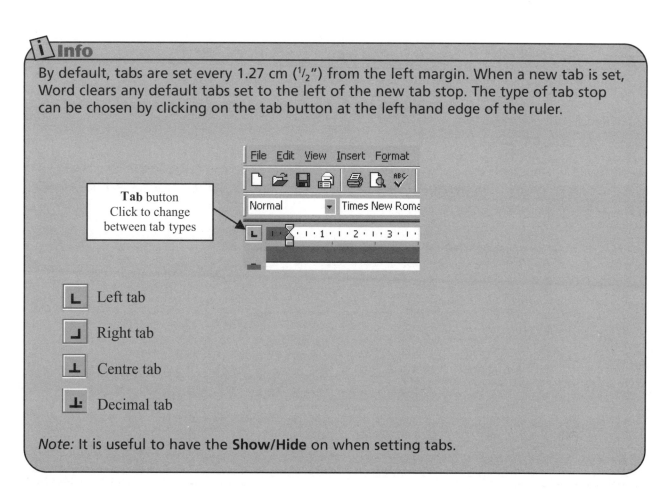

Tab button
Click to change between tab types

	L	Left tab
	⌐	Right tab
	⊥	Centre tab
	⊥.	Decimal tab

Note: It is useful to have the **Show/Hide** on when setting tabs.

📖 Method

Using preset tabs

1 Key in the text **Please contact one of the following:** in the correct position in the document.
2 Press: **Tab** once to move to the preset tab stop and key in **Mike**.
3 Press: **Tab** once and key in **ext 4448**. Press: **Enter** (Figure 3.41).

¶
Please·contact·one·of·the·following:→Mike→ext·4448¶

Figure 3.41 Using tabs

4 Press: **Tab** a number of times until the cursor is positioned lined up under the **M** of Mike.
5 Key in: **Chris**, press: **Tab** once and key in **ext 4462**. Press: **Enter**
6 Repeat Steps 4 and 5 for **Jane ext 4463** (Figure 3.42).

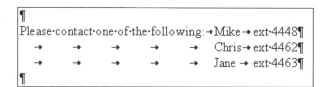

Figure 3.42 Text keyed in displaying hidden characters

ℹ️ Info

In this instance the tab stops are positioned in a convenient place and make the layout clear. Sometimes this is not the case and tab stops need to be positioned manually.

Exercise 4

Key in and position the name and extension number **Felicity ext 6884**.

Method

1   Enter the name and ext number using the above method. You will notice that, because the name Felicity is longer than the other names, the ext number is not lined up (Figure 3.43).

```
Please·contact·one·of·the·following:→Mike→ ext·4448¶
    →      →      →      →      →   Chris→ext·4462¶
    →      →      →      →      →   Jane → ext·4463¶
    →      →      →      →      →   Felicity  →   ext·6884¶
```

Figure 3.43 ext numbers are not aligned

2   To rectify this, add an extra tab space between Mike and ext, Chris and ext and Jane and ext (Figure 3.44).

```
Please·contact·one·of·the·following:→Mike→   →   ext·4448¶
    →      →      →      →      →   Chris→   →   ext·4462¶
    →      →      →      →      →   Jane →   →   ext·4463¶
    →      →      →      →      →   Felicity →   ext·6884¶
```

Figure 3.44 Extra tab spaces inserted

3   However, when you take the Show/Hide off, you will notice the ext numbers are rather a long way from the names. In order to move them closer to the names we will need to set a left tab stop.
4   Select all of the tabulated text.
5   From the **Format** menu, select: **Tabs.** The Tabs dialogue box appears (Figure 3.45).

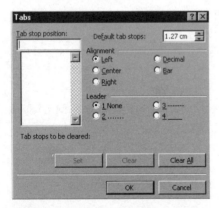

Figure 3.45 Tabs dialogue box

6   In the **Tab stop position** box, key in the first tab stop position (I am using 6.75 cm). Ensure **Alignment** is set to **Left**. Click on **Set**.
7   Key in the second tab stop position (I am using 8.25 cm). Click on **Set**.
8   Click on **OK**.
9   Your text and ruler will now look similar to that in Figure 3.46.

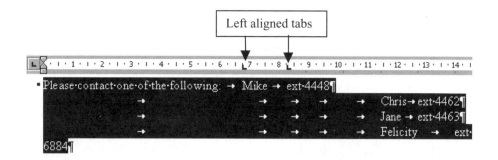

Figure 3.46 Tab set at 6.75 cm and 8.25 cm

10 To re-align the text, position the cursor before the **C** in Chris and press: the ← **Del** (**Backspace**). Repeat for Jane and Felicity. The text will now be aligned (Figure 3.47).

11 Remove the highlighting. Turn Show/Hide off.

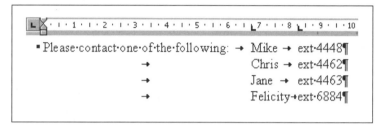

Figure 3.47 Text realigned

Info

Tabs can also be set by:

1   Selecting the tab type by clicking on the ⬛ Tab button until the type you require is showing.
2   Click once on the ruler where you want the tab stop to be.
3   Repeat as necessary.
4   To remove tabs, drag then off the ruler.

Setting leader tabs

Leader tabs have a line for the eye to follow to the tabulated entry eg

Dotted line leader ....tab

Continuous line leader _____tab

To set a leader tab:

1   From the **Format** menu, select **Tabs**.
2   In the Tabs dialogue box, set the tab as normal.
3   In the **Leader** section, set the format.
     It is well worth practising setting tabs. It is quite difficult to master.

4.3 Adding borders to a document

     ### Exercise 5

Add a border to the document.

Method

1 From the **Format** menu, select: **Borders and Shading.** The Borders and Shading dialogue box appears (Figure 3.48).

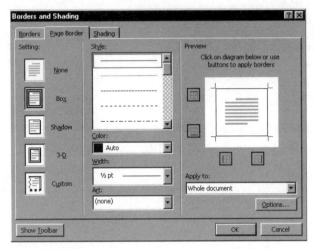

Figure 3.48 Borders and Shading dialogue box

2 Click on **Page Border** tab and make selections from the various sections (eg Box, Shadow, 3-D).
3 Click on **OK**.

 Info

You can apply borders to individual paragraphs by first selecting the relevant paragraph. Ensure the **Borders** tab is selected, format as required and make a selection in the **Apply to** section. Click on **OK**.

4.4 Saving documents under a different file format

 Exercise 6

Save the document in the normal way with the filename **Volunteers1**. Also save the file with the filename **Wanted** in a format suitable for posting on the web.

 Info

By default Word automatically saves files in the version of Word format you are using (ie WORD 97) and adds the extension .doc (eg Volunteers1.doc). However, it is possible to save documents in other formats.

 Method

1 Save the file with the filename **Volunteers1** in the normal way.

Saving a document in web format

2 From the **File** menu, select: **Save As**.
3 The Save As Dialogue box appears.
4 In the Save as type section, click on the down arrow to reveal a list. Scroll through to see the formats the document can be saved as (Figure 3.49).

5 Select: **HTML Document**. (This is a format suitable for the web.)

6 Key in the filename **Wanted**. Click on **Save**.

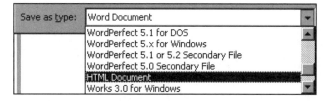

Figure 3.49 Scroll to see File formats available

Note: You can check the file format by selecting **Properties** from the **File** menu. Figure 3.50 shows the file **Wanted** has HTML encoding.

Info

File formats available

Being able to save files in different formats is extremely useful. It means that you can share files with others who do not have the same software or version of software that you are using. You can save in a previous version of Word, WordPerfect or Works format (WordPerfect and Works are other common word processors.) Other useful formats include:

Text Only – This is a basic no frills, compact text format. It can be opened and read by almost any software on any computer.

Rich Text Format – This format saves text and essential formatting. It can be opened accurately (keeping its layout) by most word processors.

Document template – This will save the style and page layout settings as the basis for another document.

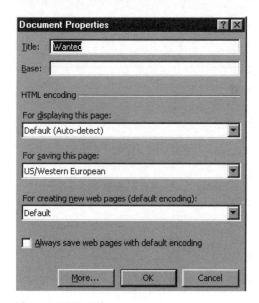

Figure 3.50 File properties

 Exercise 7

Print either of the saved files **Volunteers1** *or* **Wanted** and close both of them.

4.5 Working with templates and applying existing styles to a document

Info

Word documents are based on a template called Normal.dot. Templates act as a document model and store settings. Each template has various set styles associated with it. Normal is the default style applied to the default template for Word documents. It has the properties of being left aligned, Times New Roman, 12 pt. Other styles have their own properties, which are given next to the example text. Styles are linked to templates so Heading1 in one template may be Arial, right aligned, 16 pt, and in a different template could be Times New Roman, centred, 20 pt. You will notice that not all styles are suitable as they will upset bulleted lists, tab settings etc. Use the **Undo** button to recover original text style.

From the **Format** menu, you can experiment with **Autoformat** and **Style Gallery**. As you work through a document, styles you are using will be added to the Style list.

Exercise 8

Open the file: **Volunteers1** and format it using Word's default template existing styles.

Method

1 With the document open on screen, select the heading **VOLUNTEERS REQUIRED**.
2 Click on the down arrow in the | Normal ▼ | **Style** box.
3 Click on a suitable style.
4 Format some of the other text within the document in the same way.
5 Resave and close the document.

Exercise 9

Use a suitable Word template to produce a fax using your imagination to fill in the details.

Method

1 From the **File** menu, select **New**.
2 Click on the **Letters & Faxes** tab (Figure 3.51).

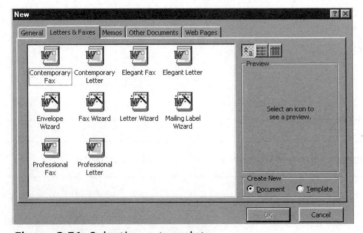

Figure 3.51 Selecting a template

3   Select a suitable template (you will see a Preview on the right-hand side) and then click on **OK**.
4   You may need to use Zoom to see all the document details.
5   Overwrite the text with your own.
6   Save the document and print one copy on A4 paper.

Info

Templates have fields that are already set up. These fields are marked in grey. If they are not marked in grey, from the **Tools** menu, select: **Options**. With the **View** tab selected, in the **Show** section, ensure that the **Field shading** box is set to **Always**. You can delete fields by selecting them and pressing **Delete**. Familiarise yourself with the different templates available in Word.

Creating a new template

 Method

1   Create the document you want to become a template.
2   From the **File** menu, select: **Save As**.
3   Key in the filename and in the **Save as type** box, select: **Document Template**.

Choosing Document Template automatically takes you to the Templates folder where it will be saved.

4   Click on **Save** and close the template document.

Opening the new template

 Method

1   From the **File** menu, select: **New**.
2   The New dialogue box is displayed.
3   With the **General** tab selected, you should be able to see your new template.
4   Click on it and then on **OK**.

4.6   Close the document and exit Word.

Section 4 word processing practice

Practice 7

Open a new Word document and key in the following text, formatting as shown:

GRAND OPENING
THE COMPUTER SHOP
SATURDAY 25 MARCH 2000

Format the three headings as follows: sans serif font, 26 pt, bold, font colour red, centre across the page

Many opening bargains including

Computers
Printers
Scanners
Modems
Software

Make into bulleted list. Format the bullets to match the theme of the flyer if possible

Come and see for yourself

Our prices are keen:
Internal Zip drives from £102.95
Hard drives 20Gb from........£129.99
Scanners from £79.99

Tabulate with decimal tab stops and leader dots

The first 10 customers will each receive boxed software of their choice up to the value of £50

We look forward to welcoming you!

All other formatting is at your discretion using styles. Add a shadow border around the whole document. Print on A4 paper in portrait display.

Save in a format suitable for posting on the web.

Practice 8

1 Load Word and the Professional Memo template. Insert the following text in the appropriate places:

   Company name: THE COMPUTER SHOP
   To: Andrea Whitely
   From: Paul Hunter
   Cc: Gita Meehan
   Today's date
   Subject: Delivery of laptops
   Message: Thank you for the delivery that I received this morning. As you know we are opening next Saturday and you would be most welcome to come and join us then. Please let me know if you can make it.
   Best Regards.

2 Save the document as **Fax laptops**.
3 Print one copy on A4 paper.

Section 5 Advanced – tables

In this section you will practise and learn how to:

* Create standard tables.

* Add/remove borders on a table.

* Change cell attributes: formatting, cell size, colour etc.

* Insert/delete columns/rows.

* Use the automatic table formatting tool.

5.1 Creating a standard table

 Exercise 1

Open a new Word document and create the following table using the Table facility.

Largest Continents	Largest Countries	Largest Oceans and Seas
Asia	Russian Federation	Pacific
Africa	Canada	Atlantic
North America	China	Indian

 Method

1 With a new document open, position the cursor where you want the top left corner of the table to be.

2 Hold down the left mouse over the ▦ **Insert Table** button: a grid appears.

3 Drag the mouse across and down the grid to result in the number of columns and rows required for the table (3 columns and 5 rows, including a blank row after the headings, Figure 3.52). Release the mouse.

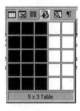

Figure 3.52 Setting cells for a new table

4 The empty table appears in your document.
5 Key in the table's text, pressing **Tab** to move to the next entry position (or use the arrow keys).

Info

If you press Enter by mistake, a line space will appear. Press: the ← **Del (Backspace)** key to remove the line space.

Working with borders

 Info

By default the table will automatically have borders around the table's cells.

 Method

6   Remove the borders on the table by positioning the cursor anywhere in the table and from the **Table** menu, select: **Select Table**.
7   From the toolbar, click on the down arrow next to the **Border** button. Click on **No Border** as shown in Figure 3.53.

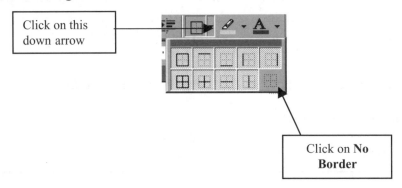

Click on this down arrow

Click on **No Border**

Figure 3.53 Deleting borders

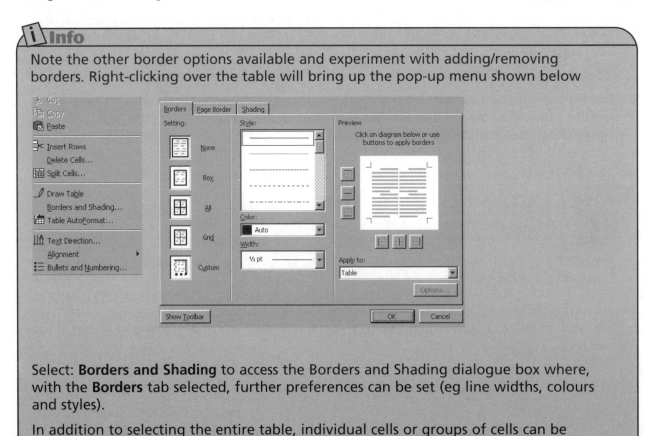 **Info**

Note the other border options available and experiment with adding/removing borders. Right-clicking over the table will bring up the pop-up menu shown below

Select: **Borders and Shading** to access the Borders and Shading dialogue box where, with the **Borders** tab selected, further preferences can be set (eg line widths, colours and styles).

In addition to selecting the entire table, individual cells or groups of cells can be selected so they can have different borders from the rest of the table.

8   Save the document with the filename **Geography**.

Info

You can also create tables manually using the Word's drawing facilities. (See section 7 for more details of how to use the drawing facilities).

5.2 Inserting/deleting rows/columns

Adding rows at the end of a table

 Exercise 2

Add a row at the bottom of the table and key in the following in the relevant places:

Antarctica   **Brazil**   **South China**

 Method

1   Position the cursor at the end of the last table entry (ie the **n** of Indian).
2   Press: **Tab**. A new row is created.
3   Key in the text and resave the document.

Inserting rows within the table

 Exercise 3

Insert a row between the one displaying North America and Antarctica and insert the text:

South America   **USA**   **Arctic**

 Method

1   Select the row below where you want to insert the new row by dragging the mouse over it.
2   From the **Table** menu, select: **Insert Cells**, then **Insert entire row** (Figure 3.54).
3   Click on **OK**.

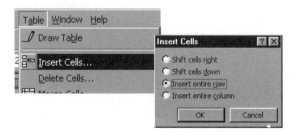

Figure 3.54 Inserting rows

4   Key in the text.

Deleting rows

 Exercise 4

Delete the row containing **Africa**, **Canada** and **Atlantic**.

Method

1   Select the row to be deleted.
2   Right-click over the selection; a pop-up menu appears (Figure 3.55).
3   Select: **Delete Cells.** The Delete Cells box appears (Figure 3.56). Click next to **Delete entire row**.

Figure 3.55 Pop-up menu   **Figure 3.56** Deleting a row

Deleting columns

 Exercise 5

Delete the middle column.

 Method

1   Select the column to delete by hovering over the top of the column. When a thick black arrow appears, click the mouse.
2   Right-click over the selection.
3   From the pop-up menu, select: **Delete Columns** (Figure 3.57).

Figure 3.57 Deleting columns

Inserting columns

 Exercise 6

Reinsert the deleted column (for practice purposes, do not use **Undo**).

 Method

1   Select the column to the right of the required position for the new column.
2   Right-click over the selection.

3 From the pop-up menu, select: **Insert Columns**.
4 Key in the text.

Inserting columns to the right of the last column in a table

Exercise 7

Insert a column, which will become the fourth column of the table and enter the following:

Largest Islands

Greenland
Borneo
Madagascar
Baffin

Method

1 Click just outside the right-hand column.
2 From the **Table** menu, select: **Select Column**.
3 Right-click over selection, select: **Insert Columns**.

Deleting an entire table

Deleting an entire table
Select the table by clicking anywhere in it and, from the **Table** menu, select: **Select, Table**.
Click on: the **Cut** button. Click on: the **Undo** button to reinstate the table!

5.3 Changing cell attributes

Exercise 8

Change the font in the heading row to Arial, 16 pt size, embolden and centre it.

Method

1 Select the heading row.
2 Format it in the usual way using the toolbar buttons.

Exercise 9

Change the background of the heading cells to a colour instead of white.

Method

1 Select the cells and right-click to bring up a pop-up menu.
2 Select: **Borders and Shading**.
3 Ensure the **Shading** tab is selected.
4 Click on a colour. Click on **OK**.

 Exercise 10

Change the width of the first column so it is narrower than the other three.

 Method

1 Select the first column.
2 Drag the right column border to the required position.

 Info

Tables are created with standard cell widths and heights. Change them by selecting them and dragging the borders, as in exercise 10. You can also use Autofit. With the table or cell(s) selected, from the **Table** menu, select: **Cell Height and Width**. With the **Column** tab selected, click on **Autofit**, then on **OK**.

5.4 Using automatic table formatting

Info

Word has several table formats to select from.

To AutoFormat a table

1 Position the cursor in the table.

2 From the **Table** menu, select: **Table AutoFormat**.

3 Select from the **Formats** list. (**Contemporary** is a good choice for the table you have just created.)

Experiment with the formats. Notice that some will not suit the table since they have headings in the first column.

5.5 Resave the document and print one copy on A4 paper

5.6 Close the document and exit Word

Section 5 word processing practice

Practice 9

1 Open a Word file.

2 Key in the following:

Earthquake Measurements

The magnitude of earthquakes is measured in units on the Richter Scale and their intensity on the Mercalli Scale.

3 Create the following table:

Mercalli	Richter	Characteristics
1	Less than 3.5	Only detected by seismograph
2	3.5	Only detected by people at rest
3	4.2	Similar to vibrations from HGV
4	4.5	Felt indoors; rocks parked cars
5	4.8	Generally felt; awakens sleepers
12	Greater than 8.1	Total destruction of area

4 Format the headings in bold, centre and make 2 pt larger than the other text.
5 Set the width of the columns so that they are in the same proportions as the columns above.
6 Delete all borders except the outside border and the bottom border of the headings row.
7 Shade the headings row cells in blue.
8 Insert a row after the one containing 5 in the Mercalli column and enter the details:

    6   **6.1**   **Causes general alarm; building walls crack**

9 Save the document with the filename **Earthquakes** and print the table only in landscape display on A4 paper.

Practice 10

1 Load Word and reload the file **Earthquakes** saved in Practice 9.
2 Delete the Mercalli column from the table (ensure an outside border is maintained).
3 Set in the left and right margins by 3 cm.
4 Change the font throughout the document (except the title) to Times New Roman, pt 16.
5 Centre the title and change to 20 pt.
6 Save the file with the filename **Earthquakes Richter**.
7 Print the file in landscape on A4 paper.

Section 6 Advanced – mail merge

In this section you will practise and learn how to:

* Create a data file for use in a mail merge.

* Merge a data file with a letter document or a label document.

What is mail merge?

Mail merge is the name given to the merging of information (usually names and addresses) with a standard document (usually a letter). The names and addresses are keyed in and stored in a database file and can be used with any standard document without having laboriously to key in the information again. Therefore it saves a lot of work. The end result of a mail merge is that the letter (or document) looks personal since it is impossible to tell that a number of other people have received the same letter.

6.1 Creating/opening a merge letter document

 Exercise 1

Open a new Word document and key in the following letter. Save the document with the filename: **Merge1**.

10 February 2000

Dear

Box Office Film Club

I am pleased to enclose details of our forthcoming film season.

All films will be shown in the Lecture Room on the Hemsley Hall Campus. Ample free parking spaces are available at both sides of the hall. If you are travelling by public transport, the nearest bus stop is in Regent Avenue. May I remind you that guest tickets will be on sale in the Hemsley Bar 20 minutes before each performance.

I look forward to welcoming you this season.

Yours sincerely

Club Secretary

Enc

Info

In this instance, since we do not already have a letter to merge, we are creating one. If the letter to merge already existed, you would open it in the normal way.

 Method

1 Key in the document, proofread, spellcheck and save it.
2 From the **Tools** menu, select: **Mail Merge**.
3 The **Mail Merge Helper** dialogue box appears (Figure 3.58).

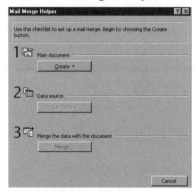

Figure 3.58 Mail Merge Helper dialogue box

4 In the **Main document** section 1, click on **Create**.
5 Select: **Form Letters** from the menu (Figure 3.59).

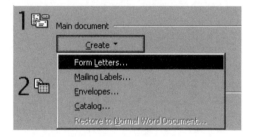

Figure 3.59 Creating form letters

6 When prompted, select: **Active window** (Figure 3.60).

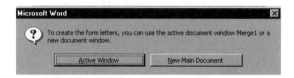

Figure 3.60 Select Active Window

7 The **Mail Merge Helper** dialogue box appears again (Figure 3.61). The filename and path of the merge document are now displayed in section 1.
8 In the **Data source** section 2, click on **Get Data**.

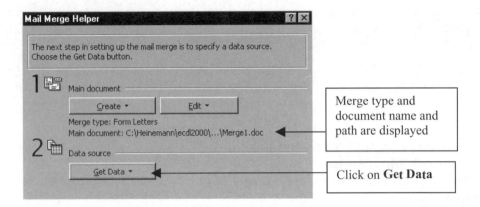

Merge type and
document name and
path are displayed

Click on **Get Data**

Figure 3.61 Mail Merge Helper dialogue box at section 2

9 Select: **Create Data Source** from the menu (Figure 3.62).

Figure 3.62 Creating a data source

10 The **Create Data Source** dialogue box appears (Figure 3.63).

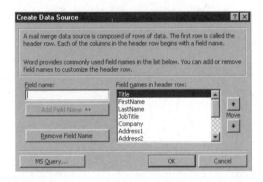

Figure 3.63 Create Data Source dialogue box

 Info

If the data source already existed, you would need to click on **Open Data Source**.

6.2 Creating a data source

Exercise 2

Use the following information to create the data source:

Mr Murray Dixon	**Miss Lynne Carter**
63 Harpur Street	**10 Brook End**
Luton	**Bedford**
LU6 1AS	**MK42 7NS**
Mr Jack Hobson	**Mrs Susi Malucci**
18 Ryton Close	**38 Sandhurst Road**
Bedford	**Luton**
MK43 6PZ	**LU5 3JU**

 Info

In the data source, each field contains the same type of information (eg in the 'Title' field Mr, Mrs, Miss etc are acceptable). Each addressee's data is called a record. By examining the data source information, you will see that the data has the following six fields: Title, FirstName, LastName, Address1, Address2 and PostalCode. Word provides commonly used field names, which are displayed in the **Field names in header row box**.

Method

1. With the **Create Data Source** dialogue box displayed (Figure 3.63), from the **Field names in header row**, delete the fields that are not relevant to our data source. To do this, click on the first field that is not required and click on **Remove Field Name**. Repeat for the other fields until the **Field names in header row** look like Figure 3.64.

Info

When a field is not displayed in the **Field names in header row**, you can add it by keying in an appropriate name in the **Field name** dialogue box (no spaces are allowed) and clicking on **Add Field Name**.

2. Click on **OK**. Save the data source when the **Save As** dialogue box is displayed.

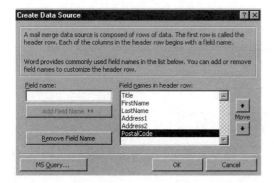

Figure 3.64 Field names in header row altered to reflect our data source

3 Click on **Edit Data Source** when the prompt box appears (Figure 3.65).

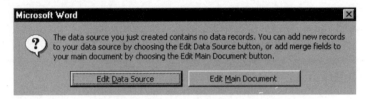

Figure 3.65 Select Edit Data Source to add data

4 The **Data Form** dialogue box appears (Figure 3.66).
5 Key in the information in the **Title** field, press: **Enter**.
6 Repeat until all the fields for the first name and address have been keyed in.
7 Press: **Enter** to move on to the next name and address.
8 Repeat until all the data has been entered.
9 Click on **OK**. Remember to press **Enter** after the final entry so it is included in the data file. The data is saved automatically.

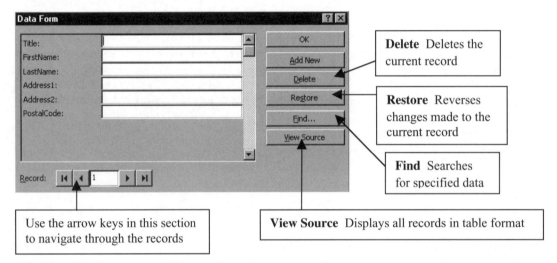

Figure 3.66 Data Form dialogue box

You are now returned to your original form letter. You will notice that the **Mail Merge** toolbar has appeared (Figure 3.67).

Figure 3.67 Mail Merge toolbar

6.3 Entering merge fields

 Exercise 3

Insert merge fields into the document.

Info

In order for Word to know where you want the data in the data source to be merged, it is necessary to insert merge fields.

Method

1   Position the cursor where you want the first merge field to be – in this case the addressee Title that will need to be placed under the date of the letter (Figure 3.68).
2   On the **Mail Merge** toolbar, click on the down arrow of the **Insert Merge Field** button (Figure 3.67).
3   Select: **field name required** (ie Title).
4   Repeat until all merge fields have been inserted.

   Note: Remember to press the space bar to leave spaces in the relevant places (eg between Title and FirstName).

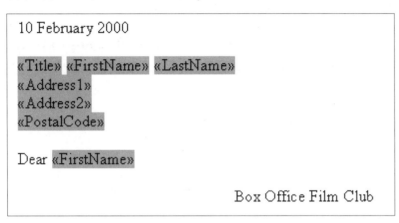

Figure 3.68 Merge codes inserted

6.4 Viewing merged document

1   To view the merged document click on the **View Merged Data** button on the Mail Merge toolbar.

2   The first merged document is displayed.

3   To view the other three, click on: the |◄ ◄ 1 ► ►| arrow buttons on the Mail Merge toolbar.

6.5 Printing the merged file

1   Click on: the ⊞ **Merge to Printer** button on the Mail Merge toolbar.
2   Print in the normal way.

6.6 Save all documents with new filenames where appropriate and exit Word

---

ⓘ Info

Use the **Merge to New Document** button to save the merged document with the current names and addresses in the database.

You can also use mail merge to produce address labels. To do this, at step 5 in 6.1, select: **Mailing Labels**. You will need to know what type of labels they are to set up the main merge document. There is a list of standard ones to choose from.

ⓘ Info

When mail merging, always proofread and spellcheck the main document carefully. One simple mistake has the potential of being duplicated many times!

Section 6 word processing practice

Practice 11

1   Key in the following letter to be used as a merge letter:

Insert date

Dear

Town and Country Enterprise AGM

Please note that the AGM will take place on Tuesday 20 June at 7.30 pm in the Coleridge Meeting Room. I am enclosing the agenda. Please let me know if you have any further items to add.

Coffee and light snacks will be provided. I look forward to seeing as many of our members as possible.

Yours sincerely

Jenny Jinx
Secretary

Enc

2   Create the data source:

Miss King	Mr Gregory	Dr Walpole
8 Wendover Place	10 George Gardens	118 Exeter Way
Kempston	Silsoe	Harrold
Bedford	Bedford	Bedford
MK32 9TG	BD27 9JU	MK55 2AS

3   Merge the letter with the data source.
4   Save all files.
5   Print the merged letters.

Practice 12

1   Use the data source created in Practice 11 to create mailing labels.
2   Print the labels on to A4 paper.

Section 7 Advanced – pictures, images and other objects

In this section you will practise and learn how to:

* Add an image to a document.

* Add AutoShapes to a document: change line colours, change AutoShape fill colours.

* Move images or drawn objects within a document.

* Resize a graphic.

* Import an image file, chart or graph into a document.

* Import a spreadsheet into a document.

7.1 Adding an image to a document

 Exercise 1

Open a new Word document and add an image suitable for a leaflet about a theatre visit.

 Method

1 Open a new Word document.
2 Position the cursor, by double-clicking the mouse, where you want the image to appear.
3 From the **Insert** menu, select: **Picture**, then **Clip Art** (Figure 3.69).

Figure 3.69 Inserting an image

 Info

Notice the other picture options here, notably **From File** (to import an existing picture file) and **Chart**, which are inserted in a similar way. As well as this method, objects including spreadsheets, graphs and graphics can be pasted in from other documents using the Cut and Paste buttons. When importing using the Insert File method, remember to set the file type to that which you are importing. As an example, if the file type is set to the Word document type and you want to insert an Excel file, the Excel file will not be displayed in the files list.

4 The **Insert Clip Art** dialogue box appears (Figure 3.70).

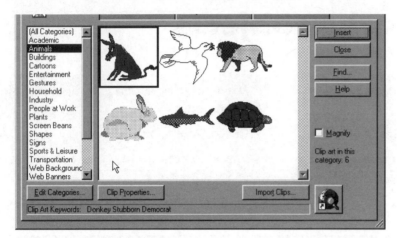

Figure 3.70 Insert Clip Art dialogue box

5 Select a suitable picture by clicking on a category and then on the Clip Art you have chosen.
6 Click on **Insert** (Figure 3.71).

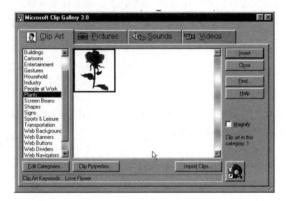

Figure 3.71 Click on Insert

7 The chosen image appears in the new document. It may be rather large!

Resizing an image

8 Click on it to select it. It will have handles on the corners and at the sides (Figure 3.72).

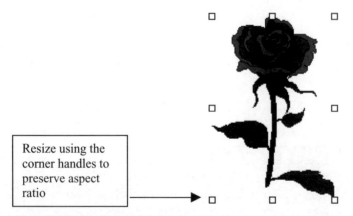

Resize using the corner handles to preserve aspect ratio

Figure 3.72 A selected image

9 Hover the mouse over a handle until a double-sided arrow appears. Drag a corner handle inwards to reduce the size of the image.

10 Drag the image to the centre using the mouse.

Info

You can also resize an image to an exact measurement by right-clicking on it and selecting: **Format Picture**. Click on the **Size** tab and key in the required measurements in the relevant boxes.

If you drag from a corner, the graphic will keep its aspect ratio (its original proportions). If you try to resize it from the side handles, it will lose its shape. Try it to see what happens. Use the **Undo** button to revert back to the original proportions.

Exercise 2

Underneath the image enter the following text. Format the text as you want.

Shakespeare Season

ROMEO AND JULIET

All this week at 7 pm in the Drama Studio

Tickets available at the door

7.2 Moving images within a document

Exercise 3

Move the image so that it appears at the bottom of the text.

Method

1   Select the image.
2   Drag the image to where you want it to appear.

7.3 Adding autoshapes to a document

Exercise 4

Using Word's drawing features, add some AutoShapes to the document.

Method

1   From the **View** menu, select: **Toolbars**, then click on **Drawing**.
2   The **Drawing** toolbar buttons are labelled in Figure 3.73 and are straightforward to use.
3   Practise adding AutoShapes, changing line colours and changing AutoShape fill colours.

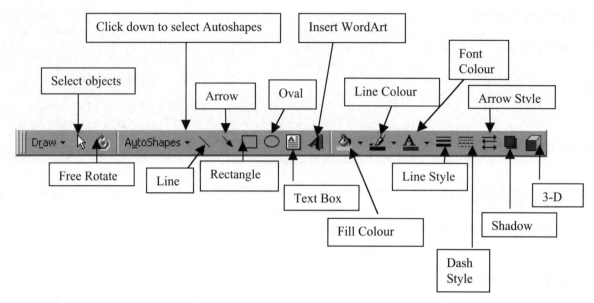

Figure 3.73 The Drawing toolbar

Adding AutoShapes

 Method

1 Click on the arrow of the **AutoShapes** button.
2 Select: a category (eg Basic Shapes).
3 Click on the shape you want to use.
4 On the document, click where you want to place the shape.
5 You can move the shape by dragging it with the mouse.

Filling a shape with colour

 Method

1 Select the shape to fill.
2 Click the down arrow on the **Fill Color** button.
3 Click on the chosen colour.

Filling a shape with a pattern

 Method

Follow steps 1 and 2 above.

1 Click on **Fill Effects**. The **Fill Effects** dialogue box appears.
2 Click on the **Pattern** tab.
3 Click on the chosen pattern. Click on **OK**.

Adding a line

 Method

1 Click on the **Line** button.
2 Position the cross hair where you want the line to start.
3 Hold down the left mouse button and drag the mouse to where you want the line to end. Release the mouse.

Formatting the line

 Method

1 Select the line by clicking on it. When it is selected, handles appear at each end.
2 Click on the **Line style** button.
3 Click on the line style you want.

Changing line colours

 Method

1 Select the line or object to change.
2 Click on the **Line color** button.
3 Click on a colour.

Adding a circle or ellipse

 Method

1 Click on the **Oval** button.
2 Hold down the left mouse button and drag out to the required shape.
3 Release the mouse.

Adding a box

 Method

Follow the method for a circle/ellipse, shown above.

> **i Info**
>
> Experiment with the other Drawing toolbar buttons to create some stunning effects. Also worth noting is the ◢ **Insert WordArt** button on the Drawing toolbar. Click on it to create special text effects.

7.4 Save, print and close the leaflet document and exit Word.

Section 7 word processing practice

Practice 13

Note: For this exercise you will need to have a simple Excel spreadsheet file to import at step 8. See Module 4.

1 Open a new Word document.
2 Key in the following text:

Working with imported objects

Possible logo idea

3 Import a piece of Clip Art in between the two headings.
4 Centre the Clip Art within the left and right margins.
5 Keeping its original aspect ratio, resize the Clip Art so it is approximately 4 cm square.
6 Insert a page break after the Clip Art.
7 At the top of the second page, key in the following text:

Inserting a spreadsheet file

8 Insert a simple spreadsheet file under the text.
9 Under the heading **Possible logo idea**, using Word's drawing features, create a simple design to be used as a logo for a sailing club, Aquamarine Sailing.
10 Number the pages at the top centre, starting at 5.
11 Copy the Clip Art and heading only to a new Word document.
12 Key in your name and the date as the first line of the first page of both documents.
13 Save and print both documents.

Note: There is no worked example of this exercise as versions will vary considerably.

Word processing quick reference guide

Action	Keyboard	Mouse	Right-mouse menu	Menu
Bold text	Select text to embolden			
	Ctrl + B	Click: the **B** **Bold** button	Font	Fo**r**mat, **F**ont
			Select: **Bold** from the **Font style:** menu	
Borders	Select text			
		Click: the ▣▾ Borders button		Fo**r**mat, **B**orders and Shading
	Select the border options you require			
Capitals (blocked)	**Caps Lock** Key in the text **Caps Lock** again to remove			Select text to be changed to capitals: Fo**r**mat, **Change Cas**e, **UPPERCASE**
Centre text	Select the text			
	Ctrl + E	Click: the ☰ **Center** button	**Paragraph** Select: **Centered** from the **Alignment:** drop-down menu	Fo**r**mat, **P**aragraph
Change case	Select the text to be changed From the **Fo**r**mat** menu, select: **Change Cas**e Select the appropriate case			
Close a file	**Ctrl + W**	Click: the ✕ **Close Window** icon		**F**ile, **C**lose
Columns		Click: the ▦ **Columns** button and drag the mouse until you have selected the number of columns		Fo**r**mat, **C**olumns Select the number of columns and options you require
Cut text	Select the text to be cut			
	Ctrl + X	Click: the ✂ **Cut** button	Cu**t**	**E**dit, Cu**t**
Delete a character	Press: **Delete** to delete the character to the right of the cursor Press: ← **(Backspace)** to delete the character to the left of the cursor			
Delete a word	Double-click: the word to select it Press: **Delete**			
Delete/cut a block of text	Select the text you want to delete			
	Delete or **Ctrl + X**	Click: the ✂ **Cut** button	Cu**t**	**E**dit, Cu**t**
Drawing features	To display the **Drawing** toolbar: From the **V**iew menu, select: **Toolbars**, **Drawing**			
	Select from the toolbar buttons (see Section 7)			
Exit Word		Click: the ✕ **Close Window** icon		**F**ile, E**x**it
Find text	**Ctrl + F**			**E**dit, **F**ind

Action	Keyboard	Mouse	Right-mouse menu	Menu
Font size	Select the text you want to change			
		Click: the ▼ down arrow next to the **Font Size** box Select: the font size you require	**Font**	**Format**, **Font**
			Select: the required size from the **Size:** menu	
Font	Select the text you want to change			
		Click: the ▼ down arrow next to the **Font** box Select: the font you require	**Font**	**Format**, **Font**
			Select: the required font from the **Font:** menu	
Formatting, copying	Select text to copy			
	Click: the 🖌 **Format Painter** button Double-click to copy to several pieces of text			
Headers and Footers				**View**, **Header and Footer**
Help	**F1**			**Help**, **Microsoft Word Help**
	Shift + F1			**Help**, **What's This?**
Hyphenation				**Tools**, **Language**, **Hyphenation**
Indenting		Click: the ⮕ **Increase Indent** button	**Paragraph**, **Indents and Spacing**	**Format**, **Paragraph**, **Indents and Spacing**
To remove indent		Click: the ⬅ **Decrease Indent** button	In the **Indentation** section, select your options as appropriate	
Insert image, file, chart, spreadsheet		Use 'Cut and paste' method	**Insert** *either* **Picture**, **Object**, **File** Resize using handles	
Insert text	Position the cursor where you want the text to appear Key in the text			
Justified margins	Select the text you want to change			
	Ctrl + J	Click: the ▤ **Justify** icon	**Paragraph**	**Format**, **Paragraph**
			Select: **Justified** from the **Alignment:** drop-down menu	
Line length, changing		Use the ruler (see below)		**File**, **Page Setup**, **Margins** (see separate table)
Line spacing			**Paragraph**	**Format**, **Paragraph**, **Indents and Spacing**
			In the **Spacing** section, select the options you require	

Action	Keyboard	Mouse	Right-mouse menu	Menu
Lists, bulleted and numbered	Click: the [icons] **Numbering** *or* **Bullets** button		**Bullets and Numbering**	**Format, Bullets and Numbering**
Load Word	In Windows 95 desktop			
		Double-click: the **Word** shortcut icon		**Start, Programs, Microsoft Word**
Mail merge	See separate section below			
Margins				**File, Page Setup, Margins**
Move a block of text	Select: the text to be moved Cut it and paste it where you want it moved to *or* Select: the text to be moved Click and drag: it to the correct position Release the mouse button			
Moving around the document	Use the cursor keys (see separate table for more)	Click: in the required position		
New file, creating	**Ctrl + N**	Click: the [icon] **New** button		**File, New**
Open an existing file	**Ctrl + O**	Click: the [icon] **Open** button		**File, Open**
	Select the appropriate directory and filename Click: **Open**			
Page break, adding	**Ctrl + Enter**			**Insert, Break, OK**
Page break, deleting	In Normal View, place the cursor on the page break Press: **Delete**			
Page display	Click: the appropriate **View** button			**View**
Page numbering				**Insert, Page Numbers** Select the required options
Page Setup				**File, Page Setup** (Choose from **Margins, Paper Size, Paper Source, Layout**)
Paper size	See Page Setup			

Action	Keyboard	Mouse	Right-mouse menu	Menu
Paragraphs – splitting/joining	*Splitting*: Move the cursor to the first letter of the new paragraph Press: **Enter** twice *Joining*: Move the cursor to the first character of the second paragraph Press : ← (**Backspace**) twice (Press: the spacebar to insert a space after a full stop)			
Print file	**Ctrl + P** Select the options you need Press: **Enter**	Click: the 🖶 **Print** button		**File**, **Print** Select the options you need and click **OK**
Print Preview		Click: the 🔍 **Print Preview** button		**File**, **Print Preview**
Ragged right margin	**Ctrl + L**	Click: the ▤ **Align Left** button	**Paragraph**	**Format**, **Paragraph**
				Select **Left** from the **Alignment:** drop-down menu
Remove text emphasis	Select text to be changed			
	Ctrl + B (remove bold) **Ctrl + I** (remove italics) **Ctrl + U** (remove underline)	Click: the appropriate button: **B** *I* U	**Font**	**Format**, **Font**
			Select **Regular** from the **Font Style:** menu	
Replace text	**Ctrl + H**			**Edit**, **Replace**
Save	**Ctrl + S**	Click: the 💾 **Save** button		**File**, **Save**
	If you have not already saved the file you will be prompted to specify the directory and to name the file If you have already done this, then Word will automatically save it			
Save using a different name or to a different directory	Select the appropriate drive and change the filename if relevant			
		Click: **Save**		**File**, **Save As**
Save file in a different file format	Save as above, select from **Save as type**			
Special characters/ symbols, inserting				**Insert**, **Symbol**
Spell check	**F7**	Click: the ✓ **Spelling and Grammar** button		**Tools**, **Spelling and Grammar**
Styles	Select from the Style box drop-down list Normal ▾			**Format**, **Style**

Action	Keyboard	Mouse	Right-mouse menu	Menu
Superscript Subscript			**Font**	**Fo**rmat, **Font**
Tables		Click: the ⊞ **Insert Table** button		**Table**, **Insert**, **Table**
	See Section 5			
Tabs	See separate information below			
Template, selecting				**File**, **New**, Select a template
Text colour	Select the text to colour			
		Click: the A· **Font Color** button	**Font, Font color**	**Fo**rmat, **Font**, **Font**, **colour**
Toolbar, modify				**View**, **Toolbars**, **Customize**
Undo	**Ctrl + Z**	Click: the ↶ **Undo** button		**Edit**, **Undo** (last action)
Widows and orphans				**Fo**rmat, **Paragraph**, **Line and Page Breaks** Select: **Widow/Orphan control**
Zoom	Click: the [100% ▼] **Zoom** button			**View**, **Zoom**

Moving around a document	
Move	**Keyboard action**
To top of document	**Ctrl + Home**
To end of document	**Ctrl + End**
Left word by word	**Ctrl + ←**
Right word by word	**Ctrl + →**
To end of line	**End**
To start of line	**Home**

Selecting text	
Selecting what	**Action**
Whole document	**Ctrl + A**
One word	Double-click on word
One paragraph	Double-click in selection border
Any block of text	Click cursor at start of text, press: **Shift**. Click cursor at end of text and click
Deselect text	Click in any white space

See Appendix for keyboard shortcuts.

Line lengths	
Line length	**Margin width**
12.7 cm (5″)	4.15 cm (1.63″)
14 cm (5½″)	3.5 cm (1.38″)
15.3 cm (6″)	2.85 cm (1.13″)
16.5 cm (6½″)	2.25 cm (0.88″)

Indentation using the ruler

Select the text you want to indent. Drag the respective markers (shown below) on the ruler to the location you want

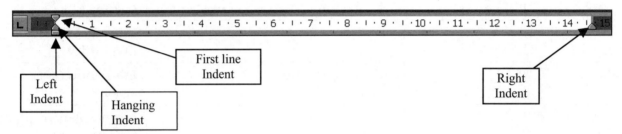

Hard spaces

It is better not to split some words at line ends (eg Mr Brown – Mr and Brown should be on the same line). A hard space, keeps the words on either side of it together. To insert a hard space, instead of just pressing the spacebar between the words, press: **CTRL + SHIFT + Spacebar**.

Mail merge

Creating and saving the merge document
1 Open a new Word file.
2 Key in the document.
3 Save the file.
4 From the **Tools** menu, select: **Mail Merge, Create, Form Letters** (or **Mailing Labels**).
5 Click on **Active Window**.

Creating and saving the data source
1 Click on **Get Data, Create Data Source**.
2 Add/Remove Field names as appropriate.
3 Click on **OK**.
4 Save the Data Source.

Editing the Data Source
1 Click on **Edit Data Source**.
2 Enter records.
3 Press: **Enter** after each record.
4 Click on **OK**.

Entering Merge Fields in merge document
1 Position the cursor where you want the first Merge Field to be.
2 On the Mail Merge toolbar click on **Insert Merge Field**.
3 Click on the field to insert.
4 Repeat until all Merge Fields are inserted.

Viewing merged document

Click on **View Merged Data** button on Mail Merge toolbar.

Printing the merged document

Click on **Merge to Printer** button on the Mail Merge toolbar.

Module 3 practice tasks

For this module you will need to have some files already set up. Ask your supervisor or tutor to prepare them for you.

Preparation

1 Create the following document and save as **Language**.

Sample extract

The people of Europe speak many different languages. English is termed a
'Germanic' language. This is because it is related to languages such as Dutch as well
as German. The links are not as easily noticed in modern day English but the
relationship is much clearer in Old English.

Old English is the name given to the English language up to $c.1150$. It was spoken
from the fifth century. It has different vocabulary, word meanings and spellings from
modern English. It even has letters, such as þ that are not found in modern English.
Its pronunciation and grammar and the ways it was used are also different. So much
so in fact that it would be most unlikely that Old English would be understood by the
average English speaker today. Although anyone speaking or writing English at the
beginning of the 21st century is using a language that dates back to Anglo Saxon
times.

There is also the subject of accents and dialects to consider. Accents can be defined
as the same language but differing in terms of pronunciation. Dialects differ in terms
of grammar and vocabulary as well.

Nearly one billion people speak different varieties of modern-day English. There are
mother tongue speakers, second language speakers and those for whom it is a foreign
language. The spread of English to different parts of the world and it being used as an
'international' language has caused much debate.

This is just a taster of course content. Please ring for details of courses in French,
German, Spanish, Welsh and Italian.

---

2 Create a name and address file and save as **Address**.

> **Title, Name, Address, Town, Postcode**
> **Miss, Smith, 29 Hobsons Way, Bristol, BS6 5ER**
> **Mr, Ahmed, 10 The Croft, Plymouth, PL2 7TR**
> **Mrs, Zwetsloot, 109 Green Lane, Oxford, OX3 9TU**
> **Dr, O'Byrne, 1 East Street, Norwich, NW8 4HR**
> **Ms, Jones, Bryn Mawr, Llanfairfechan, LL13 6AW**

Basic practice tasks

1 Start the word processor and open the file **Language**.

2 Save the document as **your initials module 3.**

3 Change the font in the document to Arial 12 pt.

4 Italicise the heading **Sample extract**.

5 Centre the heading.

6 Increase the font size of the heading to 18 pt.

7 Embolden the last paragraph.

8   Organise the courses in the last paragraph into bullet format.

9   Insert a blank line between paragraphs.

10 Insert a page break after the third paragraph.

11 Add a header **Languages Course Details** and today's date.

12 Format the header to Times New Roman 8 pt.

13 Add page numbers bottom right, starting at 5.

14 Insert your name in the first line of the document (Times New Roman 10 pt, right align).

15 Embolden all occurrences of the word **Old**.

16 Copy the first paragraph so it appears at the end of the document.

17 Change the line spacing of the first paragraph to 1.5.

18 Fully justify the second paragraph.

19 Insert the following text in the paragraph containing the bulleted list after **course content**:

    We have many others and we are confident that you will find something interesting and worthwhile.

20 Save the document with the name **your initials module 3 test1**.

21 Print the document.

22 Create a new document.

23 Copy all the text to the new document.

24 Change the font throughout to Arial 10 pt.

25 Delete the page break so that it fits on one page.

26 Set the line spacing to single throughout.

27 Set the top and bottom margins to 2 cm.

28 Save the document as **Merge**.

Advanced practice task 1

29 Working with the **Merge** document, insert the text **Ref 9054** under your name.

30 Set a left aligned tab to align the text on these first two lines at 12 cm.

31 On the line above the heading **Sample extract**, key in **Dear**.

32 At the end of the document enter the text **Yours sincerely**.

33 Insert a suitable Clip Art picture at the bottom of the document. Adjust the picture to an appropriate size so it fits neatly on the page.

34 Delete page numbers.

35 Save the document as **Merge2**.

Advanced practice task 2

1   Working with the **Merge2** document, delete the second paragraph.

2   Insert the following table after the first paragraph ending **is much clearer in Old English**.

1	Early Old English	450 – 850
2	Later Old English	850 – 1100
3	Middle English	1100 – 1450
4	Early modern English	1450 – 1750

3   Centre the table entries. Format in Times New Roman 12 pt.

4   Use the indent function to indent the last paragraph by approx 1.5 cm.

5   Set all other paragraphs with a first line indent of 0.8 cm.

6   Save the document as **Merge3**.

7   Print the **Merge3** document.

8   Open the Address file. This contains names and addresses of people who are to receive the letter. Insert merge fields for title, Name, Address, Town, Postcode. Merge the letter with the address list. Adjust the letter (if necessary) so that it fits on one page.

9   Save the file with the name **M followed by your initials**.

10   Print the merged file.

Advanced practice task 3

1   Select the **Contempory Fax** template.

2   Delete the field above *Facsimile Transmittal*.

3   In the To field, key in **Lycée la Rochelle**.

4   In the Fax field, key in **00 33 23 44 76 98 11**.

5   In the From field, key in your name.

6   In the Re field, key in **Exchange Visits**.

7   In the Pages field, key in **1**.

8   Mark the fax **Please Comment.**

9   Enter the message:

   Thank you for your interest. I will send details as soon as possible.

10   Save the fax as **Exchange** and print a copy.

Note: This is only a practice test. Successful completion does not imply certification of the module by the ECDL Foundation.

Spreadsheets

Section 1 Basics – getting started

In this section you will practise and learn how to:

* Load Excel.
* Understand the parts of the document window.
* Modify the toolbar display.
* Enter spreadsheet contents: insert text, numeric data, simple formulae.
* Understand common error messages.
* Use the Undo command.
* Delete cell contents.

* Use spellcheck.
* Save the spreadsheet structure and data.
* Print Preview and print the spreadsheet
* Display and print formulae.
* Use the page view magnification/zoom tool.
* Fit one page.
* Modify margins.
* Close the spreadsheet.
* Exit Excel.

1.1 Loading Excel

 Exercise 1

Load Excel.

 Method

Load Excel in the same way as other Office 97 applications, this time selecting:

| Microsoft Excel | from the **Start**, **Programs** menu *or* double-click on the ☒ **Excel** shortcut icon (if you have one).

1.2 Understanding the parts of Excel

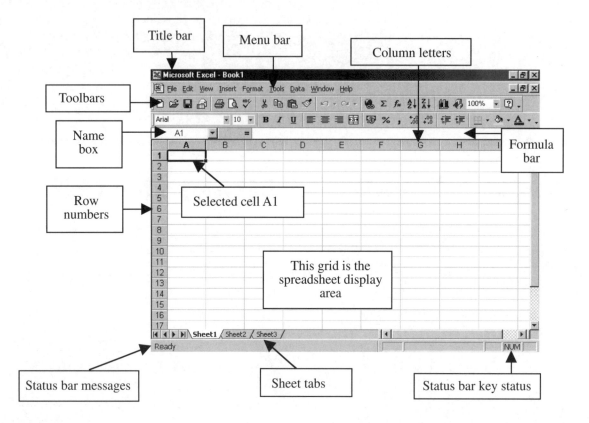

Figure 4.1 The application window

Toolbars

- The **Title bar** and **Menu bar** are at the top of the application window.

- The **Menu bar** has a set of *drop-down* menus that provide access to all Excel's features.

- The **Toolbar** is a row of buttons and selection boxes that, in most cases, provide shortcuts to the menu options or quick ways of entering values. (In Figure 4.1 the Standard and Formatting toolbars are shown.)

To modify the toolbar display

From the **View** menu, select: **Toolbars**. Click on the toolbars you want displayed so they have a tick next to them or select: **Customise** for further modifications options.

- The **Formula bar** displays the data you enter into your worksheet.

- The **Name box** displays the active cell reference.

- The **Sheet tabs** allow you to move from one spreadsheet to the next.

The **Status bar**, located at the bottom of the window, displays messages about current events. (NUM denotes the Num Lock key on your keyboard is on enabling you to use the number keys 0 to 9 to enter numbers quickly. Press the **Num Lock** key to turn Num Lock off so you can use the movement keys instead.)

The document window

This is the area between the Formula bar and the Status bar where your document (spreadsheet) is displayed. It consists of cells, each with their own cell reference (eg A1, B7, F9).

- Rows go across and are labelled 1, 2, 3, 4 ...
- Columns go down and are labelled A, B, C, D ...

Figure 4.2 shows the position of cell C6.

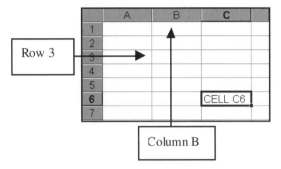

Figure 4.2 Cell references

 Info

Excel refers to a spreadsheet as a *worksheet*. When you open a new Excel document, it automatically consists of three sheets, one is displayed (Sheet1) and there are tabs for Sheet2 and Sheet3. These three sheets together are known as a *workbook*. You can add more sheets to a workbook if required. Throughout this book we will be using the word 'spreadsheet' instead of 'worksheet', and 'workbook' when more than one spreadsheet is being used in the same workbook.

Practice

Moving around the spreadsheet.

 Method

1 Move around your document using the scroll bars (Figure 4.3).

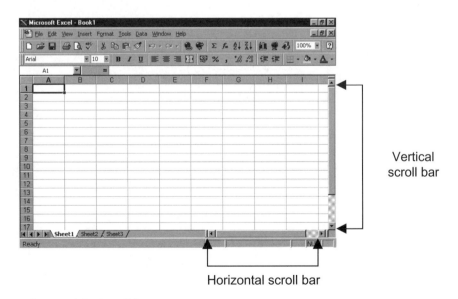

Figure 4.3 Scroll bars

2 Use navigation keys, **Page Up** and **Page Down**, to move up and down a page at a time.
3 Use the arrow keys.
4 Use the **Go To** command in the **Edit** menu. Enter the cell address (eg C5 in the **Reference** text box and click on **OK**).
5 Click in the **Name** box and key in the cell address.
6 Point to a cell with the mouse and click.
7 Pressing: **Ctrl + Home** takes you to the top of your spreadsheet. **Ctrl + End** will take you to the last entry on your spreadsheet when you have entered data.

1.3 Spreadsheet contents

You can enter:

- text
- numeric data
- formulae

(See Figure 4.4.)

Text entries are used for titles, headings and any notes. They are entries you do not want to manipulate arithmetically. Telephone numbers and stock numbers (although they contain numbers) are text entries.

Numeric data consists of numbers you want to add, subtract, multiply, divide and use in formulae.

Formulae are used to calculate the value of a cell from the contents of other cells. For instance, formulae may be used to calculate totals or averages. Formulae always start with an = sign. You must enter the formula for it to be activated by pressing: **Enter** or clicking on the ✔ **Enter** button on the Formula bar. A typical formula could look like:

$$=A1+A2 \ \ or \ =SUM(A1:A6)$$

The following operators (symbols) are used in formulae:

+ ADD   – SUBTRACT   * MULTIPLY   / DIVIDE

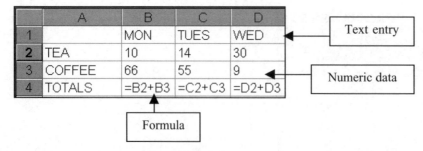

Figure 4.4 Types of spreadsheet entry

Excel follows arithmetic protocol when carrying out calculations. It will perform multiplication and division first and then addition and subtraction. Sometimes you will need to force Excel to carry out the calculation in a different order. As in arithmetic, this can be achieved by adding brackets around the appropriate part (eg when cell A1, A2 and A3 contain the numbers 4, 3 and 2, respectively).

A1+A2*A3 in numbers is 4+3×2 which Excel would calculate to be (carrying out the multiplication first) 10.

Placing brackets around the addition section forces Excel to perform the calculation differently. (A1+A2)*A3 in numbers is (4+3)×2 and gives the result 14.

1.4 Inserting text and numeric data

 Exercise 2

The spreadsheet in Figure 4.5 shows the sales figures for three different clothing companies over a four-month period. Enter the data into the spreadsheet.

 Method

1 Move to cell A1 and key in **Month**
2 Move to cell B1 and key in **Casualco**.
3 Move to cell C1 and key in **Smartco**.
4 Complete the worksheet in this way until it looks like Figure 4.5.

	A	B	C	D
1	Month	Casualco	Smartco	Partyco
2	May	990	830	770
3	June	550	880	220
4	July	330	660	700
5	August	400	550	820

Figure 4.5 Spreadsheet data

1.5 Entering simple formulae

 Exercise 3

Enter simple formulae to add up cell contents.

 Method

Remember formulae must always begin with the = sign

1 Move to cell A6 and key in **Total**
2 We wish to add up the sales figures for Casualco. These are displayed in cells B2, B3, B4 and B5. Move to cell B6 (where you want the answer to appear).

i **Info**

Notice as you key in that the formula appears on the Formula bar. It may be too long to fit the cell but you can ignore this. Cell references can be in upper or lower case. If you make a mistake use the **Undo** button or press: **Esc**.

Key in: **=B2+B3+B4+B5** and press: **Enter**.

The answer 2270 appears in cell B6.

3 Add up the sales figures for Smartco in the same way by keying in:

=C2+C3+C4+C5 and press: **Enter**. The answer 2920 appears in cell C6.

Your spreadsheet will now look like Figure 4.6:

	A	B	C	D
1	Month	Casualco	Smartco	Partyco
2	May	990	830	770
3	June	550	880	220
4	July	330	660	700
5	August	400	550	820
6	Total	2270	2920	

Figure 4.6 Totalling column B and column C

Using the built-in Sum function

On a large business spreadsheet you might need to add a huge number of cell contents and specifying each cell reference would not be practical. A quicker way to add up figures is by using one of Excel's built-in functions **SUM** to work out the formula as follows. To produce a Total for Partyco this time:

1 Move to cell D6 (where you want the answer to appear)

2 Key in **=SUM(D2:D5)** and press: **Enter**.

i **Info**

The colon between the cell references in the formula above means 'to include all the cells in between D2 and D5'

Your spreadsheet will now look like Figure 4.7:

	A	B	C	D
1	Month	Casualco	Smartco	Partyco
2	May	990	830	770
3	June	550	880	220
4	July	330	660	700
5	August	400	550	820
6	Total	2270	2920	2510

Figure 4.7 Totalling column D

Practise using the SUM function:

1 Delete the Totals of Casualco (cell B6) and Smartco (cell C6) by selecting them and pressing: **Delete**.

2 Add the Totals again this time using the SUM function, in cell B6 **=SUM(B2:B5)** and in cell C6 **=SUM(C2:C5)**

Using the AutoSum button

There is an even quicker way to add cell values using the Σ **AutoSum** button.

To practise this, let's add up the totals for the three clothing companies for each month:

1 Move to cell E1 and key in **Sales**.

2 Move to cell E2, the cell where you want the total sales for May to appear.

3 Click on the Σ **AutoSum** button. You will notice that a dotted line has appeared around cells B2 to D2.

ℹ️ Info

In this example Excel has automatically chosen the correct cells to add. Sometimes it chooses the wrong ones. If this happens you will need to select the cells you want by clicking on the cell you want to start with, holding down the left mouse and dragging the dotted line across the correct cells. Be careful you don't drag too far by mistake and include the cell where you want the answer to appear. The answer cell cannot be included in the formula. If you try to include in a formula the cell reference where you want the answer to appear, an error message will be displayed. Follow the instructions given in the error message.

Common error messages

This indicates the number in the cell is too long. Increasing the cell width will allow Excel to display the number.

#REF   A deleted cell reference may be present in your formula.

#VALUE   The formula contains text instead of number.

#DIV/0!   You have tried to divide a number by zero.

---

4 Press: **Enter**

5 The answer 2590 appears in cell E2.

6 Use this method to calculate the sales total for June, July and August.

ℹ️ Info

When adding Sales for July, you will notice Excel has mistakenly decided you now want to add the figures from above the cell and has placed the dotted line around cells E2 and E3. Move the highlight by clicking the first cell you want to add (B4) and dragging across to D4. Watch out for this.

	A	B	C	D	E
1	Month	Casualco	Smartco	Partyco	Sales
2	May	990	830	770	2590
3	June	550	880	220	1650
4	July	330	660	700	1690
5	August	400	550	820	1770
6	Total	2270	2920	2510	

Figure 4.8 Sales figures for June, July and August

1.6 Saving the spreadsheet structure and data

Exercise 4

Save the spreadsheet structure and data.

 Method

1 Spellcheck the spreadsheet using the **Spelling** button and correct any errors.
2 From the **File** menu, select: **Save As**. The Save As dialogue box appears (Figure 4.9).
3 Select the location where you want to save your file and key in **Sales** in the **File name** box.
4 Click on **Save**.

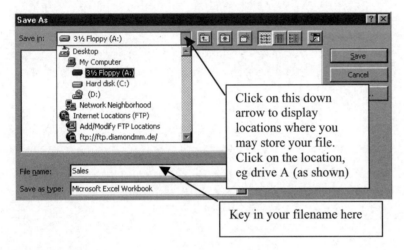

Figure 4.9 The Save As dialogue box

1.7 Printing spreadsheets

Exercise 5

Print a copy of the spreadsheet on to A4 paper.

 Method

Previewing a spreadsheet before printing

It is always wise to preview your spreadsheet before printing so you are sure it will print exactly what you want. This will save paper as well as effort.

1 Click on the [▣] **Print Preview** button.
2 Click on the **Zoom** option to see your spreadsheet contents. Click on **Zoom** again to return to default view.
3 If you are happy with the Print Preview, click on **Print**. (You can change default options here if necessary.)
4 Click on **OK**.

Info

Should you need to exit Print Preview at Step 3, press: **Esc** or click on **Close** to return to the spreadsheet.

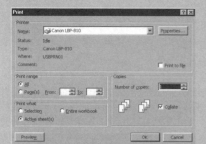

Note: In the **Print what** section of the **Print** dialogue box, you can select to print the Active sheet, the Entire workbook (when you have more than one sheet in a workbook) or a Selection (i.e. a subset of a spreadsheet that you have selected so that it is highlighted).

Printing on landscape

Info

By default the spreadsheet will print a Portrait display (the narrow edge at the top of the page). If you prefer or if your spreadsheet does not fit across the page, you can change the display to Landscape.

Portrait   Landscape

To do this from **Print Preview**, click on **Setup**:

1   Click on the **Page** tab, then on the **Landscape** option button.
2   Click on **OK**.

If not using Print Preview:

1   From the **File** menu, select: **Page Setup**.
2   Click on the **Page** tab, then on: the **Landscape** option button.
3   Click on **Print**.

1.8 Printing formulae

   Exercise 6

Print a copy of the spreadsheet showing the formulae used.

Info

It is useful to have a printout of the formulae used on your spreadsheet so you can cross-reference for accuracy.

Showing formulae on your spreadsheet

  Method

1   With your spreadsheet on screen, from the **Tools** menu, select: **Options**.
2   Click on the **View** tab (if not already selected); the Options dialogue box appears. Click on the **Formulas** check box so that a tick appears in this box. Click on **OK**. (Figure 3.10).

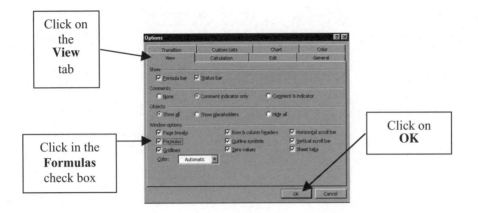

Click on the **View** tab

Click in the **Formulas** check box

Click on **OK**

Figure 4.10 Showing formulae

3 Notice that the columns have widened to accommodate the formulae.

4 If you are unable to see all the spreadsheet at once, use the ⬚ 100% ▾ **Zoom** button.

 Info

Depending on your setup, you may notice a vertical dotted line has appeared. This denotes a page break. Do not adjust the column widths, as when you take the 'show formulas' off, the cell widths will need altering again.

Info

For a quicker way to show formulae, press **Ctrl + '** (to the left of the number one key).

5 Check the spreadsheet using **Print Preview** (as above).
6 If it fits on one page, print as before.
7 If it does not fit, check it is on landscape by following the instructions above.

Info

If you really want to print in portrait display, try the following.

Fitting to 1 page
From the File menu, select: **Page Setup** *or* in **Print Preview**, click on **Setup**. With the **Page** tab selected, in the **Scaling** section, click in the option button next to **Fit to** 1 page.

Modifying margins
From the **File** menu, select **Page Setup** *or* in **Print Preview**, click on **Setup.** With the **Margins** tab selected, decrease the left and right margin settings.

 Exercise 7

Change the spreadsheet so that numbers are displayed instead of formulae.

Removing showing formulae

 Method

1 From the **Tools** menu, select: **Options**.
2 Click on the **View** tab (if not already selected), click in the **Formulas** check box so the tick is removed. Click on **OK**.

Info

A quick way to change back to values display is to press: **CTRL +**

1.9 Closing a spreadsheet file

Exercise 8

Close the spreadsheet file.

Method

From the **File** menu, select: **Close**.

1.10 Exiting Excel

Exercise 9

Exit Excel.

Method

From the **File** menu, select: **Exit**.

Section 1 spreadsheet practice

Practice 1

1   Load Excel.
2   On a new sheet enter the following data. *Leave the cells containing' formula' blank*

EXPENSES			
	AUG	OCT	NOV
RENT	350	350	350
ELEC	45	50	60
GAS	18	25	40
LOAN	55	55	55
PETROL	75	60	60
INS	20	20	20
TOTALS	formula	formula	formula

3 Enter a formula in the TOTALS row to calculate the total expenditure for AUG.
4 Save the spreadsheet as **p1 expenses**.
5 Print a copy of the spreadsheet showing values and another copy showing the formula used.
6 Close the spreadsheet file.

Practice 2

1 On a new sheet enter the following data. *Leave the cells containing 'formula' blank*

Sales						
	Tue	Wed	Thu	Fri	Sat	Total
Food	550	660	500	900	1120	formula
Menswear	200	190	300	100	780	formula
Fashions	300	625	740	800	1500	formula
Baby	200	450	380	590	213	formula
Cosmetics	77	90	65	105	280	formula
Home	500	1800	1200	954	3080	formula

2 Enter a formula to calculate the Total for the Food row.
3 Save the spreadsheet as **p2 store sales**.
4 Print a copy of the spreadsheet showing values and one showing the formula used.
5 Close the spreadsheet.

Section 2 Basics – editing

In this section you will practise and learn how to:

* Open an existing spreadsheet.

* Make alterations to cell contents.

* Select row/column.

* Delete/insert rows/columns.

* Copy or replicate formulae.

* Use find and replace.

* Understand relative and absolute cell references.

* Save existing spreadsheet to disk.

* Save the document under another file format, including saving a document for posting on the web.

* Print part of a spreadsheet.

2.1 Opening an existing spreadsheet

 Exercise 1

Recall the spreadsheet **Sales** saved in section 1.

 Method

1 With Excel loaded, click on the 📂 Open icon; the Open dialogue box appears (Figure 4.11).
2 Select the location where your file is stored by clicking on the down arrow.
3 Click on the filename **Sales**
4 Click on **Open**.

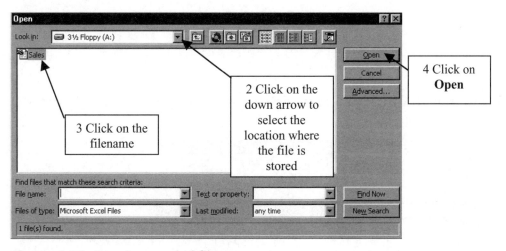

Figure 4.11 Opening a saved file

2.2 Making alterations to your spreadsheet

 Exercise 2

The Sales figures for Casualco should be **850** (not 990) in **May** and **470** (not 330) in **July**.

We need to change these entries.

Method

1 Move to cell B2 and key in: **850** and press: **Enter**.
2 Move to cell B4 and key in: **470** and press: **Enter**.

Info

Notice that the original figures are overwritten. Look what has happened to the Total for Casualco. You will see the formula has been recalculated to give a new Total. The Sales figures for May and July in column E have also updated to reflect the changes made. This will usually happen; when you change cell contents within a spreadsheet, all the formulae referring to that cell will be automatically recalculated.

Your spreadsheet will now look like Figure 4.12.

	A	B	C	D	E
1	Month	Casualco	Smartco	Partyco	Sales
2	May	850	830	770	2450
3	June	550	880	220	1650
4	July	470	660	700	1830
5	August	400	550	820	1770
6	Total	2270	2920	2510	

Figure 4.12 Updated spreadsheet

2.3 Deleting a row or column

 Exercise 3

It has been decided the figures for July are not required. Delete this row. Close up space, do not leave a blank row.

 Method

1 Click in the box to the left of the row to be deleted, (ie row 4). Row 4 is highlighted (Figure 4.13).

	A	B	C	D	E
1	Month	Casualco	Smartco	Partyco	Sales
2	May	850	830	770	2450
3	June	550	880	220	1650
4	July	470	660	700	1830
5	August	400	550	820	1770
6	Total	2270	2920	2510	

Click here →

Figure 4.13 Selecting a row

2 Right-click on the selected row; a pop-up menu appears (Figure 4.14):

Figure 4.14 Right-clicking displays a pop-up menu

3 Click on **Delete**. The spreadsheet contents move up to occupy the empty space and the figures are recalculated to reflect the change (Figure 4.15).

	A	B	C	D	E
1	Month	Casualco	Smartco	Partyco	Sales
2	May	850	830	770	2450
3	June	550	880	220	1650
4	August	400	550	820	1770
5	Total	1800	2260	1810	

Figure 4.15 Spreadsheet after deletion of the July row

Info

When you have a large spreadsheet, use **Find/Replace** from the **Edit** menu to locate/replace entries.

 Exercise 4

The figures for Smartco are no longer required; delete this column.

 Method

1 Click in the box at the top of the column to be deleted (ie C); column C is highlighted.
2 Right-click on the selection; a pop-up menu appears.
3 Click on **Delete**.

The spreadsheet now looks like Figure 4.16:

	A	B	C	D
1	Month	Casualco	Partyco	Sales
2	May	850	770	1620
3	June	550	220	770
4	August	400	820	1220
5	Total	1800	1810	

Figure 4.16 Spreadsheet after deletion of Smartco column

2.4 Copying or replicating formulae

 Exercise 5

Replicate the formula used to calculate the Total for Partyco so the Total for Sales is also calculated.

 Method

1 Move to the cell in which the formula you want to copy is stored. In this case C5.
2 Point the mouse at the bottom right of this cell until a thin black cross + appears, then holding down the left mouse, drag across cell D5 (where you want the formula copied to). Release the mouse.

The spreadsheet now looks like Figure 4.17.

	A	B	C	D
1	Month	Casualco	Partyco	Sales
2	May	850	770	1620
3	June	550	220	770
4	August	400	820	1220
5	Total	1800	1810	3610

Figure 4.17 Spreadsheet after replication of formula

 Info

If you make an error performing this procedure, click on the **Undo** button and try again.

Relative and absolute cell references

When replicating formulae, the cell references change to reflect their new position. (You can check this by looking at the formulae you have just replicated.) A relative cell reference will change relatively to its position on the spreadsheet. By contrast, an absolute cell reference will not change even if it is replicated or moved to another part of the spreadsheet. If you need to make a cell reference absolute, add a $ sign in front of the column letter and another $ sign in front of the row number or press: **F4**. (Eg cell reference C8 becomes $C$8 when it is absolute).

2.5 Adding a new column and a new row

 Exercise 6

Insert a new column, headed Jeansco, after Casualco and before Partyco. Enter the following information.

May, 600   **June, 700**   **August, 650**

Method

1 Click in the box at the top of the column after where the new column is to appear,(ie column C); column C is highlighted (Figure 4.18).

Click here

	A	B	C	D
1	Month	Casualco	Partyco	Sales
2	May	850	770	1620
3	June	550	220	770
4	August	400	820	1220
5	Total	1800	1810	3610

Figure 4.18 Selecting a column

2 Right-click on the selection; a pop-up menu appears. Click on **Insert** (Figure 4.19). An empty column appears.

	A	B	C	D	E
1	Month	Casualco	Partyco	Sales	
2	May	850	770	1620	
3	June	550			
4	August	400			
5	Total	1800			
6					
7					
8					
9					
10					
11					

Cut
Copy
Paste
Paste Special…
Insert ← Click on **Insert**
Delete
Clear Contents

Figure 4.19 Inserting a column

3 Enter the new text and data shown above.

The spreadsheet now looks like Figure 4.20.

	A	B	C	D	E
1	Month	Casualco	Jeansco	Partyco	Sales
2	May	850	600	770	2220
3	June	550	700	220	1470
4	August	400	650	820	1870
5	Total	1800		1810	5560

Figure 4.20 Spreadsheet after addition of Jeansco column and data

Calculate the Total for Jeansco, using one of the quicker methods you have learnt.

The Total is 1950.

 Exercise 7

It has been decided to reinsert the figures for July. Insert a new row for July with the following information: **Casualco 470**, **Jeansco 850**, **Partyco 700**.

Adding a new row

 Method

1 Click in the box to the left of the row below where you want the new row to appear, ie row 4. Row 4 is highlighted (Figure 4.21).

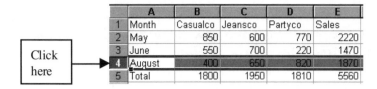

Click here

	A	B	C	D	E
1	Month	Casualco	Jeansco	Partyco	Sales
2	May	850	600	770	2220
3	June	550	700	220	1470
4	August	400	650	820	1870
5	Total	1800	1950	1810	5560

Figure 4.21 Adding a new row

2 Right-click on the highlighted row; a pop-up menu appears (Figure 4.22). Click on Insert. An empty row appears.

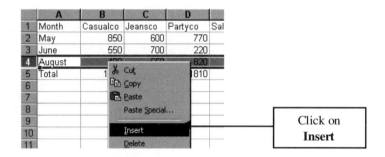

Click on
Insert

Figure 4.22 Inserting a row

3 Enter the new text and data shown above.

Replicate the formula from cell E3 to produce a Total in cell E4 for July Sales. The total is 2020.

2.6 Adding a new column or row to create new values

Exercise 8

Insert a new column for Shoesco after Partyco and before the Sales column. (see above, 2.5)

Enter the following data:

May, 621   June, 890   July, 700   August, 440

Replicate the formula from D6 to give a Total value in cell E6 for Shoesco.

Info

Note: These figures are at the end of the existing SUM cell range and are not automatically included in the Sales column figures. You will need to insert a new formula in cell F2 to reflect the new addition. This will then need to be replicated to the other cells in the Sales column. Look out for this.

Method

Follow the method in 2.5.

The spreadsheet now looks like Figure 4.23.

	A	B	C	D	E	F
1	Month	Casualco	Jeansco	Partyco	Shoesco	Sales
2	May	850	600	770	621	2841
3	June	550	700	220	890	2360
4	July	470	850	700	700	2720
5	August	400	650	820	440	2310
6	Total	2270	2800	2510	2651	10231

Figure 4.23 Spreadsheet after adding the Shoesco column

2.7 Save your spreadsheet as **Sales1** and print one copy on A4 paper

---

2.8 Saving documents under a different file format

Exercise 9

Save the spreadsheet with the filename **Clothing** in a format suitable for posting on the web.

Method

1 From the **File** menu, select: **Save as HTML**.

2 Follow the Internet Assistant Wizard's instructions.

Note: By default Excel automaticaly saves files in the version of Excel format that you are using (eg Excel 97), and adds the extension .xls (eg Sales.xls).

In Excel the **Save as type** menu in the **Save As** dialogue box (accessed through the **File** menu, Save As) includes options specific to spreadsheets (Figure 4.24). Compare this with Word in module 3, section 4.4.

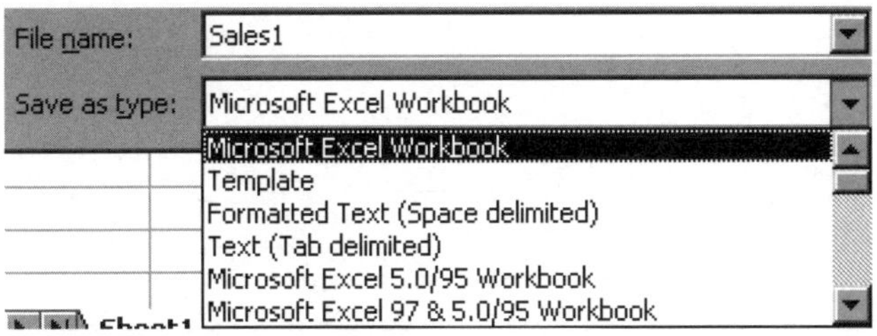

File name:	Sales1	▼
Save as type:	Microsoft Excel Workbook	▼

Microsoft Excel Workbook
Template
Formatted Text (Space delimited)
Text (Tab delimited)
Microsoft Excel 5.0/95 Workbook
Microsoft Excel 97 & 5.0/95 Workbook

Figure 4.24 Excel's Save as type menu

Info

File formats available

Being able to save files in different formats is extremely useful. It means that you can share files with others who do not have the same software or version of software that you are using. You can save in a previous version of Excel, Lotus 1-2-3 or Quattro Pro format (Lotus 1-2-3 and Quattro Pro are other common spreadsheet applications.) You can also save in dBASE format (dBASE is a common database format). Other useful formats include:

Text Only – This format saves spreadsheet contents but not formatting. The saved file can then be opened in programs that can handle text files. Note that only one sheet at a time can be saved in a text file so when saving ensure that you have the correct sheet displayed. Two commonly-used text formats include:

- **Text (Tab-delimited)** - items separated by tabs.
- **CSV (Comma delimited)** – items separated by commas.

Template – This saves text labels and formulae and formatting so that you can reuse it to create similar spreadsheets with different content.

2.9 Printing part of a spreadsheet

 Exercise 10

Print only the figures for Casualco (include the month labels).

Method

1 Select columns A and B (by dragging the mouse over the cells) to and including row 6.
2 From the **File** menu, select: **Print**
3 In the **Print what** section, click in the option box next to **Selection** (Figure 4.25)
4 Click on **OK**.

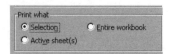

Figure 4.25 Printing a selection

2.10 Close the file and exit Excel.

Section 2 spreadsheet practice

Practice 3

1 Recall the spreadsheet **p1 expenses** saved in section 1.
2 Change the following entries:

   ELEC in **AUG** should be **35** not 45.
   GAS in **NOV** should be **54** not 40.

3 Delete the row containing the PETROL data.
4 Replicate the formula for TOTALS for the other months.
5 In a new column after the NOV column, enter the heading **TOTAL**.
6 Enter a formula to calculate the total RENT for the months shown.
7 Replicate the formula for the other costs.
8 Save the spreadsheet with the name **p3 expenses**.
9 Insert a new column headed **SEPT** after the AUG column. Enter the data:

RENT	350
ELEC	50
GAS	20
LOAN	55
INS	20

10 Adjust the spreadsheet to show the **TOTAL** for **SEPT**.
11 Calculate an overall total in the TOTALS row/TOTAL column.
12 Save the spreadsheet as **p3 expenses1** and print one copy.
13 Print the TOTAL column only showing the formulae used.
14 Close the file.

Practice 4

1 Recall the spreadsheet **p2 store sales** saved in section 1.
2 Change the following entries:

   Menswear Thu should be **350** not 300.
   Baby **Fri** should be **610** not 590.

3 Delete the Cosmetics row.
4 Replicate the formula calculating the Total for Food to all other departments.
5 Save the spreadsheet as **p4 store sales**.
6 Insert a column headed **Profit** after the Total column.
7 Calculate the profit for the Food department (20% of Total).
8 Replicate this formulae for the other departments.
9 Insert a new column headed **Mon** before the Tue column and enter the following data:

Food	25
Menswear	180
Fashions	270
Cosmetics	52
Home	25

10 Adjust the spreadsheet formulae as necessary.
11 Save the spreadsheet as **p4 store sales1** and print one copy.
12 Close the spreadsheet file.

Section 3 Basics – formatting

In this section you will practise and learn how to:

* Align cell contents.

* Modify column width and row height.

* Change text font, size and colour, italicise, embolden, change orientation.

* Use the Average function in formulae.

* Format number styles: decimal places, integers, with commas.

* Display numbers as percentages.

* Format currency symbols.

* Format different date styles.

* Use copy/cut and paste to duplicate/move cell contents in another part of the spreadsheet.

* Select non-adjacent rows or columns.

* Open several spreadsheets.

* Sort data into ascending/descending alphabetical/numerical order.

* Move cell contents between active spreadsheets.

* Use AutoFill to increment entries.

* Add borders.

* Add header/footer.

3.1 Aligning cell contents

i Info

When data is first entered, text is placed on the left of the cell and numbers line up on the right. Three toolbar buttons can be used to apply a new alignment to a range that is selected.

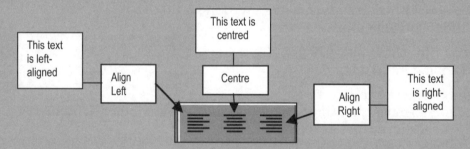

To align cell contents

Select the cells to be realigned.

Click on: the appropriate toolbar button.

 Exercise 1

1 Reload the spreadsheet **Sales1** saved at the end of section 2.

2 Display the headings: **Month, Casualco, Jeansco, Partyco, Shoesco** and **Sales** so **Month** is left-aligned and **Casualco, Jeansco, Partyco, Shoesco** and **Sales** are right-aligned.

Method

The heading Month is already left justified. To right justify the other headings:

1 Select cells B1 to F1 (Figure 4.26).

	A	B	C	D	E	F
1	Month	Casualco	Jeansco	Partyco	Shoesco	Sales
2	May	850	600	770	621	2841

Figure 4.26 Cells selected to right justify

2 Click on the **Align Right** toolbar button.

 Exercise 2

Enter a main heading **CLOTHING COMPANY SALES** and centre it across the top of the spreadsheet.

 Method

1 Insert a row at the top of the spreadsheet.
2 Key in the text.
3 Select cells A1 to F1 (ie the full extent of spreadsheet columns).
4 Click on the ▦ **Merge and Centre** button to centre the heading across the selected cells.

Info

Text can also be given a different orientation (ie text vertical instead of horizontal). To do this, from the **Format** menu, select: **Cells** (or whatever you have selected). Ensure the **Alignment** tab is selected and alter settings in the **Orientation** section.

3.2 Modifying column width/row height

Info

By default each column starts with a width of about nine numeric characters. You can adjust the column width so it accommodates the entry within.

 Exercise 3

Change the heading **Sales** so it becomes **Monthly Sales.**

 Method

1 Move to cell **F2**.
2 Click the cursor in front of the **S** of **Sales** (Figure 4.27) on the formula bar and key in **Monthly** and a space. Press: **Enter**.

Figure 4.27 Positioning the cursor to alter a heading

3 The entry is now too long to fit the cell. There are several ways to widen the column:

Info

Click on: the **Undo** button after trying each method so that you can practise.

a Position the cursor at the column border; a double arrow appears. Drag the right-hand edge of the column border (next to the column letter) to the right (Figure 4.28).

Figure 4.28 Changing column width

b Position the cursor as above and double-click the mouse (this action widens to fit the longest entry exactly).
c With the cell selected, from the **Format** menu, select: **Column, AutoFit Selection** (Figure 4.29).
d Select the column. From the **Format** menu select: **Column**, then **Width**. Key in the new width. Click on **OK**.

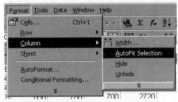

Figure 4.29 Widening a column using the menus

Info

Row height can be changed following these methods substituting Row for Column.

3.3 Changing text: size, colour, italicise and embolden

 Exercise 4

In the Total row, change the font size to 16 pt and the text colour to blue. Italicise and embolden this row only.

 Method

1 Select the row.
2 Use the **Font Size** button to change to 16 pt.
3 Use the **Font Color** button to change the text to blue.
4 Use the **Italic** and **Bold** buttons to italicise and embolden.

Info

The font type can also be altered in this way. Excel's default font is Arial, point size 10.

3.4 Using the Average function

Exercise 5

Enter a column headed **Average Sales** after the **Monthly Sales** column. Right justify this heading and widen the cell to display this heading in full. Recentre the main heading to incorporate this additional column.

In cell **G3**, enter a formula to work out the **Average Sales** for **May**. Replicate this formula to cells **G4**, **G5**, **G6** and **G7**.

Info

Excel has a built in AVERAGE function to work out averages. The syntax is:

=AVERAGE(cell ref:cell ref).

Note: In some spreadsheet applications you can shorten the word AVERAGE. Excel does not allow this.

Method

In this instance, in cell G2 the formula is =AVERAGE(B3:E3). After replicating this formula, the spreadsheet will now look like Figure 4.30:

	A	B	C	D	E	F	G
1			CLOTHING COMPANY SALES				
2	Month	Casualco	Jeansco	Partyco	Shoesco	MonthlySales	Average Sales
3	May	850	600	770	621	2841	710.25
4	June	550	700	220	890	2360	590
5	July	470	850	700	700	2720	680
6	August	400	650	820	440	2310	577.5
7	Total	2270	2800	2510	2651	10231	2557.8

Figure 4.30 Spreadsheet with the Average Sales column added

Notice there are integers (whole numbers) in cells G4 and G5. Cells G6 and G7 have 1 decimal place (one numeric character after the decimal point) and cell G3 has two decimal places (two numeric characters after the decimal point).

3.5 Using integer and decimal format to display numbers

Exercise 6

Display the numeric data in the Average Sales column as integers (whole numbers).

Method

1 Select the column entries ie cells G3 to G7.
2 Right-click the highlighted area; a pop-up menu appears (Figure 4.31).

Figure 4.31 Formatting cells

3 From the menu, select: Format Cells; the **Format Cells** dialogue box is displayed (Figure 4.32).
4 Click on the **Number** tab.
5 In the **Category** box, click on **Number**.
6 In the **Decimal places** box, use the down arrow to set to zero (0).

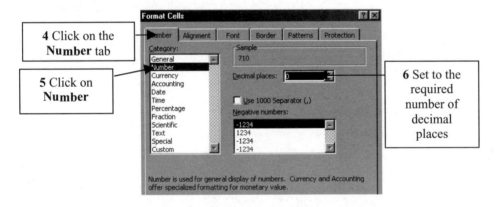

Figure 4.32 Format Cells dialogue box

7 Click on **OK**.

The Average Sales column will now look like Figure 4.33:

Average Sales
710
590
680
578
2558

Figure 4.33 Average Sales figures displayed as integers

 Exercise 7

Change the display of the numeric data in the Average Sales column to two decimal places (ie two places after the decimal point).

Info

General is the default number format in Excel and displays numbers with decimal places as in Figure 4.30. If a number has a zero positioned, as in 577.50 (the zero here is said to be 'trailing'), Excel will only display 577.5 in the General format.

You can also use the **Increase Decimal/Decrease Decimal** buttons to increase and decrease decimal places. Try this method in the following exercise.

The Average Sales column should now look like Figure 4.34.

Average Sales
710.25
590.00
680.00
577.50
2557.75

Figure 4.34 Average Sales figures displayed with 2 decimal places

---

3.6 Save the spreadsheet as **Sales2** and print one copy on A4 paper

---

3.7 Adding currency symbols

Exercise 8

In the Total row, Average Sales column, display the entry with the UK currency symbol (£).

Method

1 Select the relevant cell (ie G7).
2 Click on the **Currency** button.

Info

Excel inserts the £ symbol, a comma to denote thousands and two decimal places so pence can be displayed. Other currency options can be chosen by selecting: **Cells** from the **Format** menu.

With the **Number** tab selected, in the **Category** section, select: **Currency** and then choose from the drop-down list in the Symbol section.

Commas to denote thousands (so 1234 becomes 1,234) can be inserted in numeric data using the **' Comma Style** button.

Other symbols can be inserted as follows:

1   From the **Start** menu, select: **Programs, Accessories, System Tools, Character Map**.

2   Select the symbol required by clicking on it.

3   Click on: **Select**.

4   Click on: **Copy**.

5   Click on: **Close**.

6   In Excel click on: the **Paste** button.

3.8 Copying and pasting

Exercise 9

Copy the heading so that it appears in cell **A10**.

Using drag and drop

 Method

1 Select the cell where the heading is displayed.
2 Hover the mouse over the selection border; the mouse pointer appears.
3 Hold down the **Ctrl** key; a + appears alongside the arrow.
4 Hold down the left mouse button and drag the selection to its new position (ie cell A10).
5 Release the mouse.

Exercise 10

Copy the Month and the Shoesco columns so they appear adjacent underneath the main spreadsheet.

Copying using the Copy and Paste buttons selecting non-adjacent columns/rows

 Info

Adjacent means the cells are next to one another. Non-adjacent means that they are not. The columns in this exercise are non-adjacent.

 Method

1 Select the Month column data, hold down the **Ctrl** key and select the Shoesco column data.
2 Click on the **Copy** button. Flashing dotted lines appear around the selected columns.
3 Select the cells where you want to copy to, (eg A11 to B16).
4 Click on the **Paste** button.
5 Press: **Esc** to remove flashing lines.
6 Reformat the copied cells if necessary.

 Info

Similarly you can cut and paste. This time do not hold down the **Ctrl** key.

3.9 Displaying numbers as percentages

Exercise 11

In cell C11, enter the text **Commission rates**. Enter the following commission rates for the months of May, June, July and August respectively: **0.05**, **0.08**, **0.1** and **0.025**. Display these commission rates as percentages.

Method

1 Enter the text and data in the usual way.
2 Select the cells containing the commission rates.
3 Click on the **%** **Percent Style** button. The commission column now looks like Figure 4.35.

Commission
5%
8%
10%
3%

Figure 4.35 Commission figures changed to percentages

3.10 Save the spreadsheet as **Sales3** and print one copy on A4 paper.

3.11 Opening several spreadsheets

Exercise 12

Keeping the current spreadsheet open, open a new workbook. Copy the main heading to the new spreadsheet. Save the new workbook with the filename **Employees**.

Method

1 Click on the New button.
2 Return to the **Sales3** spreadsheet display (Window menu, click on the filename).
3 Select the cell to copy, then click on the **Copy** button.
4 Return to the new spreadsheet, select: cell A1 and click on the **Paste** button.
5 Press: **Esc** to remove the selection from the **Sales3** spreadsheet.
6 Save the new spreadsheet.

Exercise 13

Enter the following employee information:

Surname	First Name	Start Date
Jones	Julia	14/02/96
Gill	Sanjit	10/10/99
Wright	Dominic	29/09/98
Jones	Bronwen	02/05/00

Note: You can also move the contents using the **Cut** button at Step 3.

3.12 Changing date format

Exercise 14

Change the date format so that the date is displayed in the format 14-Feb-96.

 Method

1 Select the cells to format.
2 From the **Format** menu, select: **Cells**.
3 The Format Cells dialogue box is displayed (Figure 4.36).

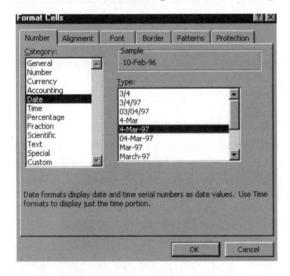

Figure 4.36 Formatting date styles

4 Ensure **Number** tab is selected.
5 In the **Category** section, click on: **Date**.
6 In the **Type** section, select the relevant format and click on: **OK**.

3.13 Sorting data into ascending/descending alphabetical/ numerical order

Exercise 15

Display the employee names in alphabetical order of surname.

Sorting using the toolbar Ascending/Descending buttons

 Method

1 Select the cell range containing the employee details (ie A3 to C6).

   Note: It is necessary to select the First Name and Start Date columns so they will be kept together when sorted.

2 Click on the **Ascending** button.

Info

The Ascending button will sort from A to Z or from the lowest number to the highest number in the selection. There is also a **Descending** button to use when necessary. This sorts from Z to A and from the highest number to the lowest number in a selection.

 Exercise 16

Sort the employee data, first by Surname, then by First Name (both in alphabetical order).

 Method

1 Select the cell range containing the employee details as before (ie A3 to C6).
2 From the **Data** menu, select: **Sort**.
3 The Sort dialogue box appears (Figure 4.37).
4 In the **Sort by** section, select: Surname.
5 In the **Then by** section, select: First Name.
6 Ensure that **Ascending** is chosen in both cases.
7 Click on **OK**.

Figure 4.37 Sorting on more than one criteria

You will notice that because Bronwen begins with a B and Julia begins with a J, Bronwen Jones is now placed above Julia Jones.

 Exercise 17

Copy the whole of the Employees spreadsheet except the main heading to a second sheet within the same workbook. Name the new sheet **Personnel data**.

 Method

1 Select the spreadsheet contents excluding the main heading.
2 Click on the **Copy** button.
3 Open a new sheet by clicking on the **Sheet2** tab (Figure 4.38).

Figure 4.38 Selecting a new sheet

4   The new sheet appears.
5   Click on the **Paste** button.
6   Reformat the cells as necessary.
7   Right-click on the new sheet tab (Sheet2) and key in the new sheet name.

3.14 Formatting numbers as text

 Exercise 18

Key in **Tel** in cell D1 and key in the employee telephone numbers as follows

Sanjit	**01234 752999**
Bronwen	**01234 621900**
Julia	**01908 554211**
Dominic	**01908 338554**

 Info

Entries such as telephone numbers or stock references, although consisting of numeric data, should be entered as text so they will be ignored in calculations.

 Method

1   Select the cells that are to contain the telephone numbers (ie cells D2 to D5)..
2   From the **Format** menu, select: **Cells**.
3   With the **Number** tab selected, in the **Category** section, select **Text** from the list.
4   Click on **OK**.
5   Key in the telephone numbers.

Note: It is essential you format the cells *before* entering the telephone numbers.

3.15 Using AutoFill

 Exercise 19

Add the following column headings after Tel:

Week1, **Week2**, **Week3**, **Week4**

 Info

If a cell contains a number, date or time period that can extend in a series, by dragging the fill handle of a cell, you can copy that cell to other cells in the same row or column. The values are incremented. For example, if a cell contains MONDAY, Excel can quickly fill in other cells in the row or column with TUESDAY, WEDNESDAY and so on.

Method

1 Enter **Week1** in cell E1.
2 Hover the mouse over the Fill handle at the bottom right of the cell; a cross appears.
3 Hold down the left mouse and drag across the cells you want to AutoFill (ie F1,G1 and H1).
4 Release the mouse.

3.16 Adding borders

Exercise 20

Add a border round the entire spreadsheet and a double line border under the heading row.

 ## Method

1 Select the spreadsheet.
2 Click on the down arrow of the ▦ **Borders** button.
3 Select: the outside Border as shown in Figure 4.39.

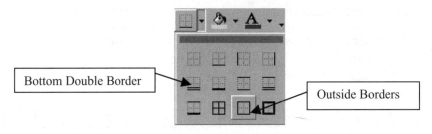

Figure 4.39 Adding borders

4 Select the heading row.
5 Using the **Borders** button, select: bottom double **Border** (Figure 4.39).

3.17 Adding headers/footers

Exercise 21

Add the header **Produced by (your name)** and the **date** to all the open spreadsheets.

 ## Method

1 With the spreadsheet displayed, from the **File** menu, select: **Page Setup**.
2 The Page Setup dialogue box appears. Click on the **Header/Footer** tab so it is displayed (Figure 4.40).
3 Click on **Custom header**.

Note: Click on Custom Footer to add information to a footer.

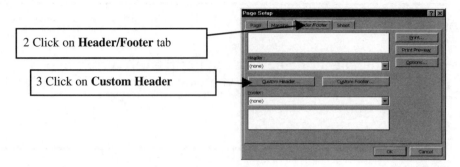

2 Click on **Header/Footer** tab

3 Click on **Custom Header**

Figure 4.40 Adding headers/footers

4 The Header dialogue box appears. Click in the **Left** section and key in **Produced by (your name)**. Click in the **Center** section and key in the date (or click the **Date** button (Figure 4.41) if you are certain your computer's date is set correctly – the actual date will not be displayed here but you can practise to see what appears on your Print Preview).

5 Click on **OK** and on **OK** again

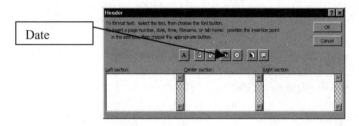

Date

Figure 4.41 Inserting an automatic date into a header

6 Switch to the next open spreadsheet and repeat.

i Info

Creating a footer. At Step 3 click on: **Custom Footer** and repeat as for Custom Header.

3.18 Save and print all your work on A4 paper

3.19 Close all files and exit Excel.

Section 3 spreadsheet practice

Practice 5

1 Recall the spreadsheet **p3 expenses1** saved in section 2.
2 Right align all the column headings.
3 Change the row headings to Times New Roman, 12 point, red, bold.
4 Display all the numeric data in the months columns to one decimal place.
5 Display the numeric data in the TOTAL column in UK pounds to two decimal places.
6 Add a new column after the TOTAL column headed **AVERAGE**.
7 Set the new column width to 10.
8 Enter a formula in the AVERAGE column to calculate the average expenditure over the four-monthly period.
9 Display the numeric data in the AVERAGE column in integer format.
10 Open another sheet in the same workbook.
11 On the new sheet, enter the heading **YEARLY EXPENSES**. Format it to bold, 18 pt.
12 Copy the row headings from the first sheet to column A.
13 Enter column headings **1 Jan 99** and increment on a monthly basis to 1 Dec 99.
14 Copy the data for AUG to NOV to the appropriate columns on the second sheet.
15 Format the dates in the column headings to Jan-99, Feb-99 etc.
16 Add a border round the whole spreadsheet.
17 Add the header **ECDL 2000** in the centre and today's date at the right.
18 Save the workbook as **p5 expenses2**.
19 Print a copy of both sheets in landscape display.
20 Close the file.

Practice 6

1 Recall the spreadsheet **p4 store sales1** saved in section 2.
2 Embolden and centre the column headings.
3 Display all the numeric data to two decimal places.
4 Enter a new row headed **Average Store Sales**. Widen the column to display the new entry.
5 In this row, enter a formula to calculate the average daily sales for Mon.
6 Replicate the formula for the other days.
7 Change the row heading Fashions to **Ladies Fashions**.
8 Copy the Food and Home rows and column headings to a new workbook file.
9 Insert a row at the top of the new spreadsheet with the title **HOUSEHOLD SALES**. Centre the heading across the cells.
10 Insert a column before the Profit column headed **Predicted Increased Sales**.
11 Enter **0.012** in the Food row and **0.035** in the Home row.
12 Format the figures in this column as %.
13 Add a border around the spreadsheet and between the cells.
14 Save the Household Sales spreadsheet file as **p6 house** and the original spreadsheet as **p6 store sales2**.
15 Print both spreadsheet files fitting them each to one page.
16 Close both files.

Section 4 Advanced – charting

In this section you will practise and learn how to:

* Produce different types of charts/graphs from spreadsheet figures to analyse data: pie charts, column charts, bar charts, line graphs, comparative charts.

* Edit or modify a chart/graph: add a title or label, change the scale, change the colours.

* Change the chart type.

* Move and delete charts/graphs.

4.1 Different types of display

There are many different ways of graphically displaying data in Excel. The main ones we will be looking at are pie charts, column/bar charts, line graphs and comparative charts.

Info

Excel uses the word 'chart' and not 'graph' for all its graphical displays. In the UK we usually tend to differentiate between charts and graphs. For our purposes we can assume they are the same thing.

4.2 Pie chart

A pie chart consists of a circle divided into a number of segments. In this example (Figure 4.42), there are three segments representing eye colours: blue, brown and green, in Tutor Group A. The largest segment is brown and it tells us that 44% of Tutor Group A have brown eyes, the next largest is green with 30%, and the smallest blue with 26%. There is a legend (key) to show us which colour or shade represents which eye colour.

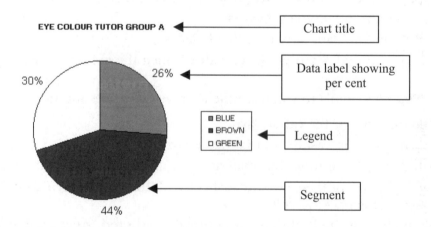

Figure 4.42 Pie chart

Chart components

* *Chart title.* The chart title should be descriptive and clear.

* *Data labels.* On a pie chart you can show percentage values or actual values. You can show the legend labels next to the segments instead of a legend.

- *Legend.* A legend is a key showing the different colours/shades that correspond to the data represented in the pie chart.

- *Segment.* The pie chart is made up of segments that represent different data types.

4.3 Column and bar charts

A column chart uses columns to represent values. The chart has two axes, the *x* (horizontal) axis and the *y* (vertical) axis. The *x* axis usually represents data that does not change, such as days of the week. The *y* axis usually represents values that fluctuate, such as monetary values or temperatures. This type of chart is useful for showing comparisons.

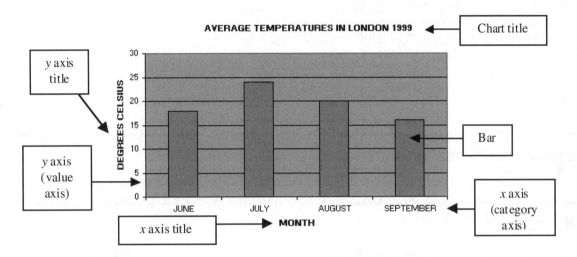

Figure 4.43 Column chart

The column chart (Figure 4.43) shows the comparison of average temperatures in London. The tallest column, July, shows the overall hottest average temperature. The shortest column, September, shows it was the coolest month of those shown.

A bar chart has the same components as a column chart but shows the categories vertically and the values horizontally (Figure 4.44).

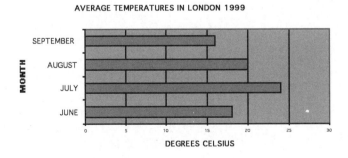

Figure 4.44 Bar chart

4.4 Line graph

A line graph (Figure 4.45) shows trends in data at equal intervals. Points on the graph are joined together to form a continuous line. It has properties in common with a column/bar chart, such as *x* and *y* axes and axes titles.

The line graph (Figure 4.45) shows the trend is up, as the line is going up and not down. Sales have been increasing steadily since 1990. I have drawn a line from the *x* axis, at the end of 1990, to the plotted line and then drawn a line to the *y* axis. Where this line joins the *y* axis the value can be read, just over £11 million. This was the value of sales at the end of 1990.

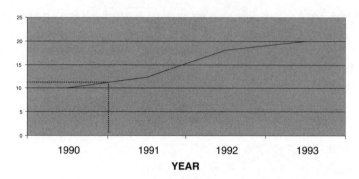

Figure 4.45 Line graph

4.5 Comparative charts

A comparative chart is used to compare sets of data. The display shows two or more columns (if a comparative column chart, Figure 4.46) or two or more lines (if a comparative line graph, Figure 4.47) of the same item.

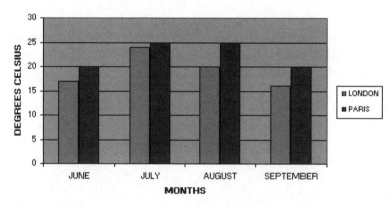

Figure 4.46 Comparative column chart

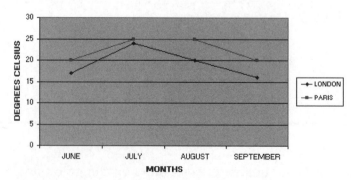

Figure 4.47 Comparative line graph

4.6 Creating a pie chart

Exercise 1

Produce a pie chart showing the branch sales percentages for Le Cafe for the months January to June 2000.

 Method

1 Load Excel as shown in section 1.
2 Enter the data so that the spreadsheet looks like Figure 4.48.

	A	B
1	BOURNEMOUTH	22
2	LUTON	28
3	MANCHESTER	19
4	READING	31

Figure 4.48 Data entered into spreadsheet

3 Save the spreadsheet as **Le Cafe**.

Now create the pie chart including labels for each of the segments. Enter the following heading **BRANCH SALES PERCENTAGES – JANUARY TO JUNE 2000**.

 Method

1 Select all of the data entered ie cells A1 to B4.
2 Click on the ▥ Chart Wizard button.
3 **Step 1 of 4 Chart Wizard** dialogue box appears: **Chart Type** (Figure 4.49).

   a The **Standard Types** tab is selected. In the **Chart type** box, click on **Pie**.
   b In the **Chart sub-type** box, click on the top left pie type, as shown. This is usually already selected as the default setting.

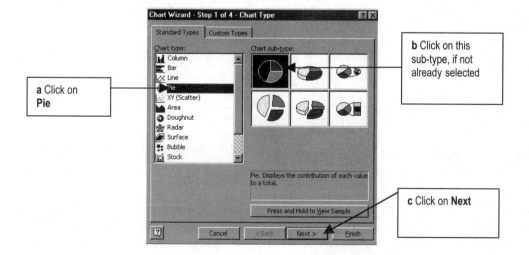

Figure 4.49 Step 1 of Chart Wizard

Info

There are many different types of pie charts you can choose. To view and learn the names of charts, click and hold the mouse on: **Press and hold to view sample**. Try experimenting with the different types.

4   **Step 2 Chart Wizard** dialogue box appears: **Chart Source Data** (Figure 4.50).

There is a preview of the pie chart together with a legend – a key to the different segments of the pie. With the **Data Range** tab selected, the data range selected is shown as:

=Sheet1$A$1:$B$4

Ignoring the $ signs, this represents Sheet1, cells A1 to B4. Click on **Next**.

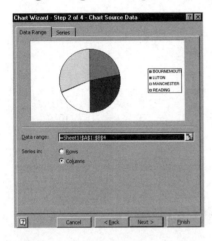

Figure 4.50 Step 2 of Chart Wizard

Data points and data range/series

Info

A data point is the name given to each plotted item and its related value eg Bournemouth 22 represents a data point. A data range/series is the name given to all the data points being plotted.

If you have made an error in selecting the data range to chart, at Step 2 of Chart Wizard, either:

1   Change the data range by clicking in the **Data range** box and keying in the correct range *or*
2   Click on the **Collapse Dialog** button, reselect the cell range and click on the **Collapse Dialog** button again.

In this example we have the data series in columns. You will need to click in the **Rows** option button if the data series is in rows. Should you need to go back a step, after Step 1 of Chart Wizard, click on **Back**.

In some circumstances Excel will automatically make assumptions about what is a data range. It will try to include, for example, years (ie 1993, 1994, 1995) since they are numerical (if they have not been formatted as text, see 3.14). In such cases you will need to carry out steps 1 and 2 (above) to overwrite Excel's assumptions. Then click on the **Series** tab. In the **Category (X) axis labels**, click on the **Collapse Dialog** button and select the cell range for year labels. Click on the **Collapse Dialog** button again.

You can chart non-adjacent rows or columns. Select the first row/column to chart, hold down **Ctrl** when selecting other non-adjacent rows/columns.

5 **Step 3 Chart Wizard** dialogue box appears: **Chart Options** (Figure 4.51).

   a With the **Titles** tab selected, click in the **Chart title** box and key in: **BRANCH SALES PERCENTAGES – JANUARY TO JUNE 2000**

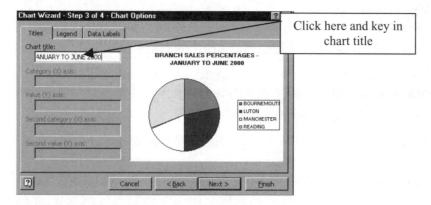

Figure 4.51 Step 3 of Chart Wizard

You will not be able to see all the title as it will scroll out of the visible section. Do not press **Enter** as this will result in moving to the next step of Chart Wizard. If you have pressed **Enter**, click on **Back**.

   b Click on the **Legend** tab (Figure 4.52).
   c Click in the **Show legend** tick box to remove the tick.

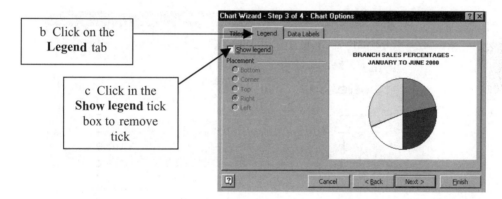

Figure 4.52 Removing a legend

---

i Info

You have been asked to show labels for each of the segments, not a legend. Having segment data labels and a legend duplicates information and will make the chart appear cluttered.

---

   d Click on the **Data Labels** tab (Figure 4.53).
   e Click in the **Show label** option button.
   f Click on **Next**.

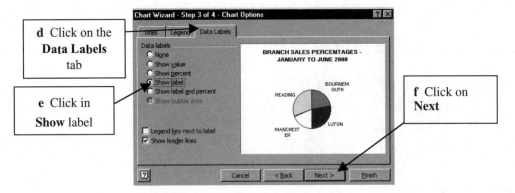

Figure 4.53 Showing labels

> **i Info**
>
> You will notice labels and choices appear on the chart preview as you work. If you make an error, carry out the instruction again.

6 **Step 4 Chart Wizard** dialogue box appears: **Chart Location** (Figure 4.54).

   a Click in the **As new sheet** option button.
   b In the box shown, key in the name **Le Cafe pie**.
   c Click on **Finish**.

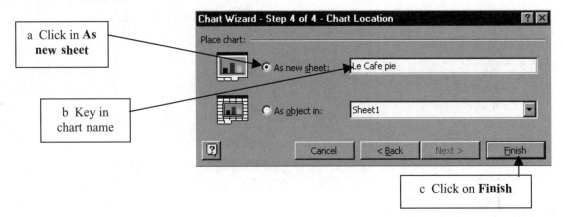

Figure 4.54 Step 4 of Chart Wizard

> **i Info**
>
> You can choose **As object in** if you want the chart to appear on the same sheet as the data. The chart will be located in the workbook (the same file) whichever option you choose.

The completed pie chart is displayed as shown in Figure 4.55.

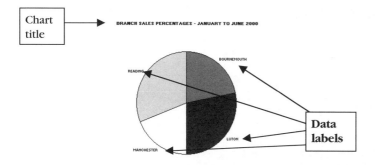

Figure 4.55 Completed pie chart

Info

Should you need to make any changes (eg to the title, labels or want to change to a different type of chart), with the chart displayed on screen, right-click in the chart area to bring up the menu shown. You will notice the menu items in the second section (ie below **Format Chart Area)**, correspond to the dialogue boxes of Chart Wizard. Choose from these options.

Note: Pie charts are generated from one data series only. You will need to bear this in mind if you are changing **Chart Type** (you may need to hide some of the original data for a correct result). **To hide data**: Select the column(s)/row(s) to hide. Right-click on the selection and select: Hide. **To unhide data**: Select the columns/rows on either side of the hidden data. Right-click on the selection, select: Unhide.

4.7 Saving the chart

 Method

Click on the **Save** button.

Info

You can use this quick saving method as you have already saved the chart as **Le cafe pie**. The chart and spreadsheet will be saved as one file.

You can swap between chart and spreadsheet display by clicking the relevant tab in the worksheet tab area at the bottom of the currently displayed spreadsheet.

▶️\ Le Cafe pie \ **Sheet1** / Sheet2 / Sheet

4.8 Printing a chart

 Method

1 With the chart displayed on screen, from the **File** menu, select **Print**. The **Print** dialogue box appears (Figure 4.56).

2   In the **Print what** section, ensure the **Active sheet** option button is selected.
3   Click on **OK**.

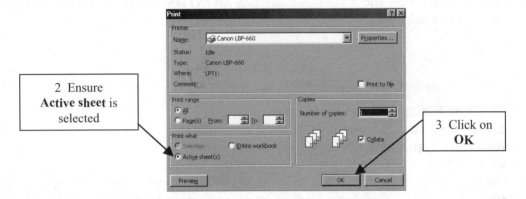

2 Ensure **Active sheet** is selected

3 Click on **OK**

Figure 4.56 Print dialogue box

Info

By default the chart will print in landscape format.

4.9 Closing the chart

 Method

From the **File** menu, select: **Close**.

Info

You can close with the display on either the chart or the spreadsheet. They will be saved together with the same filename.

4.10 Creating a column chart

 Exercise 2

Produce a column chart showing the monthly sales from January to June for the Bournemouth branch.

 Method

1   Load Excel *or* click on the **New** button if Excel is already loaded.
2   Enter the data so your spreadsheet looks like Figure 4.57.

	A	B
1	MONTH	SALES - £
2	January	25000
3	February	23000
4	March	40000
5	April	11000
6	May	24000
7	June	19000

Figure 4.57 Spreadsheet with data entered

3   Save the spreadsheet as **BOURNEMOUTH SALES.**

Now create the column chart. Title the *x* (horizontal) axis **MONTHS** and the *y* (vertical) axis £. Give the bar chart the title **MONTHLY SALES, BOURNEMOUTH BRANCH.**

Method

1   From the data entered, select all except the headings (ie cells A2 to B7).
2   Click on the **Chart Wizard** button.
3   **Step 1** (of 4) **Chart Wizard** dialogue box appears: **Chart Type**.
    a   With the **Standard Types** tab selected, click on **Column**.
    b   In the **Chart sub-type** box, click on the top left chart. (This is the default so may already be selected.)
    c   Click on **Next**.

Practise

Experiment with the different chart types.

4   **Step 2 Chart Wizard** dialogue box appears: **Chart Source Data**. Click on **Next**.
5   **Step 3 Chart Wizard** dialogue box appears: **Chart Options**.
    a   Select the **Titles** tab (if not already selected), click in the **Chart title** box and key in:

MONTHLY SALES, BOURNEMOUTH BRANCH.

    b   Click in the **Category** (*x*) axis box and key in: **MONTHS**
    c   Click in the **Value** (*y*) axis box and key in: **£**
    d   Click on the **Legend** tab.
    e   Click in the **Show legend** tick box to remove the tick.
    f   Click on **Next**.

6   **Step 4 Chart Wizard** dialogue box appears: **Chart Location**.

    a   Click on **As new sheet** option button and key in the name **SALESBAR**
    b   Click on **Finish**.

The completed column chart is shown in Figure 4.58.

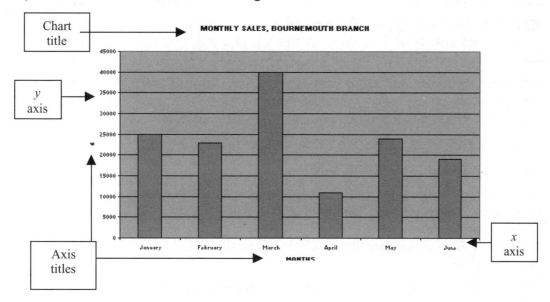

Figure 4.58 Completed column chart

7   Save the chart as in 4.7.
8   Print the chart as in 4.8.
9   Close the chart as in 4.9.

4.11 Creating a line graph

Exercise 3

Produce a line graph showing the monthly sales from January to June for the Luton branch.

 Method

1 Load Excel or click on the **New** button.
2 Enter the data so your spreadsheet looks like Figure 4.59.

	A	B
1	MONTH	SALES - £
2	January	17000
3	February	14000
4	March	26000
5	April	32000
6	May	22000
7	June	20000

Figure 4.59 Spreadsheet with data entered

3. Save the spreadsheet as **LUTON SALES**.

For the data create a line graph. Enter the *x* (horizontal) axis title **MONTHS** and the *y* (vertical) axis **£**. The title for the graph is **MONTHLY SALES – LUTON BRANCH**.

 Method

1 Select the data entered in the cells A2 to B7.
2 Click on the 📊 **Chart Wizard** button.
3 **Step 1** (of 4) **Chart Wizard** dialogue box appears: **Chart type**.

   a With the **Standard Types** tab selected, click on **Line**.
   b In the **Chart sub-type** box, click on the top left chart.
   c Click on **Next**.

4 **Step 2 Chart Wizard** dialogue box appears: **Chart Source Data**. Click on **Next**.
5 **Step 3 Chart Wizard** dialogue box appears: **Chart Options**.

   a Select the **Titles** tab, click in the **Chart title** box and key in:

   MONTHLY SALES – LUTON BRANCH

   b Click in the **Category (*x*) axis** box and key in: **MONTHS**
   Click in the **Value (*y*) axis box** and key in: **£**
   c Click on the **Legend** tab.
   d Click in the **Show legend** tick box to remove the tick.
   e Click on **Next**.

6 **Step 4 Chart Wizard** dialogue box appears: **Chart Location**.

   a Click on **As new sheet** option button and key in the name **SALES LINE**
   b Click on **Finish**.

   The completed line graph is displayed as shown in Figure 4.60.

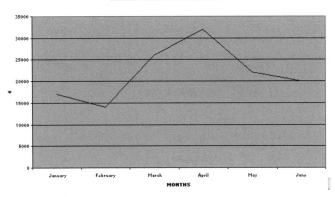

MONTHLY SALES - LUTON BRANCH

MONTHS

Figure 4.60 Completed line graph

7 Save the graph as in 4.7.
8 Print the graph as in 4.8.
9 Close the graph as in 4.9.

4.12 Creating a comparative chart

 Exercise 4

Produce a comparative column chart showing Le Cafe's daily sales of hot chocolate and cappuccino from Sunday to Saturday.

 Method

1 Load Excel *or* click on the **New** toolbar button.
2 Enter the data so the spreadsheet looks like Figure 4.61.

	A	B	C
1		HOT CHOCOLATE	CAPPUCCINO
2	SUN	100	220
3	MON	40	98
4	TUE	70	106
5	WED	103	155
6	THU	207	198
7	FRI	264	189
8	SAT	298	68

Figure 4.61 Spreadsheet with data entered

3 Save the spreadsheet as **BEVERAGES**.

Create a comparative column chart using the data entered. Enter the *y* axis title **NUMBER OF BEVERAGES**. Enter the *x* axis title **DAY**. Create a legend to show Hot Chocolate and Cappuccino. The title for the graph is **BEVERAGE SALES**.

 Method

1 Select all the data entered (ie cells A1 to C8).
2 Click on the **Chart Wizard** button.
3 **Step 1 Chart Wizard**

    a With the **Standard Types** tab selected, click on **Column**.
    b In the **Chart sub-type** box, click on the first chart at the top left.
    c Click on **Next**.

4 Step 2 Chart Wizard:
click on **Next**.

5 Step 3 Chart Wizard:

    a Select the **Titles** tab, click in the **Chart title** box and key in: **BEVERAGE SALES**
    b Click in the **Category (*x*) axis** box and key in: **DAY**
    c Click in the **Value (*y*) axis** box and key in: **NUMBER OF BEVERAGES**
    d Click on **Next**.

6 Step 4 Chart Wizard

    a Click on the **As new sheet** option button and key in **BEVERAGE COMPARISON**
    b Click on **Finish**.

The completed comparative chart is displayed as shown in Figure 4.62.

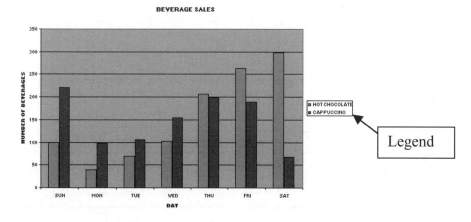

Figure 4.62 Completed comparative graph

> **i Info**
>
> In this example, we need to show a legend to indicate which colour bars represent hot chocolate and cappuccino. If you are printing in black and white, the bars and legend will display in differing patterns.
>
> If you are printing a comparative line graph to a black and white printer, be careful to choose a chart type that displays different shapes on the lines to distinguish them.

7 Save the chart as in 4.7.
8 Print the chart as in 4.8.

4.13 Changing chart colours

A pop-up menu will be displayed when you double-click on any part of the completed chart. There will be options to change colours, patterns, fonts etc. Practise this now.

4.14 Changing chart scales

To change the *y* axis value:

1 With the chart displayed on screen, double-click on the **Value Axis** (Figure 4.63).

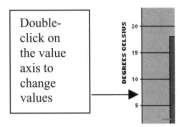

Figure 4.63 The Value Axis

2   The Format Axis dialogue box appears.
3   With the **Scale** tab selected, change the values in the **Minimum** and **Maximum** boxes.
4   Click on **OK**.

Practise this now.

4.15 Moving a chart

Click on it to select it.

Either

Use **Cut** and **Paste** to move it to another sheet or application *or*
Drag the chart using the mouse to another location on the same sheet.

4.16 Deleting a chart

1   Click on the chart to select it.
2   Press: **Delete**.

4.17   Save and close the spreadsheets and exit Excel

Section 4 Spreadsheet practice

Practice 7

1 Set up the following spreadsheet.
2 Enter the appropriate formulae in the relevant cells.

Note: To convert degrees C to degrees F: (°Cx1.8)+32.

Temperature Chart						
	Degrees C					Degrees F
	May	**June**	**July**	**August**	**4-Month Average**	**May**
Amsterdam	18	21	22	22	formula	formula
Athens	25	30	33	33	formula	formula
Berlin	19	22	24	23	formula	formula
Budapest	22	26	28	27	formula	formula
Copenhagen	16	19	22	21	formula	formula
Dublin	15	18	20	19	formula	formula
Helsinki	14	19	22	20	formula	formula
London	17	20	22	22	formula	formula
Madrid	21	27	31	30	formula	formula
Oslo	16	20	22	21	formula	formula
Paris	20	23	25	24	formula	formula
Rome	23	28	30	30	formula	formula
Stockholm	14	19	22	20	formula	formula
Vienna	19	23	25	24	formula	formula
Zurich	19	23	25	24	formula	formula

3 Working with the degrees C columns, create a 3-D column chart comparing the temperatures in Helsinki and Rome.
4 Use the chart title **Temperature Comparison (Helsinki, Rome)**.
5 Label the *x axis* **Month** and the *y* axis **Degrees C**.
6 Change the scale to display starting at 10.
7 Save the chart on a new sheet.
8 Print the chart in landscape.
9 Change the chart type to Line with markers displayed at each data value.
10 Print the Line graph.

Practice 8

1 Using the spreadsheet created in Practice 7, create a clustered bar chart with 3-D visual effect of the temperatures in May in degrees F for the cities Oslo through to Zurich.
2 Use the chart title **May Temperatures**.
3 Title the *category axis* **Cities** and the *value axis* **Degrees F**.
4 Save the chart on the same sheet as the spreadsheet data.
5 Reposition and resize the chart so it does not obscure any of the spreadsheet data and shows all the city names.
6 Save the spreadsheet file and print a copy of the data and chart on one page.

Practice 9

1   Set up the following spreadsheet:

Football attendance figures
Adult Male   16,790
Adult Female   3,791
Male under 16   10,000
Female under 16   1,199

2   Create a pie chart on a new sheet in the same workbook to display the percentage attendance.
3   Add the title **Attendance Figures**.
4   Add a legend.
5   Save and print the chart in portrait display.
6   Copy the chart to a new sheet in the same workbook.
7   Change the chart on the sheet just created to an exploded pie.
8   Colour the segments as follows:

Adult Male = black, Adult Female = red, Male (under 16) = yellow, Female (under 16) = grey.

9   Print the exploded pie chart in landscape display.
10 Save and close the file.

Section 5 Advanced – importing

In this section you will practise and learn how to:

* Import objects into a spreadsheet: image files, charts/graphs, text files etc.

* Move and resize imported objects within a spreadsheet.

5.1 Importing objects into a spreadsheet

 Exercise 1

Reload any of the spreadsheets created in section 4. Import an image file, a chart/graph and a text file.

Inserting an image file

 Method

1 With the spreadsheet displayed on screen, select the place on the spreadsheet where you want the image to appear.
2 From the **Insert** menu, select: **Object** (Figure 4.64).

Figure 4.64 Inserting an object

3 The Object dialogue box appears (Figure 4.65). In this case select: **Microsoft Clip Gallery**.

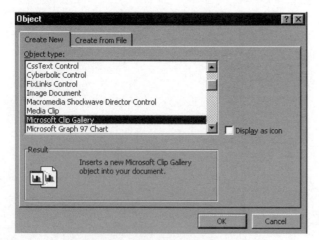

Figure 4.65 The Object dialogue box

4   The Microsoft Clip Gallery appears. Select a suitable clip and click on **Insert**. The clip is inserted on the spreadsheet.

ℹ️ Info

In the **Object type** section, scroll through to examine the different types that can be inserted. You will notice you can insert numerous objects using this method. If you are inserting an existing file (eg a Word file), click on the **Create from file** tab and locate the file by clicking on **Browse**. Double-click on the Filename and then click on **OK**.

Inserting a **graph/ chart**

To insert a graph/ chart created in another application:

1   Open the application and select the graph/ chart.

2   Click on: the **Copy** button.

3   Display the active spreadsheet by clicking on its button on the taskbar.

4   Click on: the **Paste** button.

Note: This method can also be used for other objects.

5.2 Resizing and moving imported objects

Resizing an imported object

You will notice the import has handles. Resize it using the handles. Remember, to keep its proportions, resize from a corner.

Moving an imported object

With the object selected, drag it to the required position using the mouse *or* use the cut and paste method.

5.3 Save and print the spreadsheet

5.4 Close the file and exit Excel

Section 5 spreadsheet practice

Practice 10

1   Load any Excel spreadsheet you have saved
2   Practise importing different types of files.
3   Practise moving and resizing them.

Spreadsheets quick reference guide

Action	Keyboard	Mouse	Right-mouse menu	Menu
Absolute cell reference	Add $ sign in front of the cell reference column letter and in front of the cell reference row number or press: **F4**			
Align cell entries	Select cells to align			
		Click: the relevant button: ≡ ≡ ≡ ⊞	**Format Cells**	**Format, Cells**
			Select the **Alignment** tab Select from the **Horizontal:** drop-down menu as appropriate	
Autofill	Select the first cell, drag the **Fill Handle** across the cells			
Bold text	Select cells to embolden			
	Ctrl + B	Click: the **B Bold** button	**Format Cells**	**Format, Cells**
			Select the **Font** tab Select **Bold** from the **Font style:** menu	
Borders	Select the cells you want to add a border to			
		Click on the down arrow of the ⊞▼ **Borders** button. Select the border you require	**Format Cells, Border** tab	**Format, Cells Border** tab
Capitals (blocked)	**Caps Lock** (press again to remove)			
Close a file	**Ctrl + W**	Click: the **⊠ Close window** icon		**File, Close**
Columns, adding	Select the column following the one where you want the new column to appear – by clicking on the column ref box (at top of column)			
			Insert	**Insert, Columns**
Columns, changing width of		Drag the column border C ↔ D to fit the widest entry	Select the column(s) by clicking (and dragging) on the column ref box (at top of column)	
			Column Width Key in the width you want	**Format, Column, Width** Key in the width you want *or* **Format, Column, AutoFit Selection**
Columns, deleting	Select the column you want to delete by clicking on the column ref box (at top of column)			
	Delete		**Delete**	**Edit, Delete**

Action	Keyboard	Mouse	Right-mouse menu	Menu
Commas, inserting in numbers		Click: the **,** **Comma Style** button	**Format Cells**, **Number**, **Number**, **Use 1000 Separator**	**Format**, **Cells**, **Number**, **Number**, **Use 1000 Separator**
Copy/cut and paste	Select cell(s) to copy/cut				
	Using drag and drop Copy: hold down Ctrl and drag to new position. Cut: drag to new position				
	Using Cut/Copy and Paste Click: the **Cut/Paste** button. Select where you want to cut/copy to. Click: the **Paste** button				
Copy (replicate) formulae mouse	Select cell with formula to be copied Drag the mouse from bottom right corner of cell over cells to copy to, release				
Currency symbols		Click: the **Currency** button for UK currency		**Format**, **Cells**, **Number**, **Category**, **Currency**, select: symbol to use
Date, adding	From the **View** menu, select: **Header and Footer** Click: **Custom Header** Click: where you want the date to appear Click: the **Date** button				
Date, formatting			**Format cells**, **Category**, **Date**, **Type**	**Format**, **Cells**, **Category**, **Date**, **Type**
Decimal places		Click: the **Increase Decimal** button to increase the number of decimal places Click: the **Decrease Decimal** to decrease the number of decimal places	**Format Cells** Select the **Number** tab Click: **Number** in the **Category:** menu Select the number of decimal places you need	**Format**, **Cells**
Enter text	Click: in the cell where you want text to appear Key in: the text Press: **Enter**				
Enter numeric data	Click: in the cell where you want text to appear Key in: the data Press: **Enter**				
Enter formulae	Click: in the cell where you want text to appear Key in: = followed by the formula Press: **Enter**				
Exit the program		Click: the **X** **Close Window** icon		**File**, **Exit**
Find and Replace				**Edit**, **Replace**

Action	Keyboard	Mouse	Right-mouse menu	Menu
Fit to page				**File**, **Page Setup**, **Fit to (1) Page**
Formulae, functions	Click on: the cell where the result is required			
	Use: **=SUM(cell ref:cell ref)** for adding a range of cells *or* Click: Σ **AutoSum** button Click and drag over the cell range Press: **Enter**			
	Use: **=AVERAGE(cell ref:cell ref)** to find the average value in a range of cells			
	Use: **=COUNT(cell ref:cell ref)** to count the number of cells in range			
	Use: **=LOOKUP(cell that holds the compare value, range)** to find the cell that contains the value specified			
	Use: **=IF(test, "value if true", "value if false")** to return a value for the given test			
Formulae, operators	+ add - subtract * multiply / divide			
Formulae, showing	**Ctrl +**			**Tools**, **Options**, **View** Under **Window options**, select **Formulas** so a tick appears
Formulae, printing	Ensure the formulae are showing			
				File, **Page Setup**, **Page** tab, **Landscape** or **File**, **Page Setup**, **Page** tab Under **Scaling**, select **Fit to 1 page wide** and **1 page tall**
Help	**F1**			**Help** **Microsoft Excel Help**
	Shift + F1			**Help**, **What's This?**
Hide columns	**Ctrl + 0**		**Hide**	**Format**, **Column**, **Hide**
Hide rows			**Hide**	**Format**, **Row**, **Hide**
Import/insert objects				**Insert**, **Object**
Integers (whole numbers)		Click: the .00→.0 **Decrease Decimal** button until you have reduced the number of decimal places to zero	**Format Cells**	**Format**, **Cells**
			Select the **Number** tab Click: **Number** in the **Category** menu Change the number of decimal places to zero	

Action	Keyboard	Mouse	Right-mouse menu	Menu
Moving around	Use the cursor keys	Click where you want to move to		
Move to top of document	**Ctrl + Home**			
Move to end of document	**Ctrl + End**			
Naming cells	From the **Insert** menu, select: **Name**, **Define** Key in: the name Click: **OK**			
New file	**Ctrl + N**	Click: the New button		**File**, **New**
Open an existing file	**Ctrl + O**	Click: the Open button		**File**, **Open**
	Select: the drive required Select: the filename Click: **Open**			
Page number, adding	From the **View** menu, select: **Header and Footer** Click: **Custom Header** Click: where you want the page number to appear Click: the Page button			
Page Setup	From the **File** menu, select: **Page Setup**			
Percentages, numbers as		Click: the **% Percent Style** button		
Print file	**Ctrl + P** Select the options you need Press: **Enter**	Click: the Print button		**File**, **Print** Select the options you need and click: **OK**
Printing in landscape	From the **File** menu, select: **Page Setup** Click: the **Page** tab Select: **Landscape** Click: **OK**			
Printing selected cells only	Select the cells to print			
	Ctrl + P			**File**, **Print**
	Select: **Selection** Click: **OK**			
Print Preview		Click: the Print Preview button		**File**, **Print Preview**
Remove text emphasis	Select text to be changed			
	Ctrl + B (remove bold) **Ctrl + I** (remove italics) **Ctrl + U** (remove underline)	Click: the appropriate button: **B** *I* U	**Format Cells**	**Format**, **Cells** Select the **Font** tab Click: **Regular** in the **Font Style:** menu

Action	Keyboard	Mouse	Right-mouse menu	Menu
Replicate (copy) formulae	Select: the cell with the formula to be copied Drag the mouse from the bottom right corner of the cell over the cells to copy to Release mouse			
Restore deleted input	**Ctrl + Z**	Click: the ↶ **Undo** button		**Edit**, **Undo**
Rows, adding	Select the row by clicking in the row ref box (at side of row) below the one where you want the new row to appear			
			Insert	**Insert**, **Rows**
Rows, deleting	Select the row by clicking in the row ref box (at side of row) below the one you want to delete			
			Delete	**Edit**, **Delete**
Save	**Ctrl + S**	Click: the ▣ **Save** button		**File**, **Save**
	If you have not already saved the file you will be prompted to specify the directory and to name the file. If you have already done this, Excel will automatically save it			
Save using a different name or to a different directory				**File**, Save **As**
	Select the appropriate drive and change the filename if relevant Click: **Save**			
Save file in a different file format	Save as above, select from **Save as type**			
Selecting cells Selecting non-adjacent cells Remove selection	Click and drag across cells Select the first cell(s), hold down **Ctrl** and click the others Click in any white space			
Sheets, adding, changing				**Insert**, **Worksheet**
	Click on: appropriate sheet tab			
copying		Use **Copy** and **Paste** buttons	Right-click on: sheet tab. Select: **Move or Copy**. In the **Before sheet** section, select appropriate sheet. Ensure **Create a copy** is ticked. Click: **OK**	
deleting			Right-click on: Sheet tab. Select: **Delete**	
renaming			Right-click on: sheet tab. Select: **Rename**	

Action	Keyboard	Mouse	Right-mouse menu	Menu
Sorting data	Select cells in the range to sort			
		Click: the [⬇A-Z] **Ascending** or the [⬇Z-A] **Descending** button		
Spellcheck	Move cursor to top of document			
	F7	Click: the [ABC✓] **Spelling** button		**Tools**, **Spelling**
Text formatting: font, size, colour, italicise, embolden, orientation	Select cell(s) to format			
	Ctrl + B Embolden **Ctrl + I** Italicise **Ctrl + U** Underline	Click: the relevant toolbar button on the formatting toolbar	**Format Cells**, **Font** tab For orientation: **Alignment** tab	**Format**, **Cells**, **Font** tab For orientation: **Alignment** tab
Toolbar, modify				**View**, **Toolbars**, **Customize**
Undo	**Ctrl + Z**	Click: the [↺] **Undo** button		**Edit**, **Undo**
Unhide columns	Select the columns on either side of the hidden ones			
	Ctrl + Shift + 0		**Unhide**	**Format**, **Column**, **Unhide**
Unhide rows	Select the rows on either side of the hidden ones			
			Unhide	**Format**, **Row**, **Unhide**
Zoom		Click: the [100% ▼] **Zoom** button		**View**, **Zoom**

Spreadsheet charts quick reference guide

Action	Keyboard	Mouse	Right-mouse menu	Menu
Change graphical display	*To change the scale ratios:* With the graph on screen Select: the **Plot Area** Drag the corner handles inwards (to reduce the scale) and outwards (to increase the scale) *To set upper and lower limits for* y *(vertical) axis:* With the graph on screen Double-click: the **Value Axis** In the **Format Axis** dialogue box: Click: the **Scale** tab Key in: the new values in the **Maximum** and **Minimum** boxes Click: **OK** *To set intermediate values:* With the graph on screen Double-click: the **Value Axis** In the **Format Axis** dialogue box: Click: the **Scale** tab Change the **Major** unit to the required value Click: **Close**			
Create a chart	Select the data to chart			
		Click: the ▓ **Chart Wizard** button		**Insert, Chart**

	STEP 1 Select: the chart type
	              Click: **Next**
	STEP 2 Check the source data is correct, if not change it
	              Click: **Next**
	STEP 3 Select: the **Titles** tab
	              Key in the title
	              Select: the **Legend** tab
	              Click: in the **Show legend** box to add/remove tick as appropriate
	              Select: the **Data Labels** tab
	              Click: **Show label** if appropriate
	              Click: **Next**
	STEP 4 Click: **As new sheet** or **As object in**
	              Key in: the chart name
	              Click: **Finish**			

Delete a chart	Select the chart. Press: **Delete**			
Edit a chart			Right-click on: the chart. Select from options	
Move a chart	Select the chart. Use **Cut** and **Paste** buttons or drag and drop to new location			

Action	Keyboard	Mouse	Right-mouse menu	Menu
Print a chart	With the chart displayed on screen			
	Ctrl + P Ensure **Active sheet** is selected Click: **OK**	Click: the 🖨 **Print** button (this will automatically print the sheet)		**File**, **Print** Ensure **Active sheet/ Selected chart** is selected. Click: **OK**
Save a chart	**Ctrl + S**	Click: the 💾 **Save** button		**File**, **Save**
Sheets, changing remaning, deleting	Click on: appropriate sheet tab		**Rename** **Delete**	

Module 4 practice tasks

Basic practice task 1

You work for a temporary employment agency. Create a spreadsheet to calculate weekly payments for staff on the temporary register.

1   Create the following spreadsheet. Leave the cells that contain formula blank.

Name	Hourly rate	Weekend rate	Weekly hours	Weekend hours	Hourly rate total	Weekend total	Total pay
Rachel Simms	6.80	formula	18	12	formula	formula	formula
Gareth Philips	10.50	formula	22.5	8	formula	formula	formula
Jeanna Larouse	6.80	formula	30	2	formula	formula	formula
Mark Anthony	7.80	formula	21	2	formula	formula	formula
Philip Smith	5.80	formula	10	7	formula	formula	formula
Greg Moore	6.80	formula	17	5	formula	formula	formula
Jayne Temple	7.80	formula	30	0	formula	formula	formula
Sara Janes	10.50	formula	30	0	formula	formula	formula
Tom Batco	10.50	formula	25	3	formula	formula	formula

2   Save the spreadsheet as **your initials wages**.

3   Enter your name in the upper left corner of the spreadsheet.

4   Add a header with the text centred **Spreadsheet produced by (your name)**.

5   Create a formula to calculate the Weekend rate for each employee:

Weekend rate is 20% more than hourly rate

Formula = 120/100*Hourly rate

6   Create a formula to calculate Hourly rate total *Hourly rate * weekly hours*

7   Create a formula to calculate Weekend total *Weekend rate * Weekend hours*

8   Create a formula to calculate Total pay for each employee

Hourly rate total + Weekend total

9   Format all columns with monetary amounts to £ currency two decimal places.

10 Add a title row with the text **Temporary register payments** centred across the columns.

11 Embolden the title and change the font size so it is 4 pts larger than the rest of the spreadsheet.

12 Add a row at the bottom with the heading **Total temp pay**.

13 Enter a formula in the Total Pay column to calculate Total temp pay. Use **SUM**.

14 Change the Name column width to 16.

15 Embolden the column headings.

16 Put a border around the whole table and between each cell.

17 Save the spreadsheet as **your initials wages1**.

18 Print with landscape orientation.

Advanced practice task 1

19 Create a column chart on the same sheet to show the Total pay for each employee.

20 Use the title **Employee Total Pay**.

21 Insert a new sheet in the same workbook with the name **Total Pay Bar**.

22 Copy the chart to the **Total Pay Bar** sheet.

23 Print the **Total Pay Bar** sheet only.

24 Delete the chart from the original sheet.

25 Save the spreadsheets and close the spreadsheet program.

Basic practice task 2

Create a spreadsheet to calculate currency exchanges.

1 Set up the following spreadsheet:

Your £ Buys			
No of pounds for exchange	10,190		
Country	Currency	Exchange rate	Exchange result
France (Franc)	FRF	10.47	formula
Germany (Deutsche Mark)	DEM	3.11	formula
Spain (Peseta)	ESP	276	formula
Italy (Lira)	ITL	3086	formula

2 Save the spreadsheet as **your initials Currency**.

3 In the Exchange result column, enter a formula to convert the currency (use an absolute cell reference for the pounds for conversion).

4 Format all figures in the Exchange result column to the appropriate currency format with two decimal places.

5 Centre the title **Your £ buys** across the spreadsheet.

6 Embolden all row headings and increase the font size of the headings by 2 pts.

7 Set the width of the Currency column to 10.

8 Insert a new row below the France row with the following data:

Belgium (Franc), BEF, 64.26

9 Add a thin line at the top of the spreadsheet and a thick line under the bottom cells.

10 Sort in ascending order of Country.

11 Save the spreadsheet as **your initials Currency1** and print.

Advanced practice task 2

12 Create a new workbook with the filename **Conversions**

13 Copy the original worksheet to the new workbook.

14 Delete the Italy row.

15 Insert a footer with the text **Conversions by (your initials)** on the right.

16 Create an exploded pie chart on a new sheet in the **Conversions** workbook showing the Countries and Results of exchange.

17 Include a legend for the countries.

18 Title the chart **Exchange result on 10,190GBP**.

19 On the first sheet of the conversions workbook, insert a suitable ClipArt.

20 Resize the ClipArt so it fits on one page with the data.

21 Save all documents and print both sheets in the **Conversions** file.

Note: This is only a practice test. Successful completion does not imply certification of the module by the ECDL Foundation.

Module 5

Database

Section 1 Getting started

In this section you will practise and learn how to:

* Open Access.
* Save a database.
* Close a database.
* Use Help functions.
* Modify toolbar.
* Change viewing modes.

* Design and plan a database.
* Create a table.
* Enter data.
* Define a primary key.
* Set up an index.
* Modify table layout attributes.
* Add records.
* Modify field attributes.

1.1 Understanding Access basics

Access is a very powerful database program with numerous features. We will be using only those features necessary to create simple databases and to edit, sort, search and print them. As Access is quite complicated for the new user, we will start by creating and manipulating a very small database in order to concentrate on understanding the processes involved, without hindrance of having to key in lots of data. Different facets of Access will be explained as and when we meet them.

Common database terms, which are general to all types of database applications, include the following:

* **File**. A file is a collection of related records.
* **Record**. Each collection of information for each item in a file is called a record.
* **Field**. A record is divided into separate categories, known as fields. There are different types of field. The common ones are as follows:
  - *Alphabetic* (in Access called TEXT) fields. These contain text that is manipulated alphabetically.
  - *Numeric* (in Access called NUMBER) fields. These recognise numbers and sort in ascending or descending numerical order. In Access CURRENCY and DATE/TIME fields can also be used as number fields where appropriate.

- *Alphanumeric* (in Access called TEXT) fields. These contain numbers and text that do not need to be sorted in number order (telephone numbers, for example).

An Access database file contains database objects. We will be using four database objects – tables, queries, reports and forms. We will meet all the above terms as we progress through this section.

 Exercise 1

You organise the college's fitness centre events and need to set up a database of classes.

Set up a database file using the following field titles:

CLASS	the name of the class
DAY	the day the class takes place
ROOM	the location of the class
INSTRUCTOR	the instructor's name
NUMBER OF WEEKS	the number of weeks the class runs

 Info

There are five fields in each record of this database file – four text fields, **CLASS, DAY, ROOM** and **INSTRUCTOR** and one numeric field **NUMBER OF WEEKS**.

Enter the details shown below:

CLASS	DAY	ROOM	INSTRUCTOR	NUMBER OF WEEKS
AEROBICS	**MONDAY**	**HALL**	**KENNY**	10
AEROBIKING	**WEDNESDAY**	**GYM**	**SALLY**	10
FIT AND FUNKY	**THURSDAY**	**DANCE STUDIO**	**LYNNE**	15
SYNC AND SWIM	**WEDNESDAY**	**POOL**	**DUNCAN**	5
POWER HOUR	**FRIDAY**	**HALL**	**LARRY**	10
BODY BLITZ	**TUESDAY**	**DANCE STUDIO**	**LYNNE**	20

Each row of data (above), excluding field headings, makes up one record. Therefore there will be six records in this database file.

 Info

When entering data, you can use codes instead of the full entry, for instance, in the **DAY** field, the codes **M, TU, W, TH** and **F** would be suitable codes for days of the week. This can save time and storage space. For simplicity we will create this database without codes.

1.2 Loading Access

 Exercise 2

Load Access.

 Method

Load Access in the same way as loading other Office applications, this time selecting:

from the **Start**, **Programs** menu *or* use the Access shortcut icon if you have one.

The Access window appears.

Info

You will notice that there are many similarities with other Office application windows, for example: Title bar, Menu bar and Standard toolbar. Other toolbar buttons will be displayed automatically to reflect the current task as you work through different components of the database. It is worth examining the toolbar buttons as you work through the exercises so you become acquainted with them. As in other Office applications, you can customise the toolbars to your own preferences by selecting **Toolbars** from the **View** menu. Similarly, help is accessed from the **Help** menu or by pressing **F1**.

1.3 Creating a new database

Method

On loading Access, a dialogue box also appears (Figure 5.1).

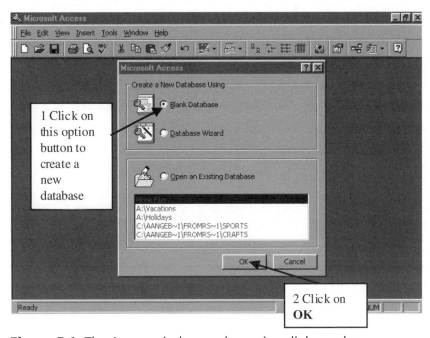

Figure 5.1 The Access window and opening dialogue box

Info

When creating a new database, you have the option of choosing a Wizard to help you. This can provide a quick way of creating databases on some occasions. However, they are not always perfect for your needs. Experiment with them when you have time so you can compare the two methods and decide for yourself which is best for you.

1 Click on the option button next to **Blank Database** in order to create a new one.
2 Click on **OK**. The File New Database dialogue box is shown (Figure 5.2).

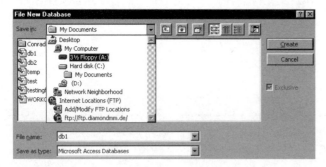

Figure 5.2 The File New Database dialogue box

3   Choose where your file will be located and then key in the filename **SPORTS** (if saving to a floppy disk, remember to have the disk inserted in the drive).

4   Click on **Create**. The SPORTS: Database window is shown (Figure 5.3).

Figure 5.3 SPORTS Database window

i **Info**

The overall database filename is **SPORTS**. There are several different objects which we will be creating and storing within this database file. They are all accessed using the tabs. The ones we will be working with are:

* *Tables.* Used to store data in rows and columns.
* *Queries.* Used when extracting data from tables.
* *Reports.* Used when printouts are required. You can print tables but have limited design options. Reports can be designed for your individual requirements.
* *Forms.* Provide a convenient way to view individual records since they display one record at a time. They do not store data but use the data stored in tables.

1.4 Designing a table

 Method

1   The **Tables** tab is chosen by default (if not, click it to choose it).
2   Click on **New**. The New Table window appears (Figure 5.4).

Figure 5.4 Creating a table in Design view

3. Click on **Design View**.
4. Click on **OK**.

The Table window in Design view is shown (Figure 5.5).

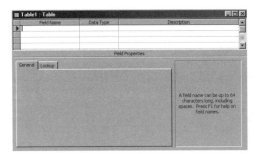

Figure 5.5 The Table window in Design view

 Exercise 3

Define the fields in the table.

 Method

1   In the **Field Name** column, with the **Caps Lock** on, key in the name of the first field, **CLASS** and press: **Enter** to move to the next column.
2   In the **Data Type** column, keep the default Text as this column will contain text entries (ie names of classes). Press: **Enter**.
3   In the **Description** column, you can type a description of the information this field will contain. This is optional, so leave it blank in this case and press: **Enter**.

Repeat steps 1 to 3 for the other fields except:

Choose Text as the Data Type for **DAY**, **ROOM** and **INSTRUCTOR**, but **NUMBER OF WEEKS** is a numeric field (ie it contains numbers). therefore choose **Number** as the Data Type. To do this:

In the Data Type column, next to the Field Name **NUMBER OF WEEKS**, click in the **Data Type** box, a down arrow appears. Click on the down arrow and click on **Number** (Figure 5.6).

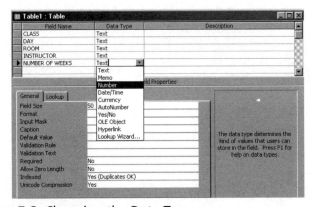

Figure 5.6 Changing the Data Type

 Info

See quick reference for different data types.

The Field Properties can then be altered to choose the field size of the number that is required (Figure 5.7).

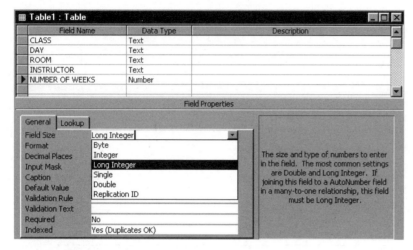

Figure 5.7 Setting Field Properties

Click in the box where **Long Integer** (the default) is displayed; a down arrow appears. Click on the down arrow to see the options available. The options we will use in this section are:

• *Long Integer.* integer means a whole number (ie no decimal places).
• *Double.* this allows decimal places.

In this case (as we do not require decimal places) we will leave the Field Size as Long Integer. Click on **Long Integer**.

The Table design should look like Figure 5.8.

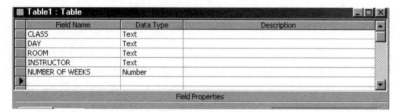

Figure 5.8 The Table design should look like this

ⓘ Info

In the Field Properties section, the field size for text entries is set at 50 characters. This will accommodate most entries and can be left as it is. Should you be very short of storage space (this is unlikely in this instance), you could save some space by reducing the field sizes as appropriate.

If you make a mistake when keying in, you can always go back and make corrections or use the **Undo** button.

ⓘ Info

If you missed out a field, see section 3 or the quick reference at the end of this chapter for the method to insert it.

1.5 Saving the table design

 Method

1 Click on the ⊠ **Close** button of the table window.
2 You are prompted to save the table design (Figure 5.9).
3 Click on **Yes**.

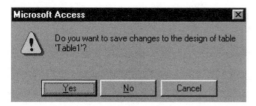

Figure 5.9 Saving a table

4 The Save As dialogue box appears (Figure 5.10).
5 Key in the Table name **CLASSES**.
6 Click on **OK**.

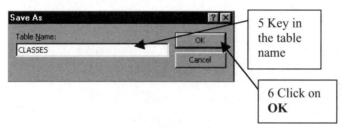

Figure 5.10 The Save As dialogue box

A message is displayed as shown in Figure 5.11:

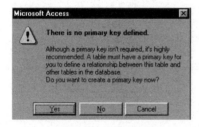

Figure 5.11 Primary Key message

7 Click on **No**.

Primary keys and indexes

 Info

A primary key is not essential. It is a field that uniquely identifies each record in a table. Examples of this type of field would be car registration numbers or unique part numbers. In some databases, there is no field that can be guaranteed not to duplicate an entry. In such cases, at the Save stage, Access can create a primary key by setting up a field called ID and allocating a number to each record.

Setting a primary key on a specific field

In Table Design view, select the field you want for the primary key and then click on the
🔑 **Primary Key** button. The primary key icon appears to the left of the chosen field as shown:

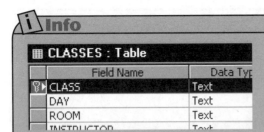

To change the primary key

Follow the instructions above again, selecting the new field. Primary keys speed up data retrieval and are useful when working with large databases or multiple databases.

Fields that have a primary key allocated are automatically indexed. With large databases, indexing fields you often sort and search is another way of speeding up data retrieval. To set up an index:

1   With the table in Design View, position the cursor in the field you want to index.

2   In the **Field Properties** section (below), and in the **Indexed** section, select: **Yes(Duplicates OK)** or **Yes(No Duplicates)**, depending on whether the indexed field entries are unique; eg car registration numbers set to **Yes(No Duplicates)**, surnames set to **Yes(Duplicates OK)**. Repeat with any other fields you want to index.

3   Save the changes to the table design when prompted.

To delete an index

In table Design view set the Indexed field property to **No**.
To view a list of indexed fields on an existing database:

With the table in Design View, click on the ⌨ Indexes button.

To remove a primary key and not set a new one:

1   Click on the ⌨ Indexes button. The Indexes dialogue box appears.
2   Select: **No** from the **Primary** menu.

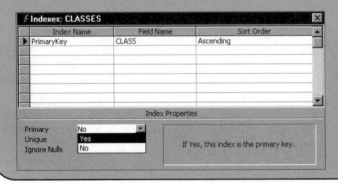

8   Close the database design window by clicking on the **Close** button (Figure 5.12).

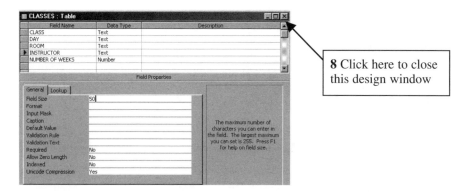

Figure 5.12 Closing the Design Window

Info

If you have not remembered to save your design, you cannot exit Design view without being prompted to save.

Should you need to make any changes to the design, click on the Design **Design** button, make the changes and click on the **Close** button. You are prompted to save the changes. Click on **Yes**.

9 You are returned to the SPORTS: Database window.

1.6 Entering data

 Exercise 4

Enter the data.

Method

See figure 5.13

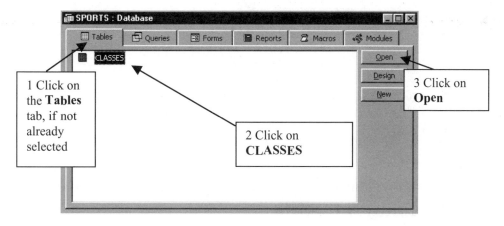

Figure 5.13 Opening a Table

4 The Table window appears (Figure 5.14). The table is now dispalyed in Datasheet view so you can enter and manipulate data.

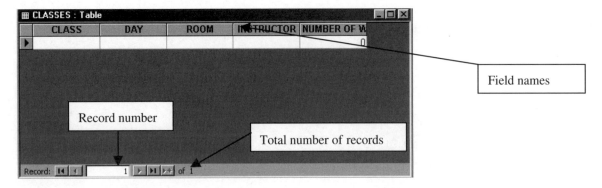

Figure 5.14 **CLASSES** table ready for data entry

5   As you can see, the **NUMBER OF WEEKS** field heading does not display in full. Widen this column by dragging the mouse, as shown in Figure 5.15.

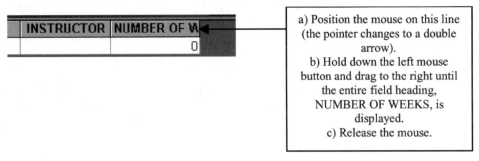

a) Position the mouse on this line (the pointer changes to a double arrow).
b) Hold down the left mouse button and drag to the right until the entire field heading, NUMBER OF WEEKS, is displayed.
c) Release the mouse.

Figure 5.15 Widening columns

Note: You can also widen the column by double-clicking where shown in Figure 5.15.

6   Key in the data in the appropriate fields as shown (Figure 5.16), pressing **Enter**, **Tab** or arrow keys to move from field to field.

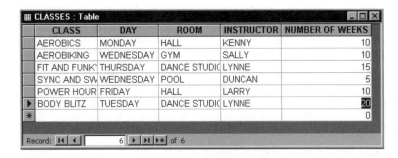

Figure 5.16 Data has been keyed in

7   You can see that **FIT AND FUNKY, SYNC AND SWIM** and **DANCE STUDIO** are too long to fit in the CLASS and ROOM field columns. Widen these columns as shown in Figure 5.15.
8   Proofread on screen against copy.
9   Correct any errors by clicking to position the cursor on the error, then correct as necessary.

1.7 Saving data and closing the table

Exercise 5

Save the data and close the table.

Method

1   Click on the **Close** button at the top right of the Table window.
2   The data is saved automatically.
3   If you have made any layout changes, you will be asked if you want to save these, Click on **Yes**.

1.8 Saving the database file

 Exercise 6

Save the database file **SPORTS**.

 Method

From the **File** menu, select: **Close**.

 Info

The database file and its components are automatically saved together. Each individual part, such as the Table **CLASSES,** has been saved as we have progressed through the exercises. If any parts are not saved, you will be prompted to save before closing.

1.9 Exiting Access

 Exercise 7

Exit Access.

 Method

From the **File** menu, select: **Exit**.

Section 1 database practice

Practice 1

1 Start up Access.
2 Set up the following database with the filename **Solicitor**.
3 Save the table as **Clients**.

Note: The TIME and PREVIOUS VISITS should be numeric fields. Use Date/Time for the TIME field data type and Field Properties format: Short Time. For more information on Data Types, see the quick reference at the end of the chapter.

> ### Info
>
> To repeat data as in the SOLICITOR field, key in the solicitor's name. Select the name by double-clicking on it. Click on the **Copy** button. Move to the cell you want to copy to and click on the **Paste** button. Move to the next cell to copy to and click on the **Paste** button. Repeat as appropriate.

SOLICITOR	CLIENT NAME	REF NO	DAY	TIME	PREVIOUS VISITS
PATEL	JONES L	J120	WED	09:30	6
PATEL	SMITH C	J561	TUE	12:00	10
PATEL	CLARKSON J	M124	SAT	16:00	4
PATEL	GRIGGS S	N6570	FRI	13:45	10
COLLINS	DENT J	C780	SAT	09:00	12
COLLINS	JENKINS Z	E120	WED	10:30	0
COLLINS	DENNIS M	L833	SAT	10:00	8
COLLINS	MOWHILL S	H777	FRI	17:45	12
McBRIDE	HARMAN D	G652	THU	11:00	12
McBRIDE	PETERS H	Y444	FRI	18:30	6
McBRIDE	CLARKE F	R567	SAT	09:30	0
McBRIDE	PAUL G	H800	SAT	11:00	6
McBRIDE	MULERO M	D437	WED	15:00	2
SIMPSON	ANDREWS C	G123	WED	10:00	6
SIMPSON	GOODYEAR K	H321	WED	11:00	6
SIMPSON	STEWART J	L909	SAT	12:00	10
SIMPSON	GREGORY A	F549	THU	16:00	10

4 Close the database file.

Practice 2

1 Start up Access.
2 Set up the following database file with the filename **Bikes**.
3 Save the table as **Stock**.

Note: The PRICE and NO IN STOCK should be numeric fields. Use Currency for the PRICE field. Data Type: Field Properties; Format: Fixed.

STORE	TYPE	MODEL	COLOUR	PRICE	NO IN STOCK
MILTON KEYNES	RACER	SPIRIT20	BLUE	359.99	10
MILTON KEYNES	RACER	SPEEDY18	GREEN	359.99	2
MILTON KEYNES	TRICYCLE	PIXIE5	YELLOW	60.50	6
MILTON KEYNES	RACER	SPIRIT18	RED	279.99	10
OLNEY	TANDEM	TWIN20	RED	399.00	1
OLNEY	MOUNTAIN	ROUGHTRACK1	BLUE	89.99	5
OLNEY	MOUNTAIN	ROUGHTRACK6	SILVER	129.99	6
OLNEY	TRICYCLE	PIXIE5	YELLOW	60.50	8
OLNEY	TRICYCLE	PIXIE10	RED	65.99	6
NEWPORT PAGNELL	RACER	SPEEDY18	SILVER	339.99	4
NEWPORT PAGNELL	TRICYCLE	PIXIE5	YELLOW	60.50	2
NEWPORT PAGNELL	MOUNTAIN	ROUGHTRACK1	BLUE	89.99	14
NEWPORT PAGNELL	RACER	SPIRIT18	BRONZE	279.99	2
CRANFIELD	RACER	SPIRIT20	BLACK	359.99	5
CRANFIELD	MOUNTAIN	ROUGHTRACK6	GREEN	129.99	6

4   Close the database file.

Section 2 Editing

In this section you will practise and learn how to:

* Open an existing database.
* Print data in table format.
* Navigate through a table.

* Modify data.
* Delete data.
* Delete/insert records.
* Add/delete a field.
* Change field order.

2.1. Opening an existing database

 Exercise 1

Load Access and the database file **SPORTS** created in the previous section.

 Method

Load Access (section 1). Follow the instructions in Figure 5.17.

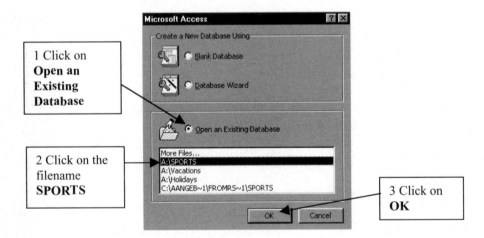

1 Click on **Open an Existing Database**

2 Click on the filename **SPORTS**

3 Click on **OK**

Figure 5.17 Opening an existing database file

2.2 Printing data in table format

 Info

The most recently used files will appear in the box. If your file is not there, click on **More Files** to locate your file.

 Exercise 2

Print the table **CLASSES**.

Method

1 Open the table, **CLASSES**:

In the Database window, ensure the **Tables** tab is selected; if not, select it. Click on **Open** (or double-click on **Classes**).

2 From the **File** menu, select: **Print**.
3 The Print dialogue box appears; we do not need to change any settings.
4 Check the printer is ready and loaded with paper.
5 Click on **OK**.

 Info

The printout will automatically print the name of the database object (in this case the table name) and the date at the top of the page.

2.3 Editing data

 Exercise 3

Some errors have been found in the data entered:

1 **AEROBICS, MONDAY** should be in the **GYM** not the **HALL**.

2 The **NUMBER OF WEEKS** for **SYNC AND SWIM, WEDNESDAY** should be 6 not 5.

Make the necessary changes.

 Method

1 Open the table **CLASSES** if it is not already open.
2 Alter the data by positioning the cursor in the place where you want to alter data, delete the incorrect data using the **Delete** key or the ← **Del (backspace)** key and key in the correct data.
3 When all editing is complete, close the table by clicking on the **Close** button.

The changes will be saved automatically.

Navigating through a table

 Info

Move through a table using the Tab or arrow keys. Move quickly to different records as shown below:

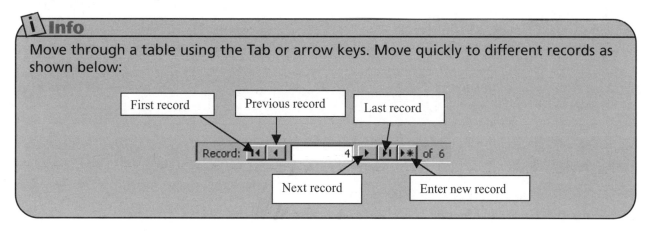

2.4 Deleting a record

Exercise 4

POWER HOUR on **FRIDAY** has been postponed. Delete all the details of this class from the database.

 Method

1 Open the table **CLASSES** if it is not already open.
2 Click the row selection box to the far left of the record (Figure 5.18).

	AEROBICS	MONDAY	GYM	KENNY	10
	AEROBIKING	WEDNESDAY	GYM	SALLY	10
▶	POWER HOUR	FRIDAY	HALL	LARRY	10
	FIT AND FUNKY	THURSDAY	DANCE STUDIO	LYNNE	15
	BODY BLITZ	TUESDAY	DANCE STUDIO	LYNNE	20
＊					0

Click in this box to select the record **POWER HOUR**

Figure 5.18 Selecting a record

3 An arrow appears in the box; the entire record is highlighted.
4 Right-click anywhere on the selection.
5 A pop-up menu appears (Figure 5.19).

Figure 5.19 Pop-up menu

6 Select: **Delete Record**
7 You will be asked to confirm you want to delete this record, click on **Yes**.

2.5 Adding a record

Exercise 5

A new class is to be started. The class name is **TONE AND TRIM**, it is to be on **FRIDAY** in the **GYM**, the instructor is **LYNNE** and it will run for **20** weeks. Add this record to the file.

 Method

1 Open the table if it is not already open.
2 Move the cursor to the last (empty) row (Figure 5.20)

	FIT AND FUNKY	THURSDAY	DANC
	BODY BLITZ	TUESDAY	DANC
▶			

Move the cursor here

Figure 5.20 Adding a record

3 Key in the data in the appropriate fields, pressing **Enter** or **Tab** after each entry.
4 Proofread on screen.
5 Close the table by clicking the **Close** button of the Table window. Data is saved automatically.

2.6 Adding a field

 Exercise 6

Add the field **MEMBER** to the database between the **ROOM** and **INSTRUCTOR** fields. Use the Yes/No data type with Yes = must be a member of the fitness centre and No = does not need to be a member, as follows:

AEROBICS	**No**
AEROBIKING	**Yes**
FIT AND FUNKY	**No**
SYNC AND SWIM	**No**
BODY BLITZ	**No**
TONE AND TRIM	**Yes**

Method

1 Open the table.
2 Change to Design view by clicking on the ⬒ **View** button.
3 Position the cursor in the field below where you want to insert the new field (ie in the **INSTRUCTOR** field).
4 Click on the ⬓ **Insert Rows** button.
5 Key in the new field name **MEMBER**.
6 Set the Data Type to **Yes/No**
7 Set the Field Properties format to **Yes/No**.
8 Save changes to the table design.
9 Enter the data in Datasheet view; clicking in the box for Yes, leaving the box empty for No.

To delete a field

 Info

1 In Design view, position the cursor in the field to delete.
2 Click on the ⬓ **Delete Rows** button.
3 You will be asked to confirm the delete.
4 Click on **Yes**.

2.7 Changing field order

   Exercise 7

Rearrange the fields so the **DAY** field is positioned after the **ROOM** field.

 Method

1   With the table in Design view, click in the selection box of the title of the field to move (ie DAY.)
2   Click in the selection box again (an arrow and dotted box appears). Using the mouse, drag the field to the new location.
3   Save the changes to the table.

2.8 Print the table on A4 paper.

 Info

You will need to change to landscape to display all the fields on one page. Use the **File** menu, **Page Setup**, **Page** tab

2.9   Close the database file and exit Access.

Section 2   Database practice

Practice 3

1   Start up Access and reload the database file **Solicitor**, saved in section 1.
2   Print out the complete file in table format.
3   Change the following records:

The appointment for Miss S Griggs to see Mr Patel should be on Saturday not Friday.

The appointment time of Miss McBride's client Dr M Mulero should be at 16.00 not 15.00.

4   Mr M Dennis who was to see Mrs Collins has cancelled. Delete his details.
5   Add the following new client for Mr Patel. His name is Mr S Samuel and he has booked an appointment for Saturday at 10 am. His reference number is D321.
6   Save the file.
7   Add a new field to the database TITLE. Enter the clients' titles as follows:

CLIENT NAME	TITLE
JONES L	MISS
SMITH C	MRS
CLARKSON J	MS
GRIGGS S	MISS
DENT J	MR
JENKINS Z	MR
DENNIS M	MR
MOWHILL S	DR
HARMAN D	MISS
PETERS H	MS
CLARKE F	MR
PAUL G	MR
MULERO M	DR
ANDREWS C	MR
GOODYEAR K	MS
STEWART J	MR
GREGORY A	MISS

8   Change the order of the fields so that the REF NO field is before the CLIENT NAME.
9   Save and print the table.
10 Close the database file.

Practice 4

1   Reload the database file **Bikes**, saved in section 1.
2   Print out the complete file in table format.
3   Change the following records:

The racer, Speedy18 bike at the Newport Pagnell store should be blue not silver.

The number of mountain, Roughtrack1s in the Newport Pagnell store should be 10 not 14.

4   Delete the red tandem, Twin20 at the Olney store.
5   Add two mountain bikes, Roughtrack3, bronze to the Cranfield store. The price is 99.99 each.
6   Save the file.
7   Add a new field to the database SALE PRICE. Enter all prices over £300 down by £30 (ie 359.99 becomes 329.99), all prices over £200 but less than £300 down by £20 and all other prices down by £10.
8   Change the field order so the COLOUR field comes before the TYPE field.
9   Save and print the table.
10 Close the file.

Section 3 Sorting and searching

In this section you will practise and learn how to:

* Find a record on given criteria.

* Create a simple query.

* Create a query with multiple criteria.

* Save a query.

* Add/remove filters.

* Add fields to a query/remove fields from a query.

* Select and sort data based on given criteria.

* Select and sort data based on common logical operators.

3.1 Sorting data

 Exercise 1

Sort the database file **SPORTS**, saved in section 2, into alphabetical order of **CLASS**.

Info

There are three main methods to sort the database. Use the toolbar button method when you do not need to save the sort. Use the filter or the query method when you want to save the sort and not overwrite any other sort.

What is filtering?

Once you have stored information in your database, you will want to sort and question the database to obtain information in different forms. When you want to see a subset of the records in a table or you want to sort the table and save it (or do all of these) you can use filtering.

What is a query?

A query is a more sophisticated method of sorting and searching a database. It has advantages over a filter as it can:

* enable you to select only certain fields to be displayed
* be used when a table is closed
* calculate sums, averages and other types of totals.

3.2 Sorting using the Sort buttons

 Method

1   Reload the saved file **SPORTS** so the SPORTS: Database window is displayed.
2   Open the table **CLASSES** in Datasheet view.
3   Click on the Field Name **CLASS** at the top of the field column so the column is selected.

4   *Click on the* *Sort Ascending button.*

Info

Use the **Sort Descending** button to sort in descending alphabetical/numerical order.

3.3 Sorting using a filter

Exercise 2

Sort the database file into descending numerical order of **NUMBER OF WEEKS** and ascending order of **INSTRUCTOR**.

 Info

Using the filtering method allows you to sort more than one field. This is called a multiple criteria sort as opposed to sorting on a single criterion, as in Exercise 1.

 Method

1 With the table **CLASSES** displayed in Datasheet view, position the cursor in the **NUMBER OF WEEKS** field.
2 From the **Records** menu, select: **Filter**, **Advanced Filter/Sort** (Figure 5.21).

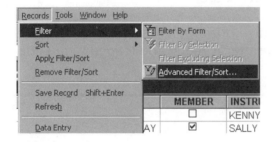

Figure 5.21 Applying a filter

3 The Filter dialogue box appears (Figure 5.22). Click in the first Field column box, click on the down arrow, and click on **NUMBER OF WEEKS**.
4 Click in the **Sort** box, click on the down arrow and click on **Descending**.
5 Click in the second field column box, click on the down arrow and click on **INSTRUCTOR**.
6 Click in the **Sort** box, click on the down arrow and click on **Ascending**.
7 From the **File** menu, select **Save As Query** and key in the query name **Weeks des and Instructor asc**. Click on **OK**.

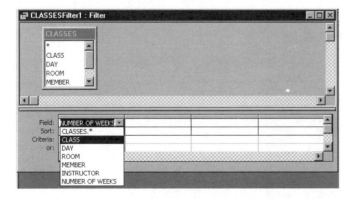

Figure 5.22 The Filter dialogue box

Info

The table is unchanged by the filtering. The filtering result saves as a query. See the next section for more information on queries.

8   To view the result of the filtering, click on the **Queries** tab in the SPORTS: Database window.
9   Double-click on the query name.

3.4 Printing a query

Exercise 3

Print the query saved as **Weeks des and Instructor asc**.

Method

1   In the SPORTS: Database window, click on the **Queries** tab.
2   Right-click on **Weeks des and Instructor asc**.
3   From the pop-up menu, select: **Print**. (If you want to print on landscape from the **File** menu select **Page Setup**, **Page** tab.) Check the printer is ready and loaded with paper.
4   Click on **OK**.

3.5 Sorting in a query

Exercise 4

Sort the database file into alphabetical order of **DAY**.

Method

1   Reload the saved file **SPORTS** so the SPORTS: Database window is displayed.
2   Click on the **Queries** tab (Figure 5.23).
3   Click on **New**.
4   The New Query dialogue box appears. Click on **Design View**, then on **OK**.

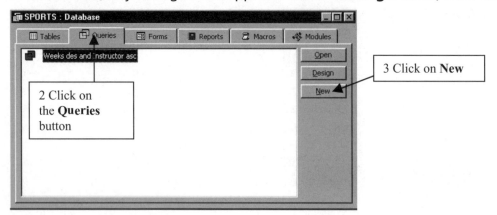

Figure 5.23 Creating a query

5   The Show Table dialogue box appears (Figure 5.24).
6   Click on **Add**, then on **Close**.

Figure 5.24 Show Table dialogue box

7 The Query – Design view window is displayed (Figure 5.25).

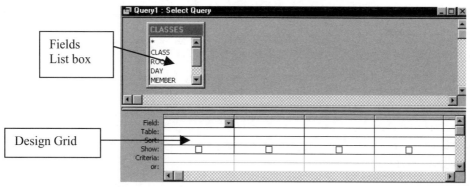

Figure 5.25 Query design

8 The fields of the **CLASSES** table are displayed in a Fields List box. Place the fields in the Design Grid as follows:

a in the Design Grid, click in the first field column.
b click on the down arrow.
c click on the name of the field you want to appear (ie **CLASS)**
d click in the next field column; click on: the down arrow.
e click on the name of the next field you want to appear (ie **DAY)**.
f repeat steps **d** and **e** until all of the fields are on the grid.

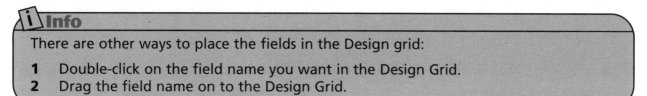

Info

There are other ways to place the fields in the Design grid:

1 Double-click on the field name you want in the Design Grid.
2 Drag the field name on to the Design Grid.

9 In the field **DAY** column, click in the **Sort** row, then click on the down arrow, then on **Ascending** (Figure 5.26).

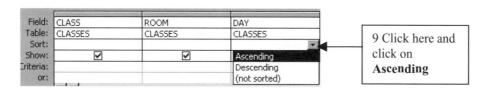

Figure 5.26 Sorting into ascending order

10 To save the query, from the **File** menu, select **Save As/Export**. Replace the default name **Query1** by deleting it and in the Within the current database as section key in the query name **Day ascending**. Click on **OK**.

11 Return to the Sports: Database window.

12 View the results of the query as in 3.3.

13 Print the query.

Info

Scan the result of the query. If there is no data or if incorrect data is displayed in Datasheet view, click on the **View** button again to return to Design view and check the query design.

The View button

You can sort on more than one field but the fields to sort must be adjacent and in order of sort preference (ie first field to sort, second field to sort etc).

You can create queries using the Query Wizard if you prefer. You will need to modify them to suit your needs. Practise this method.

14 Click on the **Close** button in the top right-hand corner of this window to return to the SPORTS: Database window.

Info

As with advanced filtering, in queries you can also do multiple criteria sorts.

3.6 Finding records specified by a single criterion

Exercise 5

Search the file for all classes taking place in the **GYM**.

Info

There are several ways to find records. You can search manually, navigating your way through the database using the methods already learnt. This is too time-consuming and not recommended for large databases. Using **Find** is a quicker method. You can also use a filter or create a query.

3.7 Finding data using Find

1 With the table displayed in Datasheet view, position the cursor in the field that you want to search on (ie **ROOM**).

2 Click on the 🔍 **Find** button. The Find and Replace dialogue box appears (Figure 5.27).

3 In the **Find What** box key in the data you want to find (ie **GYM**).

4 Ensure that **Search Only Current Field** is ticked.

5 Click on **Find Next**.

Figure 5.27 Find and Replace dialogue box

6 Access will find each record in turn.
7 When you have finished searching, close the dialogue box by clicking on the **Close** button.

Refining finds using Match

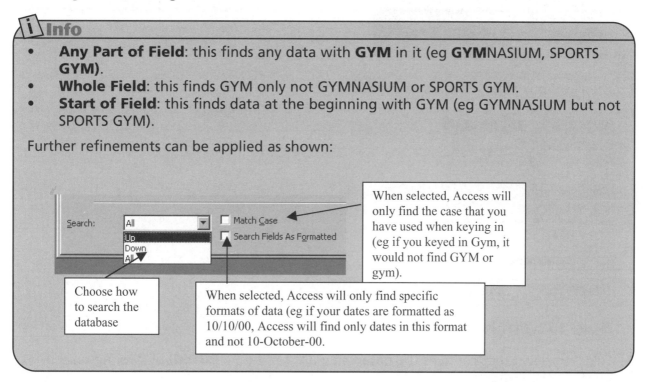

Info

- **Any Part of Field**: this finds any data with **GYM** in it (eg **GYM**NASIUM, SPORTS GYM).
- **Whole Field**: this finds GYM only not GYMNASIUM or SPORTS GYM.
- **Start of Field**: this finds data at the beginning with GYM (eg GYMNASIUM but not SPORTS GYM).

Further refinements can be applied as shown:

When selected, Access will only find the case that you have used when keying in (eg if you keyed in Gym, it would not find GYM or gym).

Choose how to search the database

When selected, Access will only find specific formats of data (eg if your dates are formatted as 10/10/00, Access will find only dates in this format and not 10-October-00.

3.8 Finding data using a filter

 Method 1

1 With the table displayed in Datasheet view, position the cursor in a cell containing the data you want to find (ie **GYM**.)
2 Click on the ⦰ **Filter** button.
3 All the records with **GYM** are displayed.

Info

You can refine your search further by selecting another data entry (eg all classes in the GYM lasting 10 weeks). With the filtered **GYM** records displayed, repeat steps 1 and 2, this time positioning the cursor in a cell containing 10.

You can also select any part of a data entry (eg if you wanted to find all records beginning with the letter G, select only the G and run the filter).

Note: If you are filtering a Yes/No field, you will change the data when you click in the cell containing it. To overcome this, click it twice so it keeps its original setting before filtering.

4 To remove the filter, click on the **Remove Filter** button.

Note: You cannot save the filter as a query using this method.

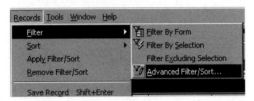 Method 2

1 With the table displayed in Datasheet view, from the **Records** menu select: **Filter, Advanced Filter/Sort** (Figure 5.28).

Figure 5.28 Adding a filter

2 The Filter box dialogue appears (Figure 5.29).

Figure 5.29 The Filter dialogue box

3 Select the field that contains the data you want to find (ie **ROOM**) by clicking on the arrow in the **Field** row.
4 In the **Criteria** row, key in **GYM**.
5 Click on the 💾 **Save As Query** button to save the filter as a query, named **GYM**.
6 Close the filter and table.
7 View the results of the filter by clicking on the **Queries** button and double-clicking on the query name.

ℹ️ Info

Quotation marks appear around the keyed text (ie **GYM**). It does not matter if you key in Gym in upper or lower case. Beware if you spell the word gym wrongly. It will not be recognised and will be unable to find any records as it looks only for an exact match.

Using Method 2, you can search with more than one specified criteria and also sort data.

3.9 Finding data using a query

 Method

Follow steps 1–8 in 3.5.

9 In the field **ROOM** column and the **Criteria** row, key in **GYM** and press: **Enter** (Figure 5.30).

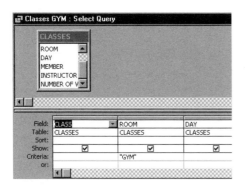

Figure 5.30 Selecting criteria

10 View the results of the query.
11 Save the query with the filename **Classes GYM**.
12 Print as in 3.4.

3.10 Selecting records specified by more than one criterion

 Exercise 6

Using the query method, find all the records for classes taking place in the **GYM** lasting less **than 15 weeks.** Print details of the selected records and show all fields.

Mathematical operators used in queries

 Info

> (greater than) symbol is obtained by holding down the **Shift** key and pressing the **full stop** key.

< (less than) symbol is obtained by holding down the **Shift** key and pressing the **comma** key.

>   greater than (or more recent than in the case of a date)

<   less than (or before in the case of a date)

>=   greater than or equal to

<=   less than or equal to

<>   not equal to

See the quick reference for a fuller table of setting criteria in queries.

Info

In this instance, as we have already created a query **Classes GYM**, we can use this as the basis for this query. You could create a completely new query for this if you wanted, but this would only duplicate effort.

 Method

1 From the SPORTS: Database window, click on the **Queries** tab, click on the query **Classes GYM**, then on the **Design** button.

2 In the field **NUMBER OF WEEKS** column and the **Criteria** row, key in **<15** and press: **Enter** (Figure 5.31).

ROOM	DAY	MEMBER	INSTRUCTOR	NUMBER OF V
CLASSES	CLASSES	CLASSES	CLASSES	CLASSES
☑	☑	☑	☑	☑
"GYM"				<15

Figure 5.31 Selecting more than one criteria

3 Save the query as **Gym less than 15 weeks** and print.

3.11 Printing specified fields from selected sorted records

 Exercise 7

Find all the records with the instructor **LYNNE lasting more than 15 weeks**. Sort the records into alphabetical order of class. Print the details of these records only. Show only the information for **CLASS, DAY** and **NUMBER OF WEEKS** fields.

 Method

Follow Steps 1–8 in 3.5.

9 In the field **INSTRUCTOR** column and **Criteria** row, key in **LYNNE** and press: **Enter**.
10 In the field **NUMBER OF WEEKS** column and **Criteria** row, key in **>15** and press: **Enter**.
11 In the **CLASS** field, **Sort** row, select **Ascending** (Figure 5.32).

Field:	CLASS	ROOM	DAY	MEMBER	INSTRUCTOR	NUMBER OF WEEKS ▼
Table:	CLASSES	CLASSES	CLASSES	CLASSES	CLASSES	CLASSES
Sort:	Ascending					
Show:	☑	☑	☑	☑	☑	☑
Criteria:					"LYNNE"	>15
or:						

Figure 5.32 Selecting more than one criteria and sorting in the same query

12 To show only the **CLASS, DAY** and **NUMBER OF WEEKS** fields, in the **Show** row and **ROOM** field column, click the tick in the box. The tick will disappear. Repeat for the **INSTRUCTOR** field. This leaves ticks in the **CLASS, DAY** and **NUMBER OF WEEKS** fields only (Figure 5.33).

CLASS	ROOM	DAY	MEMBER	INSTRUCTOR	NUMBER OF WEEKS
CLASSES	CLASSES	CLASSES	CLASSES	CLASSES	CLASSES
Ascending					
☑	☐	☑	☐	☐	☑
				"LYNNE"	>15

Figure 5.33 Showing only certain fields

13 Save the query as **Lynne more than 15 weeks**.
14 Check the result in Datasheet view.
15 Print the query.

ℹ️ Info

- You will notice that only the fields with ticks will appear on the printout.

- Remember – it is always a good idea to check your query is showing the correct result, so always view it in Datasheet view before printing. If it is not showing what you think you have asked for, return to Design view by clicking the View toolbar button and checking the details you have entered.

- You can sort and search within the same query.

Common errors

- Misspelling the criteria so the query does not find an exact match (this can also be due to a spelling error in the data in the database).

- Making the criteria plural (ie **GYMS** instead of **GYM**). The query will not find **GYMS** as this is not what was entered in the database and therefore is not an exact match.

- Leaving spaces where they should not be.

3.12 Close the database file and exit Access

Section 3 Database practice

Practice 5

1 Reload the database file **Solicitor** saved in section 2.
2 Sort the file into alphabetical order of client name and print all the details.
3 Sort the file into ascending numerical order of previous visits and print all details.
4 Search for all the clients whose appointment day is Wednesday. Print details of the selected records showing all fields.
5 Find all the records of clients whose appointments are before 12.00 and have previously visited fewer than 8 times. Print only the information in the Client Name and Time fields.
6 Save and close the file.

Practice 6

1 Reload the database file **Bikes**, saved in section 2.
2 Sort the file into alphabetical order of model and print.
3 Sort the file into descending numerical order of price and print all details.
4 Search for all the yellow bikes. Print details of the yellow bikes only.
5 Find all records of mountain bikes costing more than £100.00 (at original prices). Print only the Store, Colour, Type and Model fields.
6 Save and close the file.

Section 4 Reporting

In this section you will practise and learn how to:

* Create reports.

* Present selected data in a particular sequence on screen and in reports.

* Modify a report.

* Create and customise headers and footers

* Group data in a report-totals, sub-totals etc.

4.1 Creating a report

Exercise 1

Open the database file **SPORTS** and create a report in table format based on the table **CLASSES** displaying all the records.

Method 1 Using AutoReport

1 With the SPORTS: Database window displayed, click on the **Reports** tab.
2 Click on the **New** button.
3 In the New Report dialogue box, select **AutoReport**: **Tabular** and choose the table **CLASSES** from the drop-down list (Figure 5.34).
4 Click on **OK**.

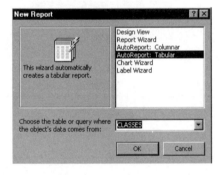

Figure 5.34 Creating an AutoReport

5 The report appears in Print Preview mode.
6 Print the report.

Info

In this instance the report looks very good. Sometimes this is not the case and you will need to use the Report Wizard to create your report. Creating reports without the aid of the wizard is very advanced and time consuming.

Method 2 Using the Report Wizard

1 With the SPORTS: Database window displayed, click on the **Reports** tab, then on the **New** button.
2 Click on **Report Wizard** and select the table **CLASSES** (Figure 5.35). Click on **OK**.

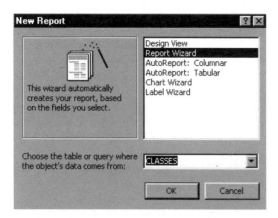

Figure 5.35 Creating a report using Report Wizard

3 The Report Wizard box appears (Figure 5.36).
4 Ensure the object the report is coming from is selected

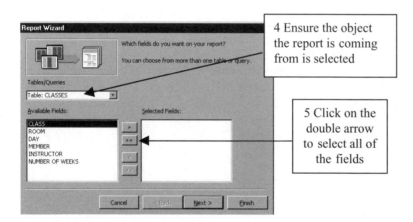

4 Ensure the object the report is coming from is selected

5 Click on the double arrow to select all of the fields

Figure 5.36 Report Wizard box

5 Choose all the fields by clicking on the **>>** button, so the **Available Fields** move to the **Selected Fields** box (Figure 5.36).

> **i Info**
>
> It is not always necessary to show all fields on a report. If this is the case, select the field you want to include and click on the **>** button to move it to the **Selected Fields** box. Repeat as required. If you make a mistake and select the wrong fields, reverse the procedure by selecting and clicking on the **<** or **<<** button as appropriate. If you want to print the fields in a different order, select them individually and move them across using the **>** button in the order you want.

6 Click on **Next**.
7 The next Report Wizard box appears. If you need to group a report, select the groupings here. Let's select grouping by **INSTRUCTOR**, so select **INSTRUCTOR** in the left box and click on the **>** button. Click on **Next** (Figure 5.37).

Figure 5.37 Selecting groupings

8 The next Report Wizard box appears. Let's sort in ascending order of **CLASS**. In box 1 click on the down arrow, then click on **CLASS** (Figure 5.38). Ensure the **A-Z** button is on A-Z. If not, click on it to reverse it.

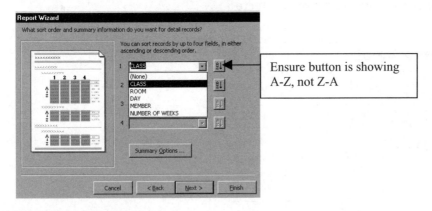

Figure 5.38 Selecting sort order

> ### ⓘ Info
>
> Sometimes it is better to ensure the data has already been sorted in the object it has come from (eg a query), because if the sort order is chosen within Report Wizard, the wizard will automatically place the sorted field in the first column of your report. This will mean moving it to the position requested. In this case it does not apply since **CLASS** is the first database field.

9 Let's show a sum of the total number of weeks for each Instructor. To do this click on **Summary Options** (Figure 5.38).
10 In the Summary Options dialogue box (Figure 5.39), click in the **NUMBER OF WEEKS** row and **Sum** column so a tick appears. (This will show a sum total for each instructor and not just the overall sum total). In the **Show** section, select **Detail and Summary**.
11 Click on **OK** then on **Next**.

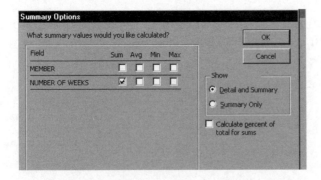

Figure 5.39 Summary Options dialogue box

12 The next Report Wizard box appears (Figure 5.40). Use your discretion for the best layout and orientation. This report, because it is going to show all the fields, will be wide; therefore it is best suited to a landscape display. Click on the **Landscape** option button. Ensure the **Adjust the Field widths** box is ticked.

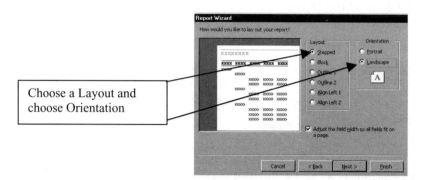

Choose a Layout and choose Orientation

Figure 5.40 Choosing Layout and Orientation

13 Click on **Next**.

14 The next Report Wizard box appears (Figure 5.41). Experiment with the styles. Each time you choose a style, example reports are displayed in the left box. **Corporate** is a good style because the layout is compact and the data will usually fit on one page.

15 Click on **Next**.

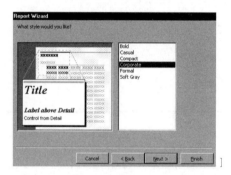

Figure 5.41 Choosing a style

16 The next Report Wizard appears (Figure 5.42). Key in a Report title.

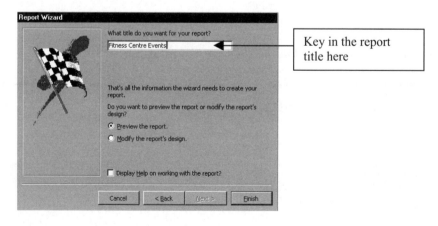

Key in the report title here

Figure 5.42 Adding a title

> **i Info**
>
> This may scroll out of view as you type. Do not worry. Always choose a descriptive title for your report. This will become the report name when it saves automatically.

17 Ensure the **Preview the report** button is selected.

18 Click on **Finish**.

19 Check the report (zoom in and out by clicking the mouse over it) to make sure all details are displayed in full as requested. Access has a habit of cutting off the edges of some of the longer entries! This will not always happen. In this case, using the **Corporate** style, my report has displayed all the entries.

20 You will notice that details of the calculations appear on the report (Figure 5.43). Since these are distracting, we can delete them.

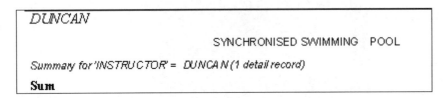

Figure 5.43 Details of calculations can be deleted

21 Click on the **View** button to switch to Design view.

22 Delete the details of calculations by clicking on the box shown below (Figure 5.44) so that it has handles. Press: **Delete**. Similarly delete **Sum** below.

◆ INSTRUCTOR Footer									
="Summary for " & "'INSTRUCTOR' = " & " " & [INSTRUCTOR] & " (" & Count(*) & " " & IIf(Count(*)=1,"d									
Sum									

Figure 5.44 Select the detail to delete it

23 Review (using the **View** button) and save the report.

4.2 Printing a report

 Exercise 2

Print the report including the field headings.

 Method

From the **File** menu, select: **Print**, then click on **OK** *or* click on the **Print** button.

4.3 Further adjusting a report design

 Exercise 3

In the Table **CLASSES**, in the **CLASS** field, change the entry **SYNC AND SWIM** to **SYNCHRONISED SWIMMING (BEGINNERS).** Review the report created in 4.1 and adjust as necessary.

i **Info**

Making this entry longer has resulted in the report not displaying the entry in its entirety ie it is not displaying (**BEGINNERS**).

Method

1 Change the entry in Datasheet view. Then change to **Report Preview** of the report created in 4.1. Click on the 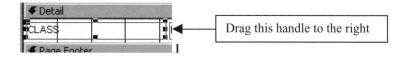 **View** button.

2 **Report Design View** will now be displayed (Figure 5.45). The report is divided into panes:

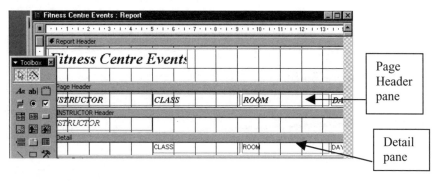

Figure 5.45 Report Design View

3 Using the scroll bars, ensure the item you want to alter is in view. In this case the item should already be visible ie **CLASS** in the Detail pane).

4 Click on the **CLASS** box to select it. Drag the handle to the right to widen the box so it is wide enough to display all the detail (Figure 5.46). (You will have to make a guess as to how wide to make the box since the detail does not appear in Report Design view.)

Figure 5.46 Widening the CLASS field

5 Unfortunately the last action has obscured some of the **ROOM** Detail. Therefore we need to resize both the **ROOM** Detail and the **ROOM** Header (so they line up). To do this, select the **ROOM** Header by clicking on it: drag the handle to the right (Figure 5.47).

Figure 5.47 Resizing the ROOM field

6 Similarly resize the **ROOM** Detail.

7 Click on the **View** button (this has now changed to a Print Preview icon) to return to Report Preview.

8 From the **File** menu, select: **Save**, to save the report design. (This is necessary, even if your report is still not perfect, as failure to save at this point will result in losing the changes you have already made.)

9 Check the Report Preview and continue to fine tune and save the design as above until you are happy with it.

4.4 Adding a header/footer

Exercise 4

Add the header: **Report produced by (your name).**

Add the footer: **Report designed to show total hours for each instructor.**

 Method

1 From the **Toolbox**, select **Label** (Figure 5.48).

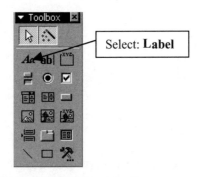

Select: **Label**

Figure 5.48 The Toolbox

2 In the **Report Header** section, click and drag out a text box.
3 Key in the header text and press **Enter**. With the text box selected, select the font, size etc.
4 Repeat for the footer text.
5 Save, preview and print the report.

 Info

You can format any of the report text by clicking on it to select it and then formatting. To select more than one text box, hold down the **Shift** key. Resize the boxes as necessary or move them by pointing to a box border until a hand appears and then drag to the new position.

4.5 Close the database file and exit Access

Section 4 database practice

Practice 7

1   Reload the database file **Solicitor** saved in section 3.
2   Produce a report as follows:

Display all the records.
Group by Solicitor.
Sort in descending order of Client Name.
Title the report **Clients grouped by solicitor**.
Add a header with your name and current time of day in Arial, bold, 14 pt.

3   Print the report.
4   Change the report title to **Client appointments this week**, **grouped by solicitor**.
5   Save and print the report.
6   Close the database file.

Practice 8

1   Reload the database file **Bikes** saved in section 3
2   Produce a report as follows:

Include all fields except Colour.
Group the report by Store.
Add totals and sub-totals for the fields Price and Sale Price and No in Stock.
Sort the report into ascending order of Price.
Add a title **Store Stock (today's date)**.
Add a footer containing the text: **Report produced by (your name)**.

3   Save and print the report.

Section 5 Forms

In this section you will practise and learn how to:

* Create a simple form.
* Enter data.
* Format text.
* Change background.
* Import an image or graphics file.
* Change arrangement of objects within a form layout.

5.1 What is a form?

Info

Once you have created an Access database table you are able to view the data in Datasheet view. There are limitations in layout design in this view and so Access provides another way to view the same data so you can see one complete record at a time, arranged to your liking, and this is called *form*. There are three ways to create a form:

1 Using AutoForm.
2 Using a Form Wizard.
3 Manually.

We will be using the first two methods as we work through this section.

5.2 Creating forms using AutoForm

 Exercise 1

Open the **SPORTS** database and create a form from the table **CLASSES**.

 Method

1 With the SPORTS: Database window open, click on the **Forms** tab.
2 Click on the **New** button.
3 The New Form dialogue box appears (Figure 5.49). Select: **AutoForm: Columnar** and choose the table **CLASSES**.
4 Click on **OK**.

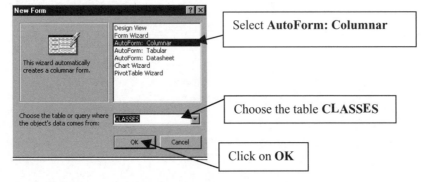

Figure 5.49 Creating a form using AutoForm

The AutoForm will appear as in Figure 5.50.

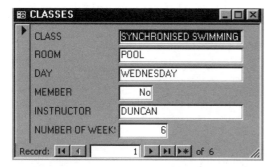

Figure 5.50 The table classes in Form layout

Info

The first record of the database is displayed (don't worry if your database is in a different order). To see the others, use the arrow buttons at the bottom as described in section 2. You can carry out all the procedures in a form you can do in a table (ie edit, add, delete records etc). When you make alterations in Form view, the contents of the table **CLASSES** will also be changed.

5.3 Creating forms using the Form Wizard

 Exercise 2

Create a form based on the table **CLASSES** using the Form Wizard. Set out the form so it is easy to read and attractive to look at.

 Method

1 With the SPORTS: Database window open, click on the **Forms** tab. Click on the **New** button. The New Form dialogue box appears. Click on **Form Wizard**. Select the table **CLASSES**. Click on **OK**.

2 A Form Wizard box appears (Figure 5.51). Ensure the table **CLASSES** is chosen. Move all the fields across to the Selected Fields section using the **>>** double arrow. Click on **Next**.

Info

As with reports, you can choose to show only some of the fields on a form.

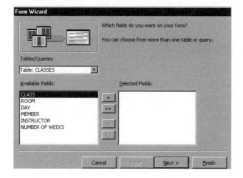

Figure 5.51 Form Wizard

3 The next Form Wizard box appears (Figure 5.52). Select the layout you require (you are given a preview in the box to the left). In this instance select: **Columnar**. Click on **Next**.

Figure 5.52 Choosing a layout

4 The Next Form Wizard box appears (Figure 5.53). Here you can choose a suitable style for your form. Examine the different styles. I will choose **Clouds**. Click on **Next**.

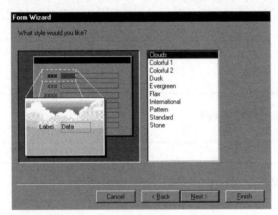

Figure 5.53 Choosing a style

5 The next Form Wizard box appears (Figure 5.54). Give the form a suitable name (eg FITNESS CLASSES) and click on **Finish**.

Figure 5.54 Giving the form a title

6 The completed form appears on screen showing the first record.
7 Save the form using **Save As** from the **File** menu.

5.4 Entering and editing data in a form

Exercise 3

Enter the following new record:

CLASS	ROOM	DAY	MEMBER	INSTRUCTOR	NO OF WEEKS
BADMINTON	SPORTS HALL	WEDNESDAY	YES	JANE	20

Method

Click on the **New Record** button and enter the data into the blank form, pressing **Enter** after each field entry.

Exercise 4

Delete the record for **BODY BLITZ**.

Method

1 Find the **BODY BLITZ** record using the **Find** button.
2 Click on the **Delete Record** button.
3 Click on **Yes** to confirm the delete.

Exercise 5

Sort the database into descending alphabetical order of **CLASS**.

Method

This is done the same way as in Datasheet view. Use the **Sort descending** button.

> **Info**
>
> You can also perform a multiple criteria sort as in datasheet view (ie from the **Records** menu, select: **Filter**, **Advanced Filter/Sort** and save it as a query).

> **Info**
>
> You can Filter by selection as in Datasheet view. The number of records found by the filtering is shown beside the navigation buttons. You can also use **Filter by Form** from the **Records** menu or by clicking in the **Filter by Form** button. In this case a blank form is displayed. Key in what you want to find, then click on the **Apply Filter** button. Click on the button again to remove the filter.
>
> You can also perform an Advanced Filter and save it as a query as in Datasheet view.

5.5 Modifying a form

Info

You can change the appearance of a form in a similar way to changing a report's appearance. The exercises below will allow you to practise this.

 Exercise 6

Change the text in the form to a different font and enlarge it.

 Method

1 In the SPORTS: Database window, click on the **Forms** tab.
2 Click on the form **FITNESS CLASSES** and click on the **Design** button.
3 The form appears in Design view (Figure 5.55).

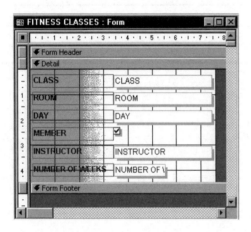

Figure 5.55 Form in Design view and Toolbox

4 As with Report designing, select the boxes containing the text to alter, holding down **Shift**.
5 Format the text using the toolbar buttons.

 Exercise 7

Change the layout of the form so the data is displayed in full (eg SYNCHRONISED SWIMMING (BEGINNERS) is currently cropped). Enlarge and rearrange the form in any order you like.

 Method

Use the methods described for reports in section 4.

 Exercise 8

Change the background colours in the text boxes.

Method

With the form in Design view, select the objects to change. Right-click the mouse to view and select from a pop-up menu.

Practise changing other options. Save the form design when you are happy with it.

5.6 Import an image or graphics file

 Exercise 9

Import a suitable image or graphics file.

 Method

1 With the form in Design view, select: **Object** or **Picture** from the **Insert** menu.
2 Select what you want to insert.
3 When the graphic appears on the form, resize and reposition it as necessary, using the same methods as in report designing.

5.7 Change arrangement of objects within form layout

 Info

As with reports you can reposition objects within the form in Design view (see section 4.3). Practise this now.

5.8 Print the file in form layout

 Method

1 Display the database form you have just created.
2 Print in the normal way.

5.9 Close the file and exit Access

Section 5 database practice

Practice 9

1   Reload the database file **Solicitor** saved in section 4.

2   Create a simple form using the table **Clients**.

3   Change the text of the Field headings to Times New Roman, italic 18 pt.

4   Change the colour of the background in the Field headings boxes to green.

5   Import a suitable graphic image and position and resize it so it fits in with the form design.

6   Enter the following new records:

SOLICITOR	CLIENT NAME	REF NO	DAY	TIME	PREVIOUS VISITS	TITLE
COLLINS	MUSGROVE D	B421	FRI	16.00	2	MR
PATEL	DANIELS Z	H555	TUE	10.00	0	MISS

7   Save the database and print the new records only in Form format.

8   Close the database file.

Practice 10

1   Reload the database file **Bikes** saved in section 4.

2   Create a simple form using the table **Stock**.

3   Change the text of the data to Arial, bold, 16pt.

4   Change the colour of the background in the data boxes to purple.

5   Import a suitable graphic image and position and resize it so it fits in with the form design.

6   Enter the following new record:

STORE	COLOUR	TYPE	MODEL	PRICE	NO IN STOCK	SALE PRICE
CRANFIELD	APACHE	RACER	SPIRIT28	489.99	1	459.99

7   Save the database and print the new record only in Form format.

8   Close the database file.

Note: No answers are given for these exercises as the form designs will vary and the answers are obvious.

Database quick reference guide

Action	Keyboard	Mouse	Right-mouse menu	Menu
Close a database	**Ctrl + W**	Click: the ✖ **Close** icon on the database window		**File**, **Close**
Close the Table window		Click: the ✖ **Close Window** icon		**File**, **Save As**
Count records in a query	In the query Design grid, select the field to count			
		Click: the Σ **Totals** button	**Totals**	
	A Totals row appears. Click: the down arrow, select: **Count**			
Create a database	Load Access Click: **Blank Access Database**, **OK** Select: the location Enter: the filename Click: **Create** Click: **Tables** tab. click: **New**. Click: **Design view, OK** Enter the field names. These will all appear (by default) as text entries under Data Type			
Data Type, change	(See separate table for Data Types) Click: in the **Data Type** box next to the field name you wish to change Click: the arrow Click: the Data Type you require (eg Number) Select the Field properties (see separate table for Field Properties) from the box below			
Primary key	If required, create a primary. Select: the field for the primary key and click: the 🔑 **Primary Key** button			
	Close the Table window by clicking the ✖ **Close** button of that window Save the table design			
Edit data	Open the table (if it is not already open)			
	Click: in the entry you want to edit Delete/overwrite the old data Key in the new data			
Enter data	In the Database window, double-click: the table name Enter the data required in the correct fields. Widen the field columns as necessary. Close the Table window as before. The data is saved automatically.			
Field, add	In Design View: Click in the field below where you want to insert a new field			
		Click: the ⇥ **Insert Rows** button	**Insert Rows**	**Insert**, **Rows**
	Add the field details. Resave the table design			
Field, delete	In Table Design View: Select: the field to be deleted by clicking to the left of it			

Action	Keyboard	Mouse	Right-mouse menu	Menu
	Delete	Click: the 🔲 **Delete Rows** button	**Delete Rows**	**Edit**, Delete **Rows**
	Click: **Yes**			
Field order, change	With the table in Design view, click: the selection box of the field to move Click: the selection box again (an arrow and dotted box appear) Drag field to new location			
Filters, add/ remove	With the object displayed in Datasheet view			
	Select what you want to filter: Click: the ▽ **Filter** button *To remove filter:* Click the **Filter** button again		**Records**, **Filter**, **Advanced Filter/Sort**	
Find a record	With the Table displayed, position the cursor in the field you want to search.			
	Ctrl + F	Click: the 🔍 **Find** button		**Edit**, **Find**
	In the **Find What** box, key in what you want to find Click: **Find Next** Continue until all records have been found *Note:* You may need to choose a field that has a unique entry to ensure you find the correct record			
Forms, create	With the database window open, click: the **Forms** tab			
	Using AutoForm Click: **New** Select: **AutoForm: Columnar** Select: object the form is based on. Click: **OK** *Using the Wizard* Select: **Form Wizard** Follow the wizard's instructions			
Headers and footers in reports	In Report Design View from the **Toolbox**, select: **Label** In the Report header/footer section, click and drag out a box Key in your text			
Index, set up	With the table in Design view, position the cursor in the field you want to index In the **Field Properties**, **Indexed** section, make selection			
deleting	Set the **Indexed** field property to **No**			
Load Access	In the Windows desktop			
		Double-click: the **Microsoft Access** shortcut icon		**Start**, **Programs**, **Microsoft Access**
Open a table in Datasheet view	In the Database window, make sure the **Tables** button is selected			
		Double-click: the table name Change to Design view by clicking: the 🔲 · **View** button		

Action	Keyboard	Mouse	Right-mouse menu	Menu
In Design view		Click: the table name Click: **Design**		
Output a report *To Word*		Ensure you are in the **Report Preview** view			
		Click: the 🔳 **Publish It with MS Word** *OR* Click the ▼ next to the 🔳 **Analyze It with MS Excel** button and select **Publish It with MS Word**		**Tools**, Office Links, **Publish it with MS Word**
to Excel		Click the ▼ next to the w🔳 **Publish It with MS Word** button and select: **Analyze It with Excel**		**Tools**, Office Links, **Analyze it with MS Excel**
Print		Select the object you want to print			
	Ctrl + P			**File**, **Print**
		Make the necessary selections From the File menu, choose **Page Setup** if you want to print landscape Make the necessary selections from the **Page Setup** dialogue box Click: **OK**			
Quick print		Click: the 🖶 **Print** button Access will automatically print the whole object		
Record, add		Click: the ▶* **New Record** button *OR* Click: in the blank cell immediately after the last record	(Right-click to the left of any record) **New Record**	**Insert**, New Record
Record, delete	colspan="4"	Select the record by clicking to the left of the first field of that record			
		Click: the ✖ **Delete Record** button	**Delete Record**	**Edit**, Delete Record
	colspan="4"	Click: **Yes** to save the change			
Replace field entries	Ctrl + H			**Edit**, Replace
Report, create		Ensure the Database window is dispalyed and that the **Reports** tab is selected			
		Click: **New** Click: **Report Wizard, OK** Select: the name of the object (e.g. query, table) that the report is to be generated from Click: **OK** Select the fields to include in the report using the [»] or [›] buttons Click: **Next**			

(If you want to group the report – select the field(s) you want to group by here)

Action	Keyboard	Mouse	Right-mouse menu	Menu
	Click: **Next** Sorting – preferably ensure the original object is sorted. However, if you want to change the sort order here select the field you want to sort by. *Note:* this could rearrange field positions in the final report Click: **Summary Options** to include calculation results on the report Click: **Next** Select Layout Select the orientation you want – **Landscape** or **Portrait** Click: **Next** Select a style Click: **Next**. Key in: the report title Click: **Finish**			
Sort records (quick sort)	Open the Table if it is not already open. Select the field you want to sort by clicking on the Field Name at the top of the field column			
Ascending order		Click: the 🔼 **Sort Ascending** button	**Sort Ascending**	
Descending order		Click the 🔽 **Sort Descending** button	**Sort Descending**	
Query, create in Design view	In the Database window ensure the **Queries** tab is selected Click: **New** Select: **Design view.** Click: **OK** Select object query is based on Click: **Add**, **Close** The fields of the table are now displayed in a list box in the Query window Place the fields you want to see in your query in the field row of the query grid by double-clicking or dragging them *Note:* Place the fields in the order you want them to appear			
Query, create a simple query using the wizard	In the database window, ensure the **Queries** button is selected Click: **New** Select: **Simple query by using Wizard**. Click: **OK** Follow the wizard's instructions			
Query, sort	Click: in the **Sort** box of the appropriate field Click: the ▾ arrow Select: **Ascending** or **Descending**.			
Specify criteria	Use the **Criteria** row in the grid to specify the conditions in a specific field – e.g. **RED** in the **Color** field. (see *Working with Queries* section)			
Print specific fields	Use the **Show** row in the grid to choose whether or not to display a particular field in the query A tick in the **Show** box means the field will show, no tick means it will not show. Click to toggle between them			
Save a query	**Ctrl + S**	Click: the 💾 **Save** button		**File, Save As**
	To see the results of your query			
		Change to Datasheet view *OR* Click: the ❗ **Run** button		**Query, Run**

Important: Always close the database file properly.

Data type	Properties
Text (the default)	No need to set, unless requested or short of storage space.
Number	*Field Size* Long Integer is the default – this is OK for whole numbers. Double – for numbers with decimal places *Format* Choose **Fixed** for 2 decimal places to show (even if the last is a zero) Choose **Decimal Places** and enter the number required (Leave the Format blank for other numbers)
Date/Time	Choose the most appropriate format for the task. (You can key in the date in any format and it will convert to the format you have set)
Currency	Choose **Format Fixed** to display 2 decimal places with no commas or £ symbol
Yes/No	No need to set
Memo	No need to set

Working with queries

When setting up queries, use the following as a guide. In the Criteria row you can enter any of the following:

- An exact match (eg SMITHSON)
- The wildcard *

The * is a wildcard that stands for any number and type of character (eg if you were unsure how to spell the name you could enter SM*THSON or SM*SON). You can place the * wildcard before, after and between characters and you can use it more than once in a single field (eg SM*TH*)

- The wildcard ?
  The ? wildcard acts as a placeholder for one character (eg SM?THSON).

- LIKE
  This tells Access not to look for an exact match (eg LIKE SMYTHSON).

- NOT
  If you want to find all the records but not SMITHSON you could enter NOT SMITHSON

- NULL
  If you have records with no value in the field, you can type NULL to find these records. For example, you may be looking for all solicitors who do not have any appointments on Wednesday and the database design has allowed no value in the day field if a solicitor does not have any appointments on Wednesday but a YES value if he or she does.

- Mathematical operators

> more than	>= more than or equal to
< less than	<= less than or equal to
= equal to	<> not equal to

- AND
  You can use AND when you need restricted results (eg if you were searching a database for certain goods costing over £5.00 but under £10.00 – use: >5.00 and <10.00).

- Fields containing YES/NO data
  If Yes the data will show as a ticked box. Use **Yes** if you want to find the ticked box data and **No** if not.

Making a copy of a table

Sometimes it is useful to save your original table intact, follow the steps below:

1 With the table name selected in the Database window, click on the **Copy** button.
2 Click on the **Paste** button.
3 In the **Paste Table As** dialogue box, key in the new table name; ensure **Structure and Data** is selected.
4 Click on **OK**.

You will now have two exact copies of the same table. Make amendments to one of them, leaving the other one intact.

Module 5 practice tasks

For this module you will need to have the following database file set up. Ask your supervisor or tutor to prepare it for you.

Preparation

Create the following database table. Save the database as **Lettings** and the table as **Properties**. Set Postcode as the primary key field.

Location	Postcode	Type	Beds	Garage	Garden	Rent £	Available
Elstow	BD41 5RW	House	3	Y	N	600	June
Bedford	BD23 1AS	Flat	1	N	N	400	July
Brickhill	MK54 3LP	House	2	Y	Y	550	June
Devonlly	MK29 7TD	Flat	2	N	Y	420	May
Goldington	BG31 8QT	House	5	Y	Y	875	August
Oakley	OS2 6RW	House	4	Y	Y	850	May
Rushden	NN14 8PT	House	2	Y	Y	500	June
Bodington	NN12 5RP	Flat	1	N	N	300	May
Carlton	MK44 9AS	House	3	Y	Y	1100	June
Harrold	MK49 4HX	Flat	2	Y	N	600	July

Practice task 1

Using the **Lettings** database and the table **Properties**:

1   Extract all records that have **three bedrooms**. Save the query as **3 bedrooms** and print.
2   Extract all records that have **Locations beginning with B**. Save the query as **Location (B)** and print.
3   Extract all records of **properties without a garage**. Save the query as **No Garage** and print the **Location, Rent** and **Availability** fields only.
4   Using a query, count the records in the database on the **Location** field.
5   Using a text editor, enter the answer to 4 and save the file as **Count**.
6   Sort the database into alphabetical order of **Type** and **Beds**.
7   Add an additional record to the database (make it up).
8   In design view, format the **Rent(£)** field to two decimal places.
9   Save and print the table.
10 Create a report titled **Types of Rental Property** showing the fields **Location, Type, Rent** and **Available**. Group by **Type**.
11 Add a header to the report with **Your name**.
12 Save and print the report.

Practice task 2

The task is to create a database of CDs.

1   Create a database table in design view with six fields. Use appropriate data types, distinguishing between text, date etc with the field sizes shown:

   Title (40), **Artist (25)**, **Release date**, **Category (15)**, **Cost**, **Top 40 (Y/N)**

2   Save the database as **Compact Disks** and the table as **CD**.
3   Create six records for any CDs (real or not) of your choice.
4   Sort the database in descending order of **Artist**.
5   Set the **Release** date field to **Long** date format.
6   Save and print the table.
7   Add a field **Label (20)** in between **Release date** and **Category**. Enter suitable label data.
8   Sort in alphabetical order of **Title**.
9   Save and print. .

Note: There is no worked example of this task as versions will vary considerably.

Note: This is only a practice test. Successful completion does not imply certification of the module by the ECDL Foundation.

Presentation

Section 1 Getting started

In this section you will practise and learn how to:

* Open PowerPoint.
* Use application help functions.
* Close PowerPoint.
* Create a new presentation.
* Choose an appropriate automatic slide layout.
• Modify slide layout.
* Add text.
* Close document.
* Save presentation
* Modify toolbar display.
* Use page view/zoom.
* Change display modes.
* Add an image, resize and move an image.
* Resize and move an image in a slide.
* Format font: italics, bold, underline, case, apply shadow, sub/superscript, apply colours.
* Align text: centre, left, right, top, bottom.
* Adjust line spacing.
* Change type of bullets.
* Resize and move text within a slide.
* Set line weights, style and colours in a text box.
* Use spellcheck.
* Preview: slide, outline, slide sorter, notes view.
* Print slides in various views.
* Select appropriate output.

1.1 Understanding PowerPoint basics

PowerPoint enables you to create, organise and design effective presentations. These can be used as handouts, overhead transparencies, 35 mm slides and automated presentations on a computer.

1.2 Loading PowerPoint

 Exercise 1

Load PowerPoint.

Method

From the **Start** menu, select: **Programs**, **Microsoft PowerPoint** *or* double-click on the **PowerPoint** shortcut icon if you have one. Either method results in the PowerPoint window being displayed on screen (Figure 6.1).

Figure 6.1 PowerPoint's opening window

1.3 Creating a new presentation

 Exercise 2

Create Slide 1.

Note: PowerPoint uses the word 'slide' for each page created, even for the production of paper printouts or overhead transparencies.

 Method

1 Click on **Blank presentation** and **OK**. The New Slide dialogue box appears (Figure 6.2).

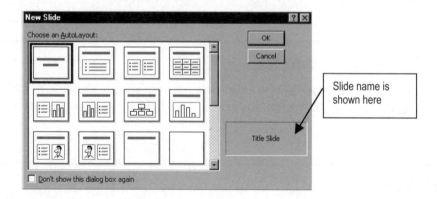

Figure 6.2 New Slide dialogue box

2 There are many different AutoLayouts to choose. In this case click the slide AutoLayout at the top left – **Title Slide** (it may already be chosen). Click on **OK**.

3 This first slide is displayed in **SlideView** (Figure 6.3).

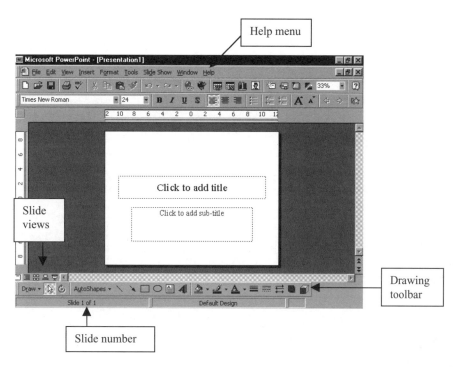

Figure 6.3 Slide in Normal View

Note: If you have selected the wrong layout, right-click in a white space on the slide (outside of the placeholders.

1 Select: **Slide Layout**.

2 Click on: a layout to select it.

3 Click on: **Reapply**.

Info

It is worth examining the PowerPoint window at this stage and noting the labels in Figure 6.3 and the following:

Modifying toolbars

The Standard and Formatting toolbars are displayed. If you want to modify the toolbar display, use the **View** menu, select: **Toolbars**, then **Customize**. Click on the **Options** tab.

Slide views

The slide is displayed in **SlideView**. This shows one slide at a time. Use this view to create/edit slides.

Other views include:

- **Outline**. Displays an outline of your presentation. You can enter/review the text in your presentation in this view.

- **Slide Sorter**

  – y ou can view all your slides in this view as miniatures (small versions or thumbnails)

  – zoom in and out for more/less detail using **Zoom** control

  – sort slides into a different presentation order by clicking on the slide you want to move and dragging it to a new location

  – add a new slide by placing the pointer between the slides where you want the new slide to appear and clicking on the **New Slide** button

  – delete a slide by selecting it and pressing the **Delete** key. Use the **Undo** toolbar button to reinstate the deleted slide.

- **Notes Page**. In this view you are able to see the slide together with a notes section where you can input any notes you want to make about the slide. These notes aid the speaker when making a presentation.
- **Slide Show**. Shows your slides on a full screen, as they will appear when you set a slide show in motion. Select the first slide. Click the **Slide Show** button. To view the next slide, press: **Page Down**. When all the slides have been viewed you will be returned to the previous view (this will be covered in more detail later).

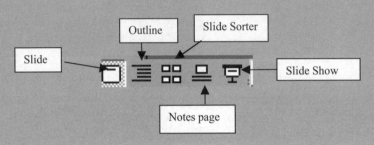

4   The slide is shown as in Figure 6.4. It has preset placeholders (boxes with dotted-line borders to hold text, bulleted lists etc).

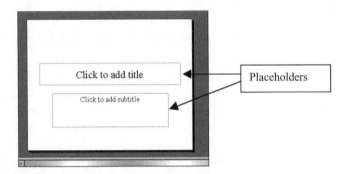

Figure 6.4 Slide View

5   In the slide window, click in the top placeholder (**Click to add title**) and key in **Learning PowerPoint**.

6   Click in the bottom placeholder (**Click to add sub-title**) and key in your name.

Info

Title and sub-title can also be referred to as heading and sub-heading. Body text is usually the text that follows the sub-heading.

    Exercise 3

Format the text on Slide 1.

Info

PowerPoint bases its default text formats on its default *master slide*. You will learn more about master slides in section 2.

    Method

As in Word, select the text you want to format and then use the **Formatting** toolbar buttons (Figure 6.5) and/or the **Format** menu, selecting **Font** to change the font type, point size, embolden, italicise or underline, apply text shadow, use sub and superscript. Change case by selecting **Change Case** from the **Format** menu.

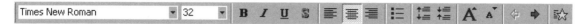

Figure 6.5 Formatting toolbar buttons

Info

Serif and sans serif fonts

Serifs are small lines that stem from the upper and lower ends of characters. Serif fonts have such lines. Sans serif fonts do not have these lines. As a general rule, larger text in a sans serif font and body text in a serif font usually make for easier reading. For example:

Times New Roman is a serif font.

Arial is a sans serif font.

1 Align the text within the placeholders using the toolbar buttons.
2 Align the text in relation to the slide:

   a   Select the placeholder box.
   b   On the **Drawing** toolbar, click on **Draw** and then select: **Align or Distribute**.
   c   Click on **Relative to Slide** so that a tick appears.
   d   Click on **Draw** again, select: **Align or Distribute** and click on the option you want ie **Align Top, Bottom, Left, Right** (Figure 6.6).

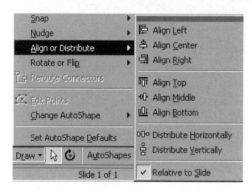

Figure 6.6 Aligning objects

3 Change the font colour by clicking the down arrow on the **Font Color** button on the **Drawing** toolbar. (By default this toolbar is at the bottom of the working area. If this is not visible, from the **View** menu, select: **Toolbars** and click on **Drawing**.)

1.4 Saving the presentation

Exercise 4

Save the presentation.

Method

1 From the **File** menu, select: **Save As**.
2 Choose where you want to save the file and key in a filename (if saving to a floppy disk, remember to have the disk inserted in the drive).
3 Click on **Save**. (if saving to a floppy disk, remember to have the disk inserted in the drive).

1.5 Bulleted lists and adding graphics to a specified slide layout

 Exercise 5

Create a second slide in the presentation.

 Method

1 Click on the  **New Slide** button.
2 Choose the AutoLayout **Text and Clip Art** as shown in Figure 6.7. Click on **OK**.

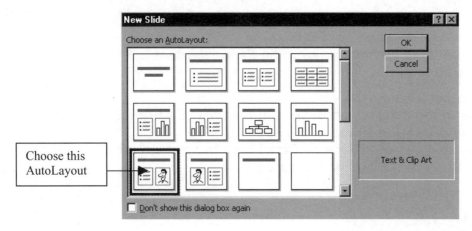

Choose this AutoLayout

Figure 6.7 Creating Slide 2

3 In the **Click to add title** placeholder, key in **Bullets and Graphics**.
4 In the left-hand placeholder, key in the numbers 1 to 7, pressing **Enter** after each number except 7 (the last one). Notice that a bulleted list has been created.

Changing bullet type

5 Select the bulleted text. From the **Format** menu select: **Bullet**.
6 Make your choices from the Bullet dialogue box by selecting the **Bullets from** list and then selecting a character for the bullet. Click on **OK**.
7 To insert a graphical image in the right-hand placeholder, double-click in the placeholder.
8 Scroll through the Clip Art and decide which one to use.
9 Click on **Insert** (Figure 6.8).

Figure 6.8 Inserting Clip Art

Slide 2 will now look something like Figure 6.9.

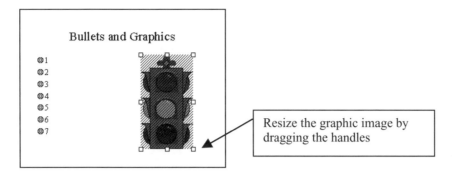

Figure 6.9 Slide 2

10 Resize the graphical image by dragging the handles.

Info

At step 6 you can select a numbered list by clicking on the **Numbered** tab. You can also add bullets and numbered lists to slides using the appropriate toolbar buttons i.e. **Bullets** and **Numbering**. Click on the relevant toolbar button before keying in text or select the text to have bullets or numbering and then click on the relevant toolbar button.

Info

If you want to preserve the proportions (aspect ratio) of the image always resize from a corner.

1.6 Moving the elements of the slide

Exercise 6

Reduce the size of the image and reposition it at the right-hand corner of the slide.

Method

1 Click on the image to select it.
2 Reduce the size as in 10 above.
3 With the graphic still selected, hover the mouse over it; an arrowhead cross appears.
4 Holding down the left mouse button, drag the graphic to the required position.

Info

This repositioning can be carried out on any of the elements following the same method, but you will notice you need to point the mouse at the border of some of the elements before the arrowhead cross appears. When this appears you can move the element.

Your slide will now look something like Figure 6.10

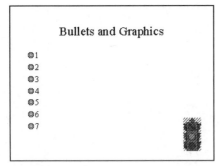

Figure 6.10 Graphic resized and repositioned

5 Save your work using the toolbar button method.

1.7 Adding text and images to a blank layout

 Exercise 7

Create Slide 3 using the blank AutoLayout. Decide on your own text for this slide.

Method

1 Click on the **New Slide** button.
2 Choose the **Blank** AutoLayout.
3 Experiment with adding your own text and graphics.

Adding text

Method

1 Click on the **Text Box** button on the Drawing toolbar.
2 Click where you want the text to start. *Note:* You need not drag out a box, as the text will expand the box to fit.
3 Key in the text and format it as required.
4 Click in any white space on the slide when finished.
5 Adjust the text box size so the text fits neatly on the slide.

Adjusting line spacing

When you have more than one line of text, you can adjust the line spacing.

Method

1 With the cursor positioned in the text box, from the **Format** menu, select: **Line Spacing**.
2 Make your choices from the Line Spacing dialogue box.

To add graphics

Method

1 From the **Insert** menu, select: **Picture** and then **Clip Art** (Figure 6.11).
2 Click on the Clip Art you want to insert. Click on the **Insert** button.

Figure 6.11 Adding a picture

Info

Notice that the menu shows other types of picture you can insert.

Note: The graphic is placed in the centre of the slide. Resize and reposition it as necessary following the method given above.

Use your imagination and practise adding and changing elements on this slide. When you are happy with the result, save your work.

You now have three slides in the presentation.

1.8 Viewing the slides

There are several ways to view your slides (see section 1.3). Practise using these views now.

Note: Press: **Esc** to exit from **Slide Show** View.

1.9 Implementing a colour scheme

Exercise 8

For all three slides, change the background colour to light blue and the title text to red.

 Method

1 In **Slide View**, from the **Format** menu, select: **Slide Color Scheme**; the Color Scheme dialogue box appears. The default here is **Standard** and you can experiment with the colour schemes provided. However to create your own scheme, ensure **Custom** is selected. Click on **Background**, then **Change Color** (Figure 6.12).

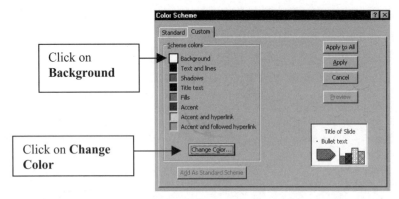

Figure 6.12 Color Scheme dialogue box

2 The Background Color dialogue box appears. With **Standard** selected, click on a shade of light blue, then on **OK** (Figure 6.13).

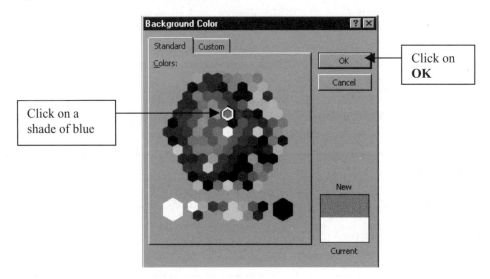

Figure 6.13 Adding a background color

3 You are returned to the Color Scheme dialogue box. This time select **Text and Lines** and follow the instructions above, choosing the colour red for the Title text.

4 When you are returned to the Color Scheme dialogue box, click on **Apply to All**. You are automatically returned to your slide.

Note: You could have chosen to apply to one slide only.

5 Change to **Slide Sorter View** and see how your slides look with this colour scheme.

Note: The text colour has not applied to the Title text. **Title Text** is not included in **Text and Lines** and must be chosen separately.

Info

PowerPoint can do design work for you by selecting **Apply Design** from the **Format** Menu, and selecting something suitable.

6 Save your work.

1.10 Spellcheck the presentation

Exercise 9

Spellcheck the presentation.

 Method

Click on the **Spelling** toolbar button. The spellcheck is consistent with other Office applications. Always resave your work after spellchecking to save any corrections.

1.11 Printing your presentation

 Exercise 10

Print the presentation of three slides, one slide per page.

 Method

1   From the **File** menu, select: **Print**. The Print dialogue box appears and printing options can be selected (Figure 6.14).

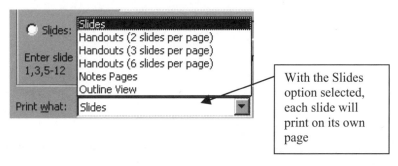

Figure 6.14 Printing options

Info

You can print slides in various views including as individual slides (one per page), as Handouts (several slides on one page, you can decide the number per page), as Notes Pages (slides and notes) or Outline View.

1.12 Closing and exiting PowerPoint

 Method

1   From the **File** menu, select: **Close**
2   From the **File** menu, select: **Exit**.

Section 1 presentation practice

1 Create a three-slide presentation as follows and format it to good effect using the layout given as a guide.

Slide 1
Using Title slide AutoLayout, enter the text shown:

> ### Multimedia on the web
> ### Multimedia Workshop 2000
>
> The Grand Hotel Conference Centre
> Bristol BS8 2TS
> Tel 0117 2102102
> *E-mail: mow@multicon.ac.uk*

Slide 2
Using the Bulleted list AutoLayout, enter the following. Format the bullets as squares. Add a suitable piece of Clip Art in the bottom right corner.

> ### The following topics will form the basis of the multimedia workshop:
>
> ✓ Text
> ✓ Graphics
> ✓ Video
> ✓ Sound

Slide 3

Using the 2 Column Text AutoLayout, enter the following text. Adjust the line spacing in the body text to 1.25 lines. *Note:* Delete the bullets by selecting them and pressing: **Delete**.

Video and Sound Workshops

Video
This will concentrate on accessing two websites with video content. The content will be compared and contrasted with a view to finding out what works and what falls flat. Website addresses will be specially selected for this workshop.

Sound
For this workshop there will be four websites to focus on. Some have streaming audio. The quality and accessibility of the sound will be judged and rated out of ten for each of the two categories.

2 Apply a light grey background to all the slides. Set all title text to dark red.
3 Save the presentation.
4 Print all slides, one per page.
5 Close the presentation file and exit PowerPoint.

Section 2 Editing and refining

In this section you will practise and learn how to:

* Open an existing presentation.
* Create and use a master slide.
* Number the slides.
* Add different types of line, move lines, change line colour/modify line width.
* Add shapes: boxes, circles etc. Rotate or flip an object. Add free-drawn lines.
* Change attributes: colour, line type, apply shadow.
* Set line weights, style and colours in a text box.

* Use copy/cut and paste to duplicate slides/text images within presentation(s).
* Use cut and paste as above.
* Reorder slides.
* Open several presentations.
* Delete an image/selected text/slides.
* Add notes to slides.
* Change slide orientation: landscape or portrait.
* Save existing presentation.
* Save under different formats and for the web.

2.1 Opening an existing presentation

 Exercise 1

Open the presentation created in section 1.

 Method

1 Open PowerPoint as in section 1.
2 Click in the option button **Open an existing presentation** and then on **OK** (Figure 6.15).
3 Click on the drive, the filename and then on **Open**.

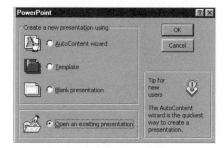

Figure 6.15 Opening an existing presentation

2.2 Creating and using a master slide

 Exercise 2

Create a master slide for the presentation, containing the date and the footer **Learning PowerPoint**.

Info

The default master slide is always present and your presentation will be based on the default settings if you do not change them. In order that your slides give a common feel to a presentation, it is a good idea to set up a master slide containing common elements you want to appear on all the slides. These elements cannot then be deleted, except from the master slide.

Method

1 From the **View** menu, select: **Master**, **Slide Master**. The master slide appears (Figure 6.16).

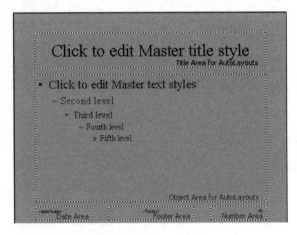

Figure 6.16 The Master slide

 Info

You can choose to leave the default settings as they are or to change them. *Note:* You can add slide numbers on a master slide or add slide numbers using the **View** menu, **Header and Footer**, **Slide** tab, **Slide number**, **Apply to all** (or choose options).

2 In this instance we will keep the default settings and enter the common information for this presentation in the **Date Area** and **Footer Area**. *Note:* You may want to increase the Zoom to be able to read the text you are working with. Change back to the default 33% when you have finished.
3 In the **Date Area**, click on **date/time** to select it and key in today's date.
4 In the **Footer Area**, key in **Learning PowerPoint**.
5 Change to **Slide Sorter View** to view the effects of creating a master slide.

 Info

You can view and edit the master slide, at any time, by selecting **Master** from the **View** menu.

2.3 Adding lines and shapes

 Exercise 3

Create a new slide and practise adding lines and shapes.

Method

1 In **Slide Sorter View**, click on the last slide in the presentation in the Outline pane. (This will ensure the new slide is correctly positioned as Slide 4 of the presentation.)
2 Click on the **New Slide** button.
3 Select **Blank** AutoLayout.
4 Ensure you are in **Slide View** with the Drawing toolbar visible. If not, from the **View** menu, select: **Toolbars**, **Drawing** so a tick appears next to it. The Drawing toolbar is shown in Figure 6.17.

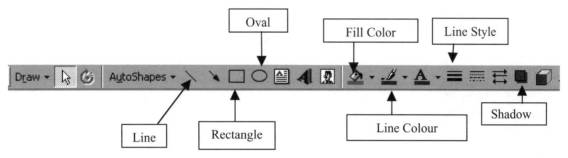

Figure 6.17 Drawing toolbar

Adding a line

1 Click on the **Line** button.
2 Position the cross hair where you want the line to start.
3 Hold down the left mouse button and drag the mouse to where you want the line to end. Release the mouse.

Formatting the line

1 Select the line by clicking on it. When it is selected, handles appear at each end.
2 Click on the **Line Style** button.
3 Click on the line style you want.
4 Click on the **Line Color** button to choose the line colour.

Changing line length and moving a line

1 Click on the line to select it.
2 Change the length by dragging the handles to the required length.
3 Move the line by holding down the mouse anywhere along its length until the arrowhead cross appears and then drag it to the new position.

Adding a circle or ellipse

1 Click the **Oval** toolbar button.
2 Hold down the left mouse button and drag out to the required shape.
3 Release the mouse.

Adding a box

Follow the method for a circle/ellipse, shown above.

Filling a shape with colour

1 Select the shape to fill.
2 Click on the **Fill Color** button.
3 Click on the chosen colour.

Filling a shape with a pattern

Follow steps 1 and 2 above.

1   Click on **Fill Effects**. The Fill Effects dialogue box appears.
2   Click on the **Pattern** tab.
3   Click on the chosen pattern. Click on **OK**.

Applying a shadow

1   Select the required object.
2   Click on the **Shadow** button.

Adding free-drawn lines

1   Click on the **Autoshapes** arrow button. Select: **Lines**, **Freeform** or **Scribble** (Figure 6.18).

Figure 6.18 Free drawn lines

2   Hold down the left mouse and draw with the 'pencil'.

Note: Check the other options on this menu – they are very useful.

Rotating or flipping an object

1   Select the object
2   Click on the **Draw** arrow, select: **Rotate or Flip** and then select from the next menu (Figure 6.19)

Figure 6.19 Rotating and flipping objects

 Info

Objects can be grouped so they stay together. To do this: hold down **Shift** and click in turn on the objects to group. From the Drawing toolbar, **Draw** menu, select: **Group**. (Ungroup from this menu.) Experiment with other Drawing toolbar buttons to create some stunning effects.

2.4 Setting line weights, styles and colours in text boxes

 Exercise 4

Create a text box at the top of the slide. Insert the text **Adding shapes and lines**. Format the text box.

 Method

1   Add a text box in the normal way and key in the text.
2   With the text box selected, format it using the Drawing toolbar buttons.

2.5 Copying/cutting and pasting within a presentation

Exercise 5

Copy the text box created in Exercise 4 so it appears centred on Slide 2 under **Bullets and Graphics**.

Method

1 In **Slide View**, select the text box.
2 Click on the **Copy** button.
3 Select Slide 2 using the **Previous Page** arrows (at the bottom of the vertical scroll bar) to move through the slides.
4 Click on the **Paste** button.
5 Position the object as appropriate.

Exercise 6

Move the graphical image on Slide 2 to a new blank slide.

Method

1 Create a new slide using the **Blank** AutoLayout.
2 In **Slide** View, move to Slide 2, and then select the image.
3 Click on the **Cut** button.
4 Move to the new slide.
5 Click on the **Paste** button.

Exercise 7

Copy the image from Slide 3 so it appears in the box on Slide 2 (in place of the moved image).

Method

1 In **Slide** View, select the image on Slide 3.
2 Click on the **Copy** button.
3 Move to Slide 2.
4 Select the image placeholder and click on **Paste**.

2.6 Duplicating whole slides

Exercise 8

Duplicate slide 1.

Method

1 In **Slide Sorter View**, select Slide 1.
2 From the **Insert** menu, select: **Duplicate Slide**.
3 The duplicate of the slide appears next to Slide 1.

Note: You can also duplicate slides by selecting the slide to copy and clicking on the **Copy** button. Click where you want the slide to appear and click on the **Paste** button. You can cut and paste whole slides using the **Cut** instead of the Copy button.

2.7 Reordering slides

 Exercise 9

Reorder the slides so the duplicate slide becomes the last slide.

 Method

In **Slide Sorter View**, hold down the left mouse on Slide 2 and drag the slide to the required position.

2.8 Opening more than one presentation

 Exercise 10

Open a new presentation and copy Slide 2 of the Learning PowerPoint presentation to the new presentation.

 Method

1 Click on the ▢ **New** button.
2 Select **Blank** slide AutoLayout, click on **OK**.
3 From the **Window** menu, click on the original PowerPoint file (Figure 6.20).

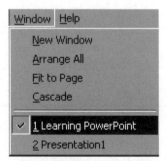

Figure 6.20 Switching presentations

4 In **Slide Sorter View** select: Slide 2.
5 Click on the **Copy** button
6 Switch to the new presentation using the **Window** menu.
7 In **Slide View**, click on the **Paste** button.
8 Resize to fit the slide if necessary.

Note: Although you have copied this slide, it will not implement the master slide for slides in this new presentation. You can use the methods in section 2.5 for copying/pasting between presentations, switching presentations using the **Window** menu.

2.9 Deleting images/text

To delete images or text from slides, select the image/text and press: **Delete**.

Practise this now.

2.10 Deleting slides

 Exercise 11

Delete Slide 3 from the presentation **Learning PowerPoint**.

 Method

1 In **Slide Sorter View**, select: Slide 3.
2 Press: **Delete**.

2.11 Adding notes to slides

 Info

You can add notes to your Slides. These are useful 'prompts' for key points when you are delivering a presentation. You can print notes for each slide together with a small version of each slide as handouts.

 Exercise 12

Add a note to Slide 1 of the new presentation '**This slide has been copied from another presentation**'. Print the slide together with the notes.

 Method

1 Ensure that the correct presentation is displayed.
2 Click on the **Notes Page View** button.
3 Key in the text in the **Notes** pane.
4 From the **File** menu: select: **Print**.
5 In the **Print what** section, select: **Notes Pages** (Figure 6.21).

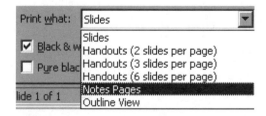

Figure 6.21 Printing notes

2.12 Changing slide orientation and sizing

Exercise 13

Print the slides in the Learning PowerPoint presentation in portrait display.

Method

1 From the **File** menu, select: **Page Setup**. The Page Setup dialogue box appears (Figure 6.22).
2 In the **Orientation**, **Slides** section, click next to **Portrait**.
3 Click on **OK**.

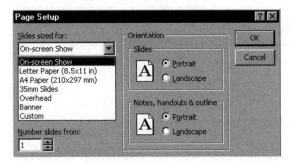

Figure 6.22 Page Setup

Info

From the Page Setup dialogue box, you can resize the slides to suit different requirements (eg 35 mm slides, overheads etc) using the **Slides sized for** drop-down list. You can also key in exact dimensions for your slides.

2.13 Saving an existing presentation and in different formats

Exercise 14

Save both presentations. Save the new presentation in a form suitable for the web.

Method

1 Save the existing presentation by clicking on the **Save** button.
2 Save the new presentation by selecting **Save as HTML** from the **File** menu.
3 Follow the instructions using Help where necessary (Figure 6.23).

Note: You can also save the presentation in other formats by selecting from the **Save as type** drop-down list in the **Save** dialogue box as shown in Figure 6.23.

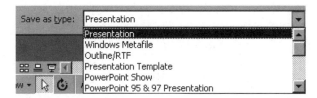

Figure 6.23 Saving in other formats

2.14 Close both presentations and exit PowerPoint.

Section 2 presentations practice

1   Reload the presentation saved in Practice Section 1.
2   Create a master slide containing the date and a footer **Created by (your name)**.
3   Add a suitable graphic to this master slide at the top left. Resize it to approximately 2 cm square (keep the original aspect ratio).
4   Add a new slide at the end of the presentation.
5   Using the Drawing toolbar buttons, create the following diagram in the centre of the newly created slide:

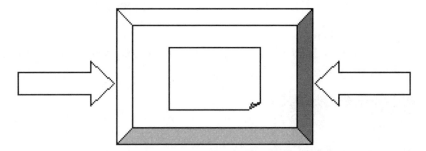

6   Add a text box below the diagram with the text **Using Multimedia**.
7   Format the text box with a background colour light green and text colour dark purple.
8   Create a new slide at the end of the presentation.
9   Copy the text box in step 7 to the new slide.
10 Open a new PowerPoint presentation and copy the last slide to become the first slide of the new presentation.
11 Add a text box to the slide in step 10 with the text **Multimedia is fun!**
12 Add a note to this slide: **Opening slide for uses of multimedia in web designs**.
13 Return to the original presentation. Reorder the slides so that Slide 1 becomes the last slide.
14 Save the original presentation and print as Handouts (all slides on one page) in portrait display.
15 Save the new presentation in a format suitable for the web.
16 Print the new presentation as Notes Pages.
17 Close both files and exit PowerPoint.

Section 3 Working with objects

In this section you will practise and learn how to:

* Create an organisational chart.

* Modify the structure of an organisational chart.

* Create different kinds of chart; bar, pies etc.

* Import images from other files.

* Copy an imported object to a master slide.

* Add borders to an object.

3.1 Creating an organisational chart

 Exercise 1

Load PowerPoint and a new presentation. On Slide 1 enter the text **Types of Chart**, add a bulleted list containing Organisational, Bar and Pie. On the master slide for this presentation, insert a footer containing your name and slide number. Save the presentation with the filename **Cybercafe Company**. On Slide 2 create an organisational chart.

 Method

1 Create Slide 1 and edit the master slide.
2 Create Slide 2 by clicking on the **New Slide** button and selecting: **Organization Chart** AutoLayout (Figure 6.24). Click on **OK**.

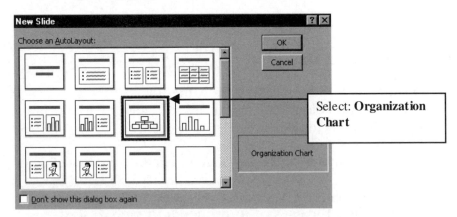

Figure 6.24 Creating an Organisational chart

3 Ensure you are in **Slide View**.
4 Key in the title **Personnel** in the Title placeholder.
5 Double-click in the chart box to add the organisational chart. The **Organization Chart** window appears (Figure 6.25).
6 Title the chart: **Cybercafe Company**. Key in the details in Figure 6.25 by clicking in the first relevant box and overwriting the original text. Click on the second relevant box and so on.

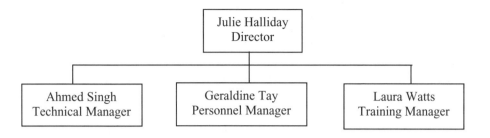

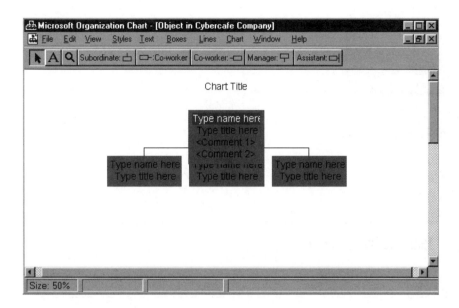

Figure 6.25 Organizational Chart window

Adding chart boxes

Exercise 2

Simeon Hardie works alongside Ahmed Singh and is also a Technical Manager. Add a Co-worker box and enter his name and his position.

Method

1 Click on the **Left Co-worker** button.
2 Click on Ahmed Singh's chart box and key in Simeon Hardie's details.

Exercise 3

Pat Hodge's line manager is Geraldine Tay. Her title is Administrator. Enter a chart box for Pat.

Method

1 Click on the **Subordinate** button.
2 Click on Geraldine Tay's chart box and key in Pat Hodge's details.

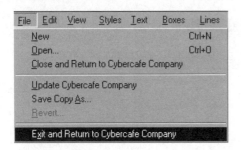

Info

You can continue adding as many boxes as necessary to complete an organisational chart. Use the menus to format the chart.

3   To return to the slide, from the **File** menu, select: **Exit and Return to Cybercafe Company** (Figure 6.26). Click on **Yes** to update the object.

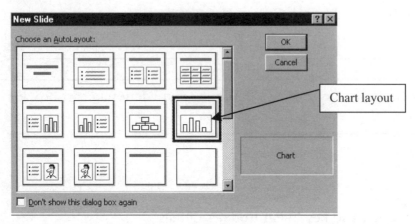

| File | Edit | View | Styles | Text | Boxes | Lines |

New   Ctrl+N
Open...   Ctrl+O
Close and Return to Cybercafe Company

Update Cybercafe Company
Save Copy As...
Revert...

Exit and Return to Cybercafe Company

Figure 6.26 Returning to the slide

3.2 Creating a bar/pie chart

Exercise 4

Create Slide 3 containing the title **Weekly Sales – January to March 2000**. Include a column chart showing the sales set out below:

	Week 1	Week 2	Week 3	Week 4
Jan	106	98	270	106
Feb	49	50	98	200
Mar	208	41	111	119

Method

1   Click on the **New Slide** button.
2   Select **Chart** AutoLayout (Figure 6.27).
3   Click on **OK**.

Figure 6.27 Chart layout

4   Key in the title in the Title placeholder.
5   Double-click to add the chart. A datasheet (Figure 6.28), a column chart and charting menus and toolbar buttons appear (Figure 6.29).
6   Key in the data above in the appropriate cells overwriting the sample data.

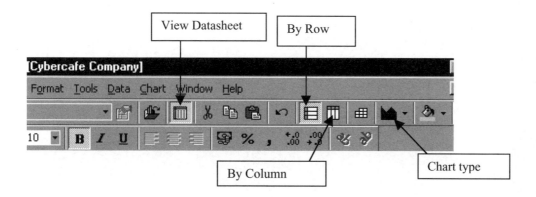

		A	B	C	D	
		1st Qtr	2nd Qtr	3rd Qtr	4th Qtr	
1	East	20.4	27.4	90	20.4	
2	West	30.6	38.6	34.6	31.6	
3	North	45.9	46.9	45	43.9	
4						

Figure 6.28 Datasheet

Figure 6.29 Charting menu and button options

7   Click on the **View Datasheet** button (Figure 6.29) to display the chart only.

Exercise 5

Change the bar chart to a column chart.

 Method

1   With the chart selected, click on the **Chart Type** button arrow and select: **3-D Bar Chart**.
2   The chart changes into the requested chart.

Info

Depending on how you lay out the data you can use the toolbar buttons to plot by row or by column. Add/delete rows or columns and format as in Excel. You can also create other types of chart (eg pie). Remember that pie charts use only one data series so you may need to hide data on the datasheet to get an accurate result. **To hide data**: Select the column(s)/row(s) to hide. Right-click on the selection and select: **Hide**. **To unhide data**: Select the columns/rows on either side of the hidden data. Right-click on the selection, and select: **Unhide**.

3.3 Importing objects and images from other files

Info

Sometimes you will want to import objects and images from other files (eg a company logo) and add it to the master slide so it will be visible throughout the presentation. If you have an image to import practise with it now. If not, make a note of the methods used below.

You can use the copy and paste methods described in section 2. You can also use:

1 The **Insert** menu and select: **Object** (Figure 6.30).

Figure 6.30 Inserting objects

2 The Insert Object dialogue box is displayed (Figure 6.31).
3 Click in the **Create from file** button.
4 Click on **Browse** to locate the file.
5 Click on **OK**.

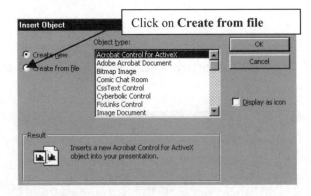

Figure 6.31 Insert Object box

6 The file is inserted into your presentation.
7 Resize and reposition it as appropriate.

Info

If you want to add it to the master slide, first from the **View** menu, select: **Master, Slide Master**. Then follow the method above.

3.4 Adding borders to an object

Exercise 6

Add a border to the imported object.

 Method

1 Select the object by clicking on it. On the Drawing toolbar, click on the **Line Color** button arrow (Figure 6.32).
2 Click on the colour you want.
3 Use the **Line Style** button to alter the line's format.

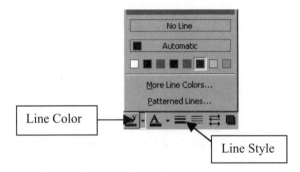

Figure 6.32 Adding a border

3.5 Save and print the presentation (as slides).

3.6 Close the presentation and exit PowerPoint.

Section 3 presentations practice

1 Open a new PowerPoint presentation, choose a suitable template background to be used throughout and create the following three slides:

Slide 1

Using the Title slide layout enter the title **Arts Department, North Weston College** and the sub-title **Friarsmith Mansion, Heathcliff Road, Leeds LS6 9YQ e-mail <u>arts@nwc.ac.uk</u>**.

Slide 2

Using the Organisation chart layout, enter the title **Structure of Arts**. Enter the organisational chart with the title **Current Staff** as shown:

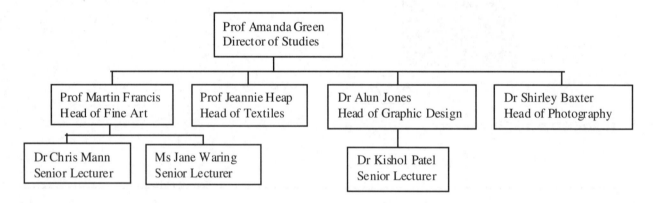

Slide 3

Using the Chart slide layout, add the title **Number of Students**. Use the following chart data to produce a 3-D column chart.

	Art	Text	Graphics	Photo
TERM 1	28	36	20	18
TERM 2	61	43	39	50
TERM 3	25	41	60	70

2 Insert a footer on all three slides: **Arts Department**, **your initials** and **the date**.
3 Insert a suitable piece of Clip Art on the first slide.
4 Change the text in the title of Slide 2 to **March 2000 – Structure of the Arts Faculty**.
5 Save the presentation and print the Slides as handouts (all on the same page).
6 Close the presentation.

Section 4 Automating a presentation

In this section you will practise and learn how to:

* Add slide transitions.
* Start a slide show.

* Add preset animation effects.
* Change preset animation effects.
* Use on-screen navigation tools.
* Hide slides.

4.1 Creating transitional timings

 Info

In **Slide Show View** you can see how the slides look on a full screen moving to the next/previous slide using the **Page Up/Page Down** keys (other keys will also perform the same task. Pressing the **Home** key will take you to Slide 1 and pressing the **End** key will take you to the last slide). The slides do not run automatically. In order for them to do this you need to set up transitional timings (slide durations) that automatically show the next slide after a set number of seconds.

 Exercise 1

Load PowerPoint and load one of the presentations you have created in the last sections. Create an automated presentation with slide durations shown below:

SLIDE NO	SLIDE DURATION
Slide 1	5 secs
Slide 2	7 secs
Slide 3	15 secs
Slide 4	10 secs

 Method

1 In **Slide Sorter View**, click on Slide 1 to select it.
2 Click on the 🖵 Slide Transition button.
3 The Slide Transition dialogue box appears (Figure 6.33).

Figure 6.33 Slide Transition box

4 In the **Advance** section, click in the box **On mouse click** so there is no tick in the box. Click in the box **Automatically after** so a tick is shown, and in the box beneath, key in the slide duration for Slide 1 (ie 5) (Figure 6.34).

Figure 6.34

5 Click on **Apply**. Slide 1 now has the duration (05) shown underneath at the left-hand side (Figure 6.35).

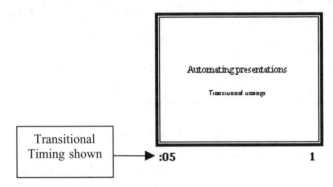

Figure 6.35 Transitional timing

6 Repeat steps 2–5 for each of the other slides ensuring you have selected the timing requested.
7 Save the presentation.

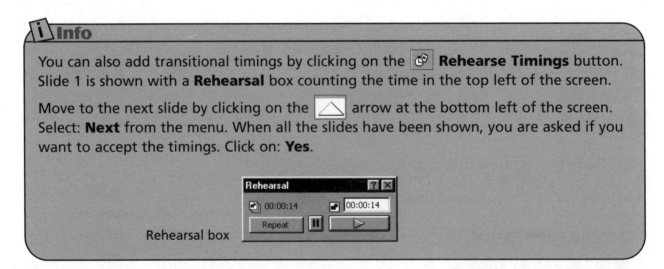

Info

You can also add transitional timings by clicking on the [icon] **Rehearse Timings** button. Slide 1 is shown with a **Rehearsal** box counting the time in the top left of the screen.

Move to the next slide by clicking on the [arrow] arrow at the bottom left of the screen. Select: **Next** from the menu. When all the slides have been shown, you are asked if you want to accept the timings. Click on: **Yes**.

Rehearsal box

4.2 Starting a slide show

Exercise 2

Start the slide show created in 4.1.

Method

1 From the **Slide Show** menu, select: **View Show**.
2 The presentation will run automatically with the timings that have been set.

4.3 Changing transitional timings

 Info

If you are not happy with the timings set, change them by selecting the slide with the time you want to change. Click on the **Slide Transition** button; edit the time next to the **Automatically after** box. Click on **Apply**. Repeat for any other slides you want to change.

4.4 Creating transitional effects

 Info

Transitional effects control how slides appear on the screen during a presentation. They are used to enhance the display and to ensure the audience of the presentation stays interested in it.

 Exercise 3

Create different transition effects for each of the slides.

 Method

1 Click on the **Slide Sorter View** button.
2 Click on Slide 1 to select it.
3 Click on the down arrow on the **Slide Transition Effects** toolbar box (Figure 6.36).

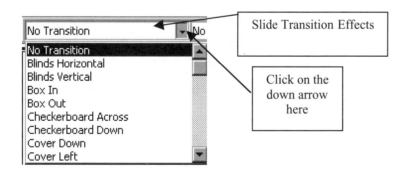

Figure 6.36 Creating slide transition effects

4 A drop-down list appears. There are many transition effects to choose from – you can scroll down for more. Click on a transition effect – you will see a preview of the effect on Slide 1. Experiment with the different effects. When you find one you like, click on that one so it remains visible in the Slide Transition Effects box.
5 An icon appears beneath the slide to show it has a transition effect applied to it (Figure 6.37).

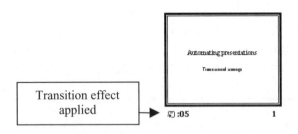

Figure 6.37 Applying a transition effect

6 Repeat for the other slides, choosing a different transitional effect for each one.
7 Save the presentation.
8 You can now run the presentation so you can view how the transitional effects look.

Info

If you want to apply the same transition effect to more than one slide in the presentation, select more than one slide by holding down the **Shift** key whilst selecting them. It is best not to apply too many transition effects to an automated presentation. Stick to the ones you think work best. You can define the transition effect further by clicking the **Slide Transition** button so the Slide Transition dialogue box appears. Here you can choose the speed of the effect and add sound!

4.5 Creating preset animation effects

Info

Preset animation effects determine the way text is revealed on a slide. They are usually very effective when applied to bulleted lists but can be applied to any slide.

Exercise 4

Add different preset animation effects to all the slides except slide 4.

Method

1 Click on the **Slide Sorter View** button.
2 Click on Slide 1 to select it.
3 Click on the down arrow on the **Text Preset Animation** toolbar box (see Figure 6.38).

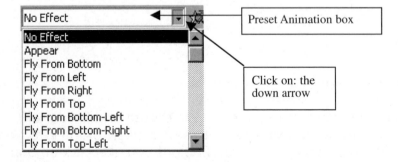

Figure 6.38 Setting a Build Effect

4 A drop-down list appears. There are many effects to choose from – you can scroll down for more. Click on an effect. You will not see a preview, as with transition effects.

5 An icon appears beneath the slide to show an animation effect has been applied to it (Figure 6.39).

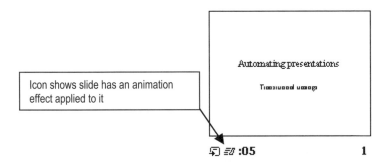

Icon shows slide has an animation effect applied to it

Figure 6.39 Preset animation effect applied

6 To view the animation effect, change to **Slide Show View**. The presentation will begin. To exit the slide show, press: **Esc**.

7 Add preset animation effects to the other slides as appropriate.

8 Save the presentation.

9 View the automated presentation.

Note: to change animation effect, repeat the method above selecting a different effect.

---

i **Info**

To start the slide show at a slide other than the first slide, select: **Set Up Show** from the **Slide Show** menu. The Set Up Show dialogue box is displayed. In the Slides section, key in the slides to view. Note the other options available in this dialogue box.

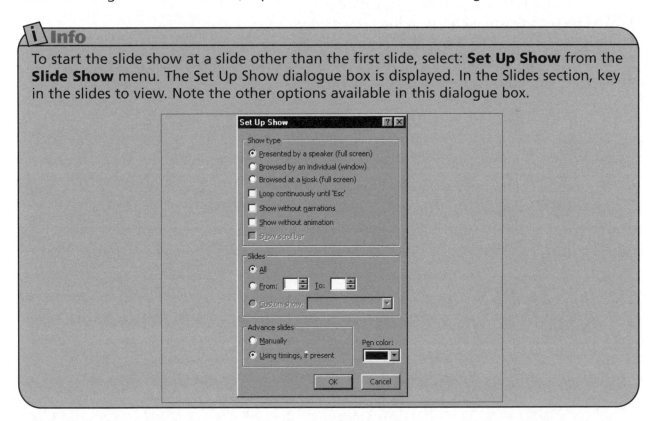

---

i **Info**

When presenting a show, you can navigate through as follows:

With the slide show running, right-click.

From the pop-up menu, select: **Go**, then: **Slide Navigator**.

Click on the slide to show next, then on: **Go To**.

4.6 Hiding slides

 Exercise 5

Hide one of the slides in your show.

 Method

1   In **Slide Sorter View**, select the slide to hide.

2   Click on: the ⬚ **Hide Slide** button.

Hidden slides have a cross through their number – eg 🔲

4.7 Save and close the presentation and exit PowerPoint

Section 4 presentations practice

1   Reload the presentation saved in Practice Section 3.
2   Add transitional timings to the presentation.
3   Add preset animation effects to the presentation.
4   Hide Slide 3.
5   Review the slide show and reset timings and effects as necessary.
6   Save the presentation.

Presentation quick reference guide

Action	Keyboard	Mouse	Right-mouse menu	Menu
Alignment, in relation to slide		Select object **Drawing** toolbar, **Draw**, **Align or Distribute**, **Relative to Slide** then **Draw**, **Align or Distribute**, select option you want		
Bold text	**Ctrl + B**	Click: the **B** **Bold** button	**Font** Select: **Bold** from the **Font style:** menu	**Format**, **Font**
Borders		Select object Drawing toolbar Click: ✏️▾ **Line Color** button Click: ≡ **Line Style** button		
Bullets, changing type			**Bullets**	**Format**, **Bullets**
Capitals (blocked)	**Caps Lock** Key in the text **Caps Lock** again to remove			Select text to be changed to capitals: **Format**, **Change Case**, **UPPERCASE**
Centre text	Select the text			
	Ctrl + E	Click: the ≡ **Center** button		**Format**, **Alignment**, **Center**
Change case	Select the text to be changed From the **Format** menu, select: **Change Case** Select the appropriate case			
Chart, inserting data organisation	Select appropriate slide AutoLayout, ie chart or organisation chart Data chart – overwrite sample data, click: 📋 **View Datasheet** button Organisation – key in text. **File** menu, **Exit and Return to (presentation)**			
Close a file	**Ctrl + W**	Click: the **X** **Close** icon		**File**, **Close**
Colours, slide				**Format**, **Slide Color Scheme**
Cut text	Select the text to be cut			
	Ctrl + X	Click: the ✂️ **Cut** button	**Cut**	**Edit**, **Cut**
Delete a character	Press: **Delete** to delete the character to the right of the cursor Press: ← (Backspace) to delete the character to the left of the cursor			
Delete an image	Select the image, press: **Delete**			
Delete a word	Double-click: the word to select it Press: **Delete**			
Delete a slide	Select the slide in Slide Sorter View. Press: **Delete**			

Action	Keyboard	Mouse	Right-mouse menu	Menu
Delete/cut a block of text	Select the text you want to delete			
	Delete *or* **Ctrl + X**	Click: the ✂ **Cut** button	**Cut**	**Edit**, **Cut**
Duplicate slide	**Insert** menu, **Duplicate Slide**			
Effects, transitional timings	In **Slide Sorter** view			
		Click: the 🔲 **Slide Transition** button	**Slide Transition**	**Slide Show**, **Slide Transition**
	In the **Advance** section Select: the timing you require			
Effects, transitional effects	In **Slide Sorter** view			
		Click: the ▾ down arrow next to the **Slide Transition Effects** box	**Slide Transition**	**Slide Show**, **Slide Transition**
			In the **Effects** section	
	Select: the effect you want			
Effects, preset animation	In **Slide Sorter** view			
		Click: the ▾ down arrow next to the **Text Preset Animation** box	**Preset text Animation**	**Preset Animation**
	Select: the effect you want from.			
Exit PowerPoint		Click: the ✕ **Close Window** icon		**File**, **Exit**
Font size	Select the text you want to change			
		Click: the ▾ down arrow next to the **Font Size** box Select: the font size you require	**Font**	**Format**, **Font**
			Select: the required size from the **Size:** menu	
Font	Select the text you want to change			
		Click: the ▾ down arrow next to the **Font** box Select: the font you require	**Font**	**Format**, **Font**
			Select: the required font from the **Font:** menu	
Serif	Serif fonts have small lines at upper and lower ends of characters – eg **Times New Roman**			
Sans serif	Sans serif fonts do not have lines – eg **Arial**			
Headers and footers				**View**, **Header and Footer**
Help	**F1**			**Help**, **Microsoft PowerPoint Help**
	Shift + F1			**What's This?**
Hide a slide		Click: the 🔲 **Hide Slide** button		**Slide Show**, **Hide Slide**

Action	Keyboard	Mouse	Right-mouse menu	Menu
Importing	From the **Insert** menu, select: **Picture** or **Object**			
graphic extract text, Excel graph or other object	Use copy (in the source application) and paste into PowerPoint			
Insert text	Position the cursor where you want the text to appear Key in the text			
Lines, adding formatting	Use the relevant Drawing Toolbar buttons			
Load PowerPoint	In Windows 95 desktop			
		Double-click: the **PowerPoint** shortcut icon		**Start**, **Programs**, **Microsoft PowerPoint**
Master slide setup				**View**, **Master**, **Slide Master**
New presentation, creating	**Ctrl + N**	Click: the ☐ **New** button		**File**, **New**
New slide	**Ctrl + M**	Click: the 🗗 **New Slide** button		**Insert**, **New Slide**
Notes, adding	In **Normal View,** add to the **Notes** pane			
Numbering slides				**Insert**, **Slide Number**
Open an existing file	**Ctrl + O**	Click: the 📂 **Open** button		**File**, **Open**
	Select the appropriate directory and filename Click: **Open**			
Orientation of slides				**File**, **Page Setup**
Print – slides, handouts, notes pages, Outline view	**Ctrl + P**			**File**, **Print**
	Select from the **Print what**: drop-down menu			
Remove text emphasis	Select text to be changed			
	Ctrl + B (remove bold) **Ctrl + I** (remove italics) **Ctrl + U** (remove underline)	Click: the appropriate button: **B** *I* U	**Font** Select: **Regular** from the **Font Style**: menu	**Format**, **Font**
Resize objects	Select the object. Resize using the handles. To preserve aspect ratio, resize from a corner			

Action	Keyboard	Mouse	Right-mouse menu	Menu
Run automated presentation		Click: the 🖳 **Slide Show** button at the bottom left of the screen		**V̲iew**, **Slide Sho̲w**
Save	**Ctrl + S**	Click: the 💾 **Save** button		**F̲ile**, **S̲ave**
	If you have not already saved the file you will be prompted to specify the directory and to name the file			
Save using a different name or to a different directory or in a different format				**F̲ile**, **Save A̲s**
	Select the appropriate drive and change the filename and file type if relevant. Click: **Save**			
Shadow, adding	On the Drawing toolbar, click: the ■ **Shadow** button			
Slide order	In **Slide Sorter** View Click and drag the slide to required position			
Spellcheck	**F7**	Click: the ✓ **Spelling** button		**T̲ools**, **S̲pelling**
Superscript and subscript text			**F̲ont, Effects**	**Fo̲rmat**, **F̲ont, Effects**
Templates, using				**F̲ormat**, **Apply Design Template**
Toolbars modifying	**V̲iew**, **T̲oolbars**, **C̲ustomize**			
Undo	**Ctrl + Z**	Click: the ↶ **Undo** button		**E̲dit**, **U̲ndo**
View		Click: a **View** button		**V̲iew**, **make selection**
Zoom		Click: the 100% ▼ **Zoom** button		**V̲iew**, **Z̲oom**

Module 6 practice tasks

Practice tasks 1

Make a 3-page presentation for Chellington Car Sales.

1. First slide is the Title slide. Key in the text: **Summer Madness 2000**.
2. Add your name and date in the bottom centre and ensure it appears on all three slides.
3. Insert a suitable piece of Clip Art on Slide 1. Resize and centre it so it looks effective.
4. On Slide 2 key in the text: **Many models on offer**:
5. Underneath key in the bulleted list:

   - **Vauxhalls**
   - **Fords**
   - **Toyotas**
   - **Volkswagens**

6. Format the bullets as ticks.
7. On Slide 3 create an organisational chart entitled **Meet the Team** as follows:

   Jean Moneypenny – Managing Director, Jack Quincy and Jill Bailey are Sales Managers immediately subordinate to Jean MoneyPenny. Paul Jones and Kiki Young are co-workers subordinate to Jill Bailey.

8. Create a slide show.
9. Save the presentation and print slides as Handouts (all three on one page).

Practice tasks 2

Make a three-page presentation for Gardening World.

1. Select a template (background) you think will be appropriate.
2. Key in the following on Slide 1 (the Title Slide): **Gardening World, Annual Report**.
3. At the bottom left corner, add your initials and a relevant piece of Clip Art (resize to fit in the corner) so they appear on all three slides.
4. Slide 2 will contain text and a chart. Key in the text: **Performance**.
5. Create the column chart using the data below:

	Qtr 1	Qtr 2	Qtr 3	Qtr 4
Plants	1900	2380	1700	4000
Trees	2000	4000	6000	3000
Equipment	5500	3322	6622	1890

6. Enter the following text on Slide 3:

   We strive to provide the very best for all your gardening needs. We are always ready to provide information and advice that will turn your fingers green.

7. Centre the text on the slide.
8. Italicise the words **fingers green** and change the text colour to green (if it is appropriate for the design).
9. Create the following graphic (use the Drawing toolbar). Centre it under the text.

10 Add a note to Slide 2: **Figures do not include bedding plant sales**.

11 Create a slide show and save it with an appropriate name.

12 Set the slide orientation to Portrait.

13 Print the slides as Notes Pages.

14 Save the presentation.

Note: This is only a practice test. Successful completion does not imply certification of the module by the ECDL Foundation.

Module 7

Information and Communication

Section 1 Getting started with the World Wide Web

In this section you will practise and learn how to:

* Open a web browsing application.
* Understand the make-up and structure of a web address.
* Display a given web page.
* Change the web browser home page.
* Save a web page as a file.
* Use application Help functions.
* Close the web browsing application.
* Change view/display modes.
* Modify toolbar display.
* Display images on web page.
* Not display image files on a web page.

1.1 What is a web browser?

A web browser is software that allows you to view, navigate and interact with the World Wide Web. Currently, the two most commonly used browsers are Internet Explorer and Netscape Navigator. In this chapter the examples use Internet Explorer. You will need to check which browser your ECDL test centre uses. If it uses Netscape Navigator, this can be downloaded free from the Internet. There are some differences between them but check you know how to transfer the skills practised in Internet Explorer.

1.2 Opening Internet Explorer

 Exercise 1

Open Internet Explorer.

 Method

From the **Start** menu, select **Programs, Internet Explorer** *or* click on the **Internet Explorer shortcut** icon.

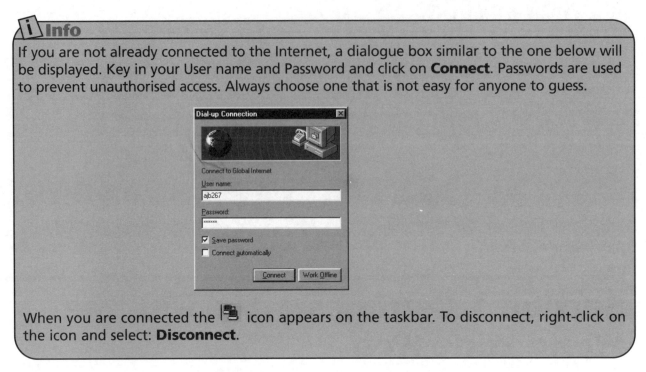

i Info

If you are not already connected to the Internet, a dialogue box similar to the one below will be displayed. Key in your User name and Password and click on **Connect**. Passwords are used to prevent unauthorised access. Always choose one that is not easy for anyone to guess.

When you are connected the 🖳 icon appears on the taskbar. To disconnect, right-click on the icon and select: **Disconnect**.

Either method will result in the Internet Explorer window being displayed (Figure 7.1). Toolbar buttons are labelled in Figure 7.2

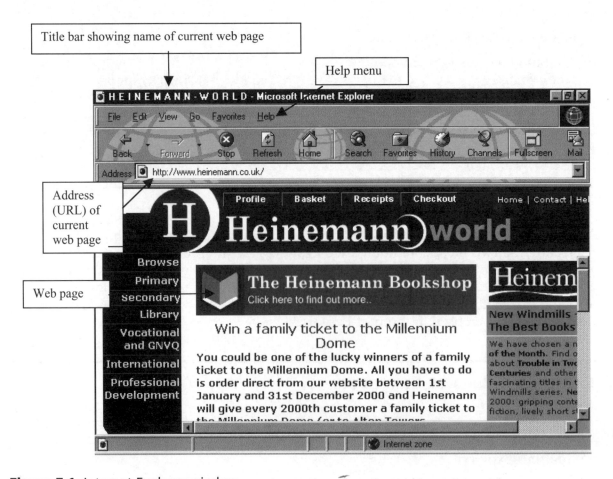

Figure 7.1 Internet Explorer window

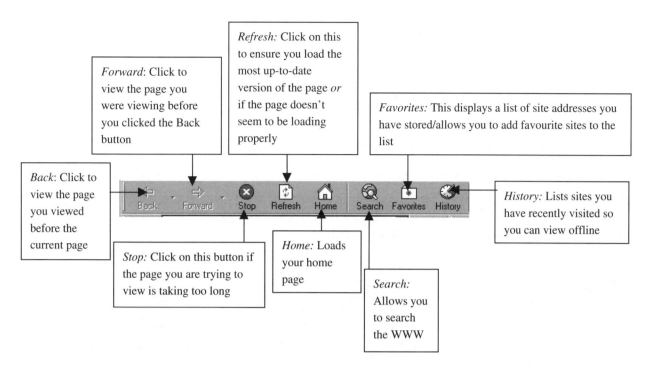

Back: Click to view the page you viewed before the current page

Forward: Click to view the page you were viewing before you clicked the Back button

Refresh: Click on this to ensure you load the most up-to-date version of the page *or* if the page doesn't seem to be loading properly

Favorites: This displays a list of site addresses you have stored/allows you to add favourite sites to the list

History: Lists sites you have recently visited so you can view offline

Stop: Click on this button if the page you are trying to view is taking too long

Home: Loads your home page

Search: Allows you to search the WWW

Figure 7.2 Internet Explorer toolbar buttons

1.3 What is a web address?

A *website* is a collection of pages on the web owned by an individual or organisation. The first page of a website is the *home page*. Every web page has a unique address. This is known as an **URL** (**U**niform **R**esource **L**ocator). It usually begins with 'http://www.' (http stands for *HyperText Transfer Protocol* and tells the web browser it is looking for a web page). Most modern browsers have 'http://' stored so you can start at 'www'. Some URLs include:

http://www.bbc.co.uk
http://www.bargainholidays.com
http://www.nhm.ac.uk

The text after the www shows the *domain name,* the organisation's name – eg BBC, bargainholidays and nhm (Natural History Museum), the type of site (eg .co and .com are commercial companies; .ac is an academic community), and the country (eg uk is United Kingdom). If there is no country name this often means the website is American.

Note: The dots are important in a web address and the address must be spelt correctly.

Sometimes URLs are longer because they include the pathname to the web page for example:

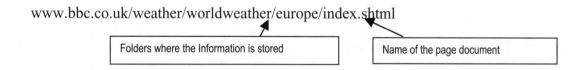

www.bbc.co.uk/weather/worldweather/europe/index.shtml

Folders where the Information is stored

Name of the page document

1.4 Displaying a given web page

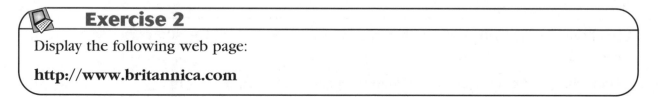

Exercise 2

Display the following web page:

http://www.britannica.com

Method

1   Key in the web address in the address box. Press: **Enter**.
2   The first page of the Encyclopaedia Britannica website is displayed.

1.5 Changing your web browser's home page

 Exercise 3

Change your web browser's home page so it is the home page of 'This is London'. The
address is: **http://www.thisislondon.co.uk**

 Info

Notice I have used the words *Home page* twice in the exercise above. A home page can
mean the page your browser displays when it first starts up *or* it can mean the first page
of a website. The home page of the 'This is London' website is the first page you see
when you enter its address.

 Method

1   Go to the 'This is London' home page by keying in the web address.
2   The 'This is London' home page appears.
3   From the **View** menu, select **Internet Options**. The Internet options box is displayed
    (Figure 7.3).
4   With the **General** tab selected, in the **Home Page** section, click on **Use Current**.
5   Click on **Apply** and then on **OK**.

Figure 7.3 Setting a browser's home page

1.6 Displaying/not displaying images

 Info

It is quicker to load a web page when you do not load the images contained in it since
image files are quite large. You are able to set up your browser so that it does not
display images.

 Exercise 4

Load the Natural History Museum home page without images. The address is
http://www.nhm.ac.uk

Then change the settings back to load the page with images.

Method

1 From the **View** menu, select: **Internet Options**.
2 Click on the **Advanced** tab.
3 In the **Multimedia** section, click in the boxes next to **Show pictures**, **Play videos**, **Play Animations** so there are no ticks.
4 Click on **Apply** and then on **OK**.
5 Key in the Natural History Museum address.
6 The Natural History Museum home page is displayed without images.

Re loading with images

7 Follow steps 1 to 5 again, this time placing ticks where they were removed.
8 Click on the **Refresh** button to redisplay the page with images.

1.7 Changing view/display

Info

You may find you want to change the look of web pages to suit your needs (ie colours, fonts etc which you find easier to read. To change settings:

1 From the **View** menu select: **Internet Options**.
2 With the **General** tab selected, click on **Colors** and make your choices. Similarly, click on **Fonts** to set your preferences.
3 Click on **Apply** and then on **OK**.

Changing text size

From the **View** menu, select: **Fonts**. Select the size you prefer.

1.8 Saving a web page as a file

 Exercise 5

Save one of the web pages you have visited as a file.

 Method

1 Load the web page by keying in the address in the **Address** box.
2 From the **File** menu, select **Save As**.
3 The **Save As** dialogue box is displayed.
4 Select the location where you want to save the web page and key in a filename.
5 In the **Save as type** section, select from the list (Figure 7.4).
6 Click on **Save**.

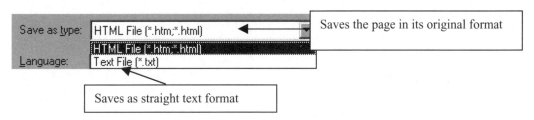

Figure 7.4 Saving a web page

1.9 Closing Internet Explorer

 Method

From the **File** menu, select: **Close**.

Section 1 information and communication practice

Practice 1

1 Open a web browser.
2 Display one of the following website home pages:

 http://www.bbc.co.uk
 http://www.channel4.co.uk

3 Set one of the site home pages as your web browser home page.
4 Save the web page as a file.
5 Change the browser's settings so images are not loaded.
6 Display the following website home page

 http://www.thisisbritain.co.uk

7 Change the browser's settings so images are displayed.

Section 2 Browsing and favorites

In this section you will practice and learn how to:

* Browse a specific site and collect data.

* Open a hyperlink or an image link and return to the original page.

* Add a web page to favorites.

* Add web pages to a favorites folder.

* Open a favorites web page.

2.1 Using hyperlinks

Web pages have links (called *hyperlinks*) you can click on to take you to other places within the current site or to other web sites. Links can take the form of underlined text, text in a different colour or they can be image links. When you hover over a link a hand (usually) appears. The home page of the Natural History Museum site has text and image links (Figure 7.5).

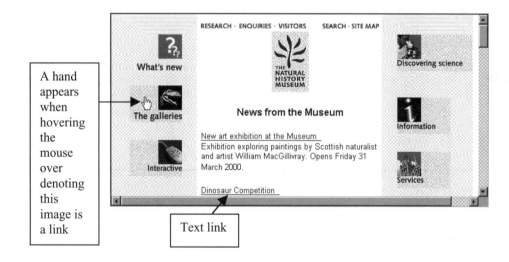

A hand appears when hovering the mouse over denoting this image is a link

Text link

Reproduced with permission from the
Natural History Museum, London

Figure 7.5 Text and image links

 Exercise 1

Follow one of the links on the Natural History Museum home page to find out specific information, (eg what galleries are there? What is new)?

 Method

1 Click on the link. Another page of the site is displayed. Notice the address and Title bar have changed to reflect you are viewing another page.

2 Collect the information you are looking for.

   a) Select the data so that it is highlighted.

   b) Click on: the **Copy** button.

   c) Open an application to copy it to e.g. Word.

   d) Click on: the **Paste** button.

3 Return to the original page by clicking on the **Back** button.

2.2 Saving a list of your favourite websites

Info

When you find a site you would like to visit again, or a site you visit often, it is a good idea to save the address of the site to make it easier to revisit in the future. These sites are then known as *Favorites* or *Bookmarks*. Note: The US spelling 'favorites' is followed here as this is how it appears in most software programs.

Exercise 2

Save the Natural History Museum site in your **Favorites** list.

 Method

1 With the home page of the site displayed, from the **Favorites** menu, select: **Add to Favorites**.
2 The **Add Favorite** dialogue box is displayed.
3 A default name already appears in the **Name** box. Change the name if you want to.
4 Click on **OK**.

Accessing Favorites

 Method

From the **Favorites** menu, click on the website name.

2.3 Organising favorites

So your list of favorites does not become unmanageable, you can organise it by creating folders to store similar content pages.

 Method

1 From the **Favorites** menu, select: **Organize Favorites**.
2 The **Organize Favorites** dialogue box is displayed (Figure 7.6).
3 Click on the **Create New Folder** button.
4 Key in a name for the new folder and press: **Enter**.
5 Drag the relevant favorites into the folder.
6 Click on **Close**.

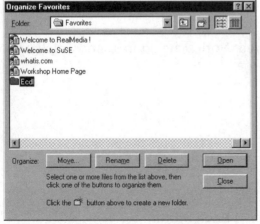

Note: Use the **Move** button when moving multiple favorites.

Figure 7.6 Organize favorites

Section 2 information and communication practice

Practice 2

1   Access one of the sites listed below:

The Louvre	**http://www.louvre.fr**
Good Book Guide	**http://www.good-book-guide.com**
British Space Centre	**http://www.bnsc.gov.uk**
The Guardian	**http://www.newsunlimited.co.uk**
ITN Online	**http://www.itn.co.uk**

2   Using hyperlinks, find out some information that is not available on the home page.

3   Add the home page of your chosen website to your favorites in a folder with the name **ECDL practice**.

Section 3 Searching

In this section you will practise and learn how to:

* Define search requirements.
* Use a key word in a search.
* Use common logical operators in a search.

* Modify page setup options.
* Print a web page.
* Present a search report as a printed document.

3.1 Searching the web

There are many ways you can find information on the web:

* If you know the web address of the site where you can find the information, go straight to the site by keying in the address and using hyperlinks to navigate through the site (or use the site's search box if it has one).

* Using Internet Explorer's **Search** button enables you to key in a word(s) (known as a **key word**) or phrase. It then uses a search engine that will look for the key word(s) on a database of websites. A search engine looks like a normal web page with a form to enter key words that you are looking for. It runs a program that searches its own database (an up-to-date list of web sites), and provides you with a list of 'hits' (ie sites that contain the keyword(s)).

* Using a chosen search engine. You may find a particular search engine usually finds what you are looking for or/and you find it easy to use. Common search engines include:

    http://www.altavista.com
    http://www.hotbot.com
    http://www.excite.co.uk
    http://www.infoseek.com
    http://www.ask.co.uk
    http://www.google.com
    http://www.raging.com
    http://www.alltheweb.com

* Using a search directory. A search directory sets out information in subject categories. This is useful if you are conducting a broad search. Currently, the most common search directory is Yahoo **http://www.yahoo.com**. Other common search directories include:

    | Magellan | **http://www.mckinley.com** |
    | Lycos | **http://www.lycos.com** |
    | LookSmart | **http://www.looksmart.com** |
    | What's New | **http://www.whatsnew.com** |
    | UK Online | **http://www.ukonline.com** |

 Exercise 1

Find the addresses of ECDL test centres using the different search methods. Compare the different methods as you progress (ie time taken, usefulness of results, ease of use).

3.2 Using the Search button

 Method

1 Click on the **Search** button.
2 Key **ECDL** into the **Search** box and enter it by clicking on **Search**.
3 My search revealed four possible links (Figure 7.7).
4 Follow the links for information.

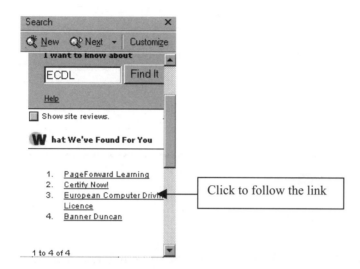

Figure 7.7 Finding Information using Search

3.3 Using a search engine

 Method

1 Access the Altavista website.
2 Key **ECDL** into the **Search** box and enter it by clicking on **Search**.
3 My search resulted in the following (Figure 7.8).
4 Follow up the links.

Figure 7.8 Using a search engine

I clicked on ECDL test and found 142 pages (Figure 7.9).

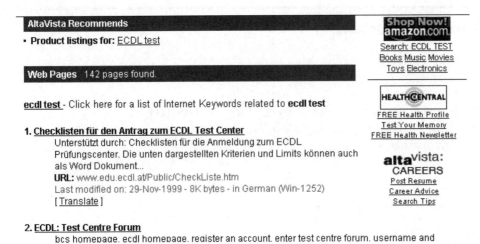

AltaVista Recommends

- **Product listings for:** ECDL test

Shop Now!
amazon.com.

Search: ECDL TEST
Books Music Movies
Toys Electronics

HEALTH C ENTRAL

FREE Health Profile
Test Your Memory
FREE Health Newsletter

altavista:
CAREERS
Post Resume
Career Advice
Search Tips

Web Pages 142 pages found.

ecdl test - Click here for a list of Internet Keywords related to **ecdl test**

1. **Checklisten für den Antrag zum ECDL Test Center**
   Unterstützt durch: Checklisten für die Anmeldung zum ECDL
   Prüfungscenter. Die unten dargestellten Kriterien und Limits können auch
   als Word Dokument...
   URL: www.edu.ecdl.at/Public/CheckListe.htm
   Last modified on: 29-Nov-1999 - 8K bytes - in German (Win-1252)
   [Translate]

2. **ECDL: Test Centre Forum**
   bcs homepage, ecdl homepage, register an account, enter test centre forum, username and

Figure 7.9 Following a link in Alta Vista

3.4 Using a search directory

 Method

1 Log in to the Yahoo site. Figure 7.10 shows some of the site's categories.

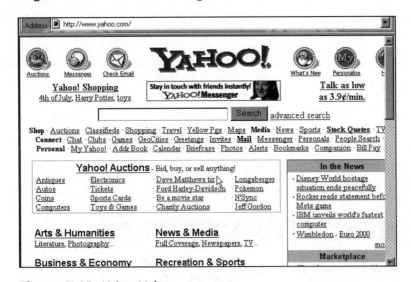

Reproduced with permission of Yahoo! Inc '
2000 by Yahoo! Inc. Yahoo! and the Yahoo!
logo are trademarks of Yahoo! Inc.

Figure 7.10 Using Yahoo

2 Click on links in the directory you think are appropriate.

3.5 Using logical operators

You can refine your searches by keying in more than one word and using logical operators:
AND, NOT (or their equivalents AND, +, &; NOT, -) and OR. Different search engines have
slightly different rules about how you enter searches with logical operators.

Using AND

Use AND or one of the symbols when searching for more than one word. Results will list sites
that contain all the search words. For example:

You are interested in finding information on football and, in particular, Everton. In the Search box, key in **Football + Everton**.

You are interested in finding information about Oscars and Disney. In the Search box, key in **Oscars + Disney**.

Using NOT

Use NOT or the minus sign when searching for information but omitting certain information. For example:

You are interested in finding information on football but not on Everton. In the Search box, key in **Football - Everton**.

You are interested in finding information about Oscars but not Disney. In the Search box, key in **Oscars - Disney**.

Using OR

You are interested in finding information about cameras. You could key in **Camera OR photography**, since both these might find useful information.

Info

For some search engines, quotation marks can be used to group words together (eg "motor racing" may find more confined results than motor racing).

Try out some other searches with logical operators. Note the different search format requirements and which methods give the most relevant results.

3.6 Modifying page setup ready for printing

 Method

1 From the **File** menu, select: **Page Setup** (Figure 7.11).
2 Change the paper size, orientation and margins.
3 Use Internet Explorer Help if you want to set headers and footers.
4 Click on **OK**.

Figure 7.11 Page Setup

3.7 Printing a web page

 Method

1 From the **File** menu, select: **Print**.
2 The Print dialogue box is displayed (Figure 7.12).

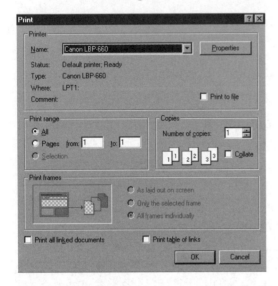

Figure 7.12 Printing

3 Make selections as appropriate.
4 If the web page is divided into frames, enter your choices in the Print Frames section.
5 Click on **OK**.

Info

You can also choose to print a table of links. This is useful for reference.

Warning

Remember anyone can set up a website and information may not always be correct or may be misleading. Always check information is from a reliable source.

3.8 Exit Internet Explorer

Section 3 information and communication practice

Practice 3

1 Using a search engine or a search directory, find answers to some of the following questions:

What is the current line-up of the Leicester City football team?
What is on BBC1 and ITN at 8 pm this evening?
What is the population of the UK?
What time do trains depart from Bristol tomorrow morning (leaving at approx 9.30 am), destination Leeds? Are there any changes en route?

2 Print out the results of your searches detailing the information requested.

Section 4 Getting started with e-mail

In this section you will practise and learn how to:

* Open an electronic mail application.
* Use application Help functions.
* Change display modes.
* Modify toolbar display.
* Create a new message.
* Insert a mail address in the Mailto box.
* Insert a title in the subject field.
* Use a spell checking tool (if available).
* Send a message with low/high priority.
* Copy a message to another address.
* Use blind copy tool.
* Receive messages.
* Add an auto-signature to a message.
* Close the electronic mail application.

Introduction

The following sections focus on sending and receiving e-mail using Microsoft Outlook Express. By demonstrating the methods used by Outlook Express you will gain an insight into the procedures involved even though you may be using a different e-mail system. It should be relatively easy to apply what you learn here to your own e-mail system.

Note: Since Outlook Express can be configured to suit your needs, the Outlook Express settings used in the examples may differ slightly from your settings. This could result in some of the methods given not conforming exactly to those you may see on your computer.

4.1 Opening Outlook Express

Exercise 1

Open Outlook Express.

Method

From the **Start** menu, select: **Programs, Internet Explorer, Outlook Express** *or* click on the **Outlook Express** shortcut icon.

Either method will result in the Outlook Express window being displayed on screen (Figure 7.13).

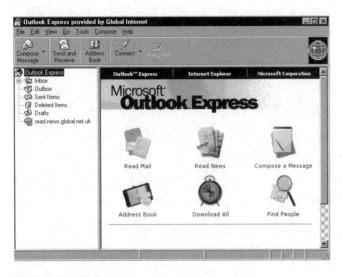

Figure 7.13 Outlook Express 4 window

The Folders list contains:

- **Inbox** folder – where incoming messages are stored.
- **Outbox** folder – where outgoing messages are stored.
- **Sent Items** folder – where sent messages are stored.
- **Deleted Items** folder – where deleted items are stored.
- **Drafts** folder – where draft messages are stored.

Info

You can change the layout and modify the toolbar to suit your needs by selecting: Layout from the **View** menu. The Window Layout Properties box is displayed as shown below:

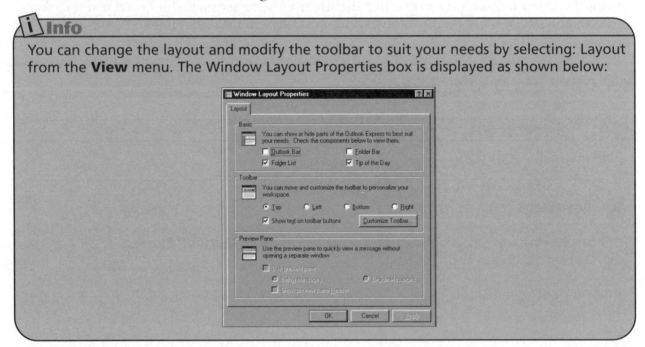

4.2 Creating messages

Exercise 2

Create the message (shown below) and send it to someone you know who has an e-mail address.

Note: If you do not have anyone to send it to, then send it to your own e-mail address.

Hi there [insert person's name]

I am learning how to use e-mail. Please let me know if you have received this message.

Thanks.

Method

1 Click on the **Compose Message** button.
2 The New Message window appears (Figure 7.14).
3 Click in the **To**: box and key in the e-mail address of the person you are sending the message to. Check you have keyed in the address correctly.

Header section:
Click in the boxes and key in the e-mail address(es) of recipient(s) and subject here

Message section:
Click in this area and key in your message here

Figure 7.14 Creating a message

Info

It is very important the address is keyed in correctly, otherwise it will not reach its destination. Each dot (full stop) is important. If you have made an error, you can delete it and key it in again.

E-mail addresses are made up of:

the user's name, followed by the @ symbol, followed by the address of the user's service provider. This includes the domain category. In this example co (meaning a company or commercial organisation in the UK), followed by the country, uk (United Kingdom). For example:

A.Smith@somewhere.co.uk

i Info

Common domain categories include the following:

ac = academic community (in the UK)
co = company or commercial organisation (in the UK)
com = company or commercial organisation
edu = educational institution
org = non-profit organisation

Each country has its own unique code (eg fr = France, ca = Canada, se = Sweden).

4 Click in the header section, subject line and key in: **Just testing**.

5 Click in the message section underneath and key in the message.

Note: The subject of your message 'Just testing' has replaced 'New Document' on the Title bar.

i Info

At this stage you can use:

• From the **Tools** menu, **Spelling** option to check spelling.

• From the **Tools** menu, **Set Priority** to determine the priority of the message. The default is Normal. A High Priority message has a red exclamation mark and a low priority message has a down arrow.

6 Click on the ⌸Send **Send** button.

Note: This will not send the message at this stage but will transfer it to your **Outbox** folder.

7 You are returned to the original Outlook Express window with the Outbox contents displayed (Figure 7.15). If the Outbox contents are not displayed, click on **Outbox**.

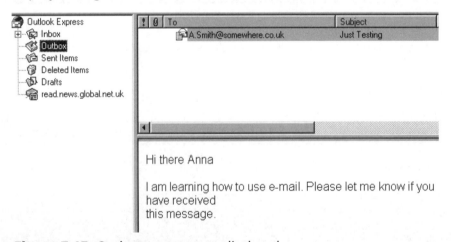

Figure 7.15 Outbox contents are displayed

i Info

You have composed your message 'offline' (ie not connected to the phone line and therefore not incurring phone costs). When you have learnt how to use e-mail, it is a good idea to compose several messages and then send them all at the same time since currently there is a minimum phone call charge. They will be stored in your **Outbox** folder until you are ready to send them, but in this example we are sending just one message. Outlook Express will automatically check if there are any incoming messages at the same time as sending messages.

4.3 Transmitting and receiving messages

Exercise 3

Transmit the message you have prepared.

 Method

1   Click on the **Send and Receive** button.
2   Outlook Express will send the message automatically and will display it is sending the message.
3   When it has been transmitted, it is placed in the **Sent Items** folder. Click on the folder to check.

> **i Info**
>
> Outlook Express can be set up to connect/disconnect automatically from the phone line. If this is not set you will need to do this manually and you should be prompted to do so. When you are connected to the phone line, an icon is placed on the taskbar. Click the right mouse button on this icon for a menu with the option to disconnect.

4.4 Copying messages

The same message can be sent to more than one address at a time.

Sending the message on equal terms to more than one address

In the **To**: box, key in the e-mail addresses and separate them with semicolons.

For example: **A.Smith@somewhere.co.uk;J.Jones@somewhereelse.ac.uk**

Note: You don't need a space after the semi-colon.

Sending 'carbon copies'

1   In the **To**: box, key in the first person's e-mail address.
2   In the **Cc**: box, key in the second person's e-mail address.

The main recipient(s) is the person in the To: box, with a 'carbon copy' sent to the second addressee(s).

Sending blind copies

Sometimes you may want to send a copy of the e-mail to an addressee(s) without other recipients' knowledge. To do this, Enter the recipient's address(es) in the **Bcc** box.

Note: With all of the above, the message is again placed in your **Sent Items** folder and is still treated as one message, even though it has been transmitted to more than one e-mail address.

4.5 Setting up an auto-signature

An auto-signature consists of text you want to include at the end of your message (and saves keying it in each time). You can set up more than one signature for different types of recipient.

Setting a signature

1 In the main Outlook Express window, from the **Tools** menu, select: **Stationery**.

2 In the Stationery dialogue box, click on **Signature** (Figure 7.16).

3 Key in your text in the Text box.

4 Click on **OK**.

5 Click on **Apply**, then on **OK**.

Inserting a signature in a message

You can select **Add signatures to all outgoing messages** by clicking in the box next to this option (Figure 7.16)

OR

In the **New Message** window, after you have keyed in your message, from the **Insert** menu, select: **Signature**.

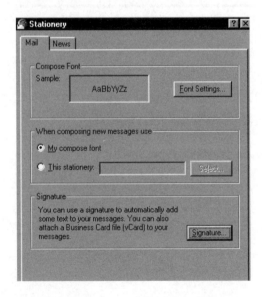

Figure 7.16 Setting up a signature

4.6 Close Outlook Express

 Method

From the **File** menu, select: **Exit** *or* click on the **Close** button.

Section 4 information and communication practice

Practice 4

1 Open an electronic mail application.
2 Send the following message with high priority to someone you know and a copy to someone else. Give the message the title **Seminar**.

Hello

Thank you for letting me know about the seminar. I will certainly be there. Perhaps we could meet in the cafeteria afterwards?

Regards

[Add an auto-signature]

Auto-signature should include your name, job title and ext no.

Section 5 Organising messages

In this section you will prastice and learn how to:

* Open a mail message.

* Open a mail inbox for a specified user.

* Attach a file to a message.

* Delete text in a message.

* Delete a file attachment from a message.

* Open and save an attachment.

* Use reply to sender/reply to all.

* Reply with/without original message insertion.

* Forward a message.

* Use copy and paste to duplicate text within a message or to another active message.

* Use cut and paste to insert text from another source into a message.

* Use cut and paste to move text within a message or to another active message.

* Create a new mail folder.

* Delete a message.

* Sort messages by name, subject, date etc.

* Move messages to a new mail folder.

* Mark/highlight a message in a mail folder.

* Search for a message.

5.1 Opening received mail messages

 Exercise 1

Open messages received.

Note: If you have not yet received replies to your e-mails then you will need to send an e-mail to your own e-mail address so there is a message received.

 Method

1 Load Outlook Express as in section 4.1 (if not already loaded).
2 You will notice there is a number (in this example, 2) next to your **Inbox** folder, indicating two messages have been received (Figure 7.17).

Figure 7.17 Messages have been received

3 The message(s) are displayed in the right-hand window.
4 Click once on the message to see it in the Preview window (bottom right), or double-click it to see it in a separate window (Figure 7.18).

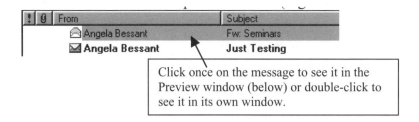

!	0	From	Subject
		Angela Bessant	Fw: Seminars
		Angela Bessant	**Just Testing**

Click once on the message to see it in the
Preview window (below) or double-click to
see it in its own window.

Figure 7.18 Viewing a received message

5.2 Opening another user's Inbox messages

Creating folders for other users

There may be several people accessing mail on the same account. If this is the case, you can add sort users' messages so they are delivered to their own individual folders.

 Method

Creating folders for users

1 From the **File** menu, select **Folder** then **New Folder**.
2 The Create Folder dialogue box is displayed
3 Click on the **Inbox** folder.
4 Key in the new name in the **Folder name** box.
5 Click on **OK**.

Now you need to sort the incoming messages so they are delivered to the correct folder(s).

Sorting incoming messages

6 From the **Tools** menu, select **Inbox Assistant**.
7 Click on **Add**.
8 Key in the relevant details in the appropriate boxes.
9 Click on **OK**.
10 Repeat these steps until all users have been entered.

Opening a user's inbox

If another user wants you to check his or her mail, look to see if he or she has a number next to his or her folder. If so, click on the folder so the messages appear in the right-hand pane. Access as in section 5.1.

5.3 Attaching files to messages

Sometimes you may want to enclose something with your message, (eg a picture or a different type of file). In such cases you can add a file to your message. This is called an attachment. You can add more than one file. These then are called attachments.

 Exercise 2

Create a simple Excel or a Word file. Save the file with the filename **TEST**. Send a message, together with the file **TEST** (the attachment), to an e-mail address. Ask the recipient to send you an attachment.

Method

1   Create a simple file and save it with the name **TEST** in a place you will know where to find it (eg on a floppy disk in Drive A).
2   Load Outlook Express and key in the following new message:

Hi [name of recipient]

I am practising sending and receiving attachments to e-mail messages. Please find the attached file TEST.

Please could you let me know you have received this and also please could you send me an example attachment?

Thanks.

[Your name]

Note: DO NOT CLICK SEND YET

3   Click on the **Insert File** button.
4   The Insert Attachment dialogue box appears (Figure 7.19).

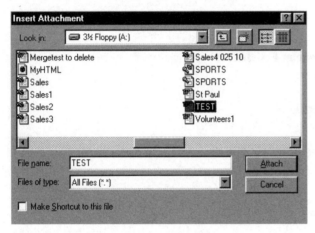

Figure 7.19 Insert Attachment dialogue box

5   Select the drive where the file is located (eg Drive A). Click on the file so it appears in the File name box (or key in the filename).
6   Click on **Attach**.
7   You will notice your attachment is now shown in the pane below the main message section (Figure 7.20).

TEST.doc
(19.0 KB)

Figure 7.20 E-mail attachment

8   You can now send the e-mail file in the normal way.

> **i Info**
>
> You can attach more than one file to a message by repeating steps 3–6 for each extra file.

5.4 Viewing attachments

Exercise 3

View an attachment you have received.

 Method

When you receive a message with an attachment, the message has a paperclip icon next to it (Figure 7.21).

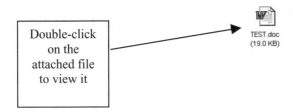

Figure 7.21 Receiving attachments

1 Double-click on the message to view it in a separate window.
2 Double-click on the attached file (Figure 7.22). The file will appear in its own program window.

Figure 7.22 Viewing an attachment

3 When you have finished viewing the file, close its window in the normal way. You are returned to Outlook Express.

5.5 Saving a file attachment

1 Double-click on the message with the attachment so it appears in its own window.
2 From the **File** menu, select: **Save Attachments**, select: the attachment. (If there is more than one, select **All** to save all of them.)
3 The Save Attachments As dialogue box is displayed (Figure 7.23).

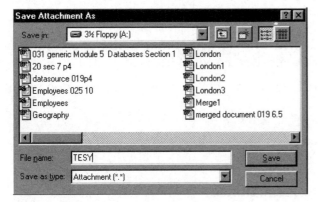

Figure 7.23 Saving attachments

4 Select the drive where you want to save it.
5 Key in the filename and click on **Save**.

or

Right-click on the attachment and select: **Save As (Figure 7.24)**.

Figure 7.24 Saving the attachments by right-clicking

5.6 Deleting a file attachment from a message

When sending attachments, if you have chosen the wrong one or need to delete one for any other reason, select the attachment by clicking on it. Press: **Delete**.

5.7 Replying to a message

 Method

1 With the message selected, click on the [Reply] **Reply to Author** button. The address and subject are already entered.
2 Key in your reply.
3 If you want to delete the original message, select it and press: **Delete**.
4 Send the message in the usual way.

> **i Info**
>
> Click on the [icon] **Reply to All** button if you want to reply to multiple e-mail addresses that were on the original message.
>
> Click on the [icon] **Forward** button to forward the message on to another e-mail address(es). Key in the e-mail address of the recipient(s). You can also add your own personal message to the new recipient(s) by clicking in the message pane and keying in the text.

5.8 Using cut/copy and paste

You can use the **Cut/Copy** and **Paste** from the **Edit** menu, as in other Office applications, to move and duplicate text within a message or to another active message.

You can also **Cut/Copy** and **Paste** to insert text from another source (eg a Word document or web page).

5.9 Deleting a mail message

In the main pane, select the message to delete. Press: **Delete**.

To select adjacent messages, hold down **Shift** when selecting.

To select non-adjacent messages, hold down **Ctrl** when selecting.

Info

Deleted messages are sent to the **Deleted Items** folder. You can recover deleted messages from here. It is a good idea to empty this folder from time to time. To do this right-click on the folder and select: **Empty Folder**. You can also delete messages by selecting them and pressing: **Delete**

5.10 Sorting messages

When you have numerous messages, you may want to sort them so they are easier to locate. To sort by name, subject or date, click on the relevant heading at the top of the messages window (Figure 7.25). In Figure 7.25 there is a down arrow next to **Sent** indicating the messages are sorted in descending date order.

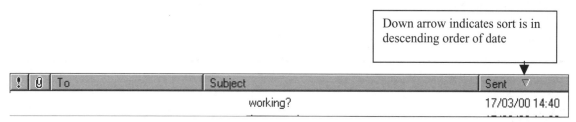

Figure 7.25 Sorting messages

Figure 7.25 Sorting messages

For a more comprehensive sort, from the **View** menu, select: **Sort By**. Options available are shown in Figure 7.26

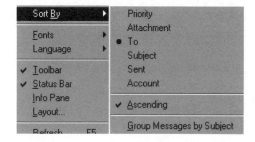

Figure 7.26 Sorting messages using the View menu

5.11 Moving/copying messages to a new mail folder

To move messages

 Method

1 Select the message(s) to move.
2 From the **Edit** menu, select: **Move to Folder** or **Copy to Folder**.
3 The Move or Copy dialogue box is displayed (Figure 7.27)

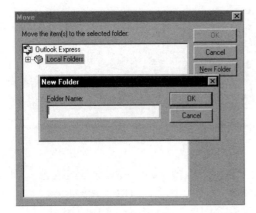

Figure 7.27 Moving messages to a new folder

4   Click on **New Folder** and key in a name for the folder.
5   Click on **OK**.
6   The message(s) is moved or copied to the new folder.

5.12 Searching for a message

 Method

1   Select the folder where you think the message is saved.
2   From the **Edit** menu, select: **Find Message**.
3   The Find Message dialogue box appears (Figure 7.28).

i Info

In this example, I have selected the **Inbox folder** at step 1. This method searches the **Inbox** folder and its subfolders when the **Include subfolders** box is ticked.

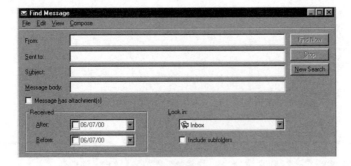

Figure 7.28 Finding messages

4   Key in details of your message in the appropriate boxes and then click on **Find Now**.

5.13 Close Outlook Express as shown in section 4.6.

Section 5 information and communication practice

Practice 5

1   Access any received message and forward it to someone.

2   Copy one sentence from a received message to a new e-mail message.

3   Title the new message **Attachments**.

4   Send it to someone and send a blind copy to someone else.

5   Create a short Word file and send it as an attachment with the e-mail.

6   Save any received e-mail to a folder named **ECDL**.

7   Set a rule so all messages relating to ECDL are highlighted.

8   Save a received attachment on to a floppy disk.

9   Look for all messages from a particular person using **Find**, **Message**.

10   Sort your emails into date order.

11   Delete an old message you don't need to keep.

Section 6 The Address Book

In this section you will practise and learn how to:

* Add a mail address to an address list.

* Update an Address Book for incoming mail.

* Delete a mail address from an address list.

* Create a new address list/distribution list.

* Reply to a message using a distribution

6.1 About the Address Book

The Outlook Address Book enables you to store addresses you use often. Using the Address Book means you do not have to remember all those cumbersome e-mail addresses and saves you having to key in addresses each time you send messages.

6.2 Adding an address to the Address Book

 Method

1 Click on the 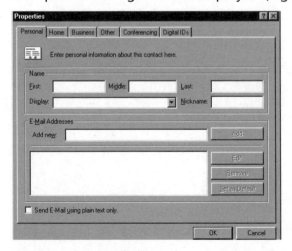 **Address Book** button.
2 The Address Book – Main Identity dialogue box is displayed (Figure 7.29).

Figure 7.29 Displaying the Address Book

3 Click on the **New Contact** button.
4 The Properties dialogue box is displayed (Figure 7.30).

Figure 7.30 Properties dialogue box awaiting new contact details

5 With the **Personal** tab selected, key in the details of your contact.

Note: By selecting other tabs you can enter further details of your contact as appropriate.

6 Click on **OK**. The new contact is added to your Address Book list.

> **ⓘ Info**
>
> Outlook Express can automatically add addresses to your Address Book when you send e-mail. To set this option:
>
> **1** From the **Tools** menu, select: **Options**.
> **2** Click on the **General** tab.
> **3** Click next to **Automatically put people I reply to in my Address Book**.
>
> Outlook Express can add addresses to your Address Book by the following method:
>
> **1** Open the mail message from the contact.
> **2** From the **Tools** menu, select **Add to Address Book** and **Sender**.

6.3 Deleting an address

 Method

1 Open the Address Book as in 6.2.
2 Select the address to delete.
3 Press: **Delete**.
4 You will be asked to confirm the delete. Click on **Yes**.

6.4 Creating an address list

If you want to send a message to people who belong to a certain group, you can create a group address list. When you have set up the group list you will need to key in the name of the group only to send the message to all members.

 Method

1 Click on the **Address Book** button.
2 Click on the **New Group** button. The Properties dialogue box is displayed (Figure 7.31).

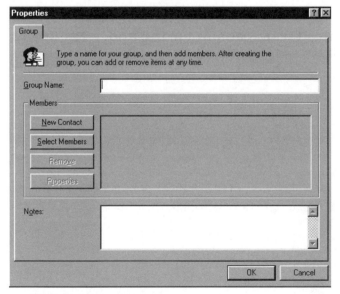

Figure 7.31 Adding a group

3 In the **Group Name** box, key in the name of the new group.
4 Click on **Select Members** to add addresses already in your address book.
5 Click on **New Contact** to add new addresses to both the list and your address book.
6 When you have completed the group entries, click on **OK**.

6.5 Sending messages using the Address Book

 Method

1 Click on the **Compose Message** button.
2 In the header section, click on the **To**: section.
3 The Select Recipients dialogue box is displayed.
4 Click on the recipient's name or the group name and click on the button.
5 Click on **OK**.

ⓘ **Info**

You can select as many recipients as you want and add them to the To, Cc or Bcc boxes.

6.6 Close Outlook Express

Section 6 Information and Communication practice

Practice 6

1 Add the following contact to the Address Book:

Jackie Louise Watson, Ms:
J.L.Watson@anywhere.com

2 Delete one of the names in your address book.

3 Set up a new group called **Sports**. Include the following in the group:

Jackie Watson and two other contacts in your address book.

4 Send a message to the Sports mailing list with the title **Newsflash** as follows:

NEWS JUST IN

Carl De Vere has just been announced team captain for the under 18s Rugby Club. I think you will agree that it is justly deserved.

Your name

5 Close the electronic mail application.

World Wide Web quick reference guide

Action	Keyboard	Mouse	Right-mouse menu	Menu
Access a website	Key in the web address (URL) in the address box			
Change View/ display				**View**, **Internet Options**, **General** and make selections from **View**
Exit Internet Explorer		Click: the ☒ Close button		**File**, **Close**
Favorites, add to open			**Add to Favorites**	**Favorites**, **Add to Favorites**
Folder, create favorites folder				**Favorites**, **Organize Favorites**
Help	**F1**			**Help**, **Contents and Index**
Hyperlink, following		Click: the hyperlink		
Images Display Do not display				**View**, **Internet Options**, **Advanced** Select from **Multimedia** section
Open Internet Explorer	In Windows 95 desktop			
		Click: the **Internet Explorer** shortcut icon		**Start**, **Programs**, **Internet Explorer** **Internet Explorer**
Page setup				**File**, **Page Setup**
Print	**Ctrl + P**	Click: the 🖨 **Print** button	**Print**	**File**, **Print**
Return to original page		Click: the **Back** button		
Searching, using common logical operators	Use **Search** button *or* a Search Engine Use **AND**, **+**, **&**, or **NOT**, **-**, or use **OR**			

Electronic mail quick reference guide

Action	Keyboard	Mouse	Right-mouse menu	Menu
Access received messages		Click: **Inbox** in left-hand window Click: the message (to view in Preview) *or* Double-click: the message (to view in own window)		
Address Book, Open		Click: the 📖 **Address Book** button		**Tools, Address Book**
Add address	Open Address Book.			
		Click: the 📇 **New Contact** button		**File, New Contact**
	Click: the **Personal** tab. Enter details. Click: **OK**			
Delete address	Open Address Book, select the contact			
	Delete	Click: the ✕ **Delete** button	**Delete**	**File, Delete**
Create address/ distribution list	Open Address Book Click: the **New Group** button Enter **Group Name** Select **Members** to add addresses already in the Address Book **New Contact** to add new addresses Click: **OK**			**File, New Group**
Attach files to messages		Click: the 📎 **Insert File** button		**Insert, File Attachment**
Attachment, delete	Double-click the message with the attachment so it appears in its own window. Select attachment			
	Delete	Click: the ✕ **Delete** button		
Attachments, save	Select the attachment			
			Save As	**File, Save Attachments**
Auto-signature, add				**Tools, Stationery, Signature**
Copy/paste	**Ctrl + C** **Ctrl + V**			**Edit, Copy** **Edit, Paste**
Copy/move messages to folders			**Copy To** **Move To**	**Edit, Move to Folder** **Copy to Folder**
Create messages		Click: the **Compose Message** button		

Action	Keyboard	Mouse	Right-mouse menu	Menu
Delete message	Select message			
	Delete	Click: the ✕ **Delete** button	**Delete**	**Edit**, **Delete**
Delete text	Select text			
	Delete			
Exit Outlook Express		Click: the ☒ **Close** button		**File**, **Exit**
Folders, create new			**New**, **Folder**	**File**, **Folder**, **New Folder**
Forward a message	**Ctrl + F**	Click: the 📧 **Forward Message** button	**Forward**	**Forward**, **Compose**
Help	**F1**			**Help**, **Contents and Index**
Load Outlook Express	In Windows 95 desktop			
		Click: the **Outlook Express** icon		**Start**, **Programs**, **Internet Explorer**, **Outlook Express**
Print messages	(With transaction details and message visible in its own window)			
	Ctrl + P	Click: the 🖨 **Print** button		**File**, **Print**
Prioritise messages				**Tools**, **Set Priority**
Reply to all	**Ctrl + Shift + R**	Click: the 📧 **Reply to All** button	**Reply to All**	
Reply to sender	**Ctrl + R**	Click: the 📧 **Reply to Author** button	**Reply to Author**	
Route/address messages	Key in the address in the **To:** box			
Multiple recipients	Separate addresses with semicolons (;) Use **Cc** box to send a 'carbon copy'. Use **Bcc** box to send a 'blind' copy			
Search for a message				**Edit**, **Find**, **Message**
Sort messages	Click on: the relevant heading at the top of the messages window			
Spellcheck	**F7**			**Tools**, **Spelling**
Transmit messages		Click: the **Send and Receive** button		**Tools**, **Send and Receive**
View attachments	(With message in its own window – attachment visible)			
		Double-click: the attachment		

Module 7 practice tasks

Answers to the following questions can be found in Module 7 or Module 1 text.

1   What is a *web browser*?
2   Explain what a hyperlink is.
3   Give an example of a web address (real or made up). Explain how each part is derived. What is another name for a web address?
4   *Home page* can have two different meanings. Explain.
5   When carrying out a search, what is a *key* word?
6   Explain how a *search engine* would help you find something on the web.
7   Why are passwords used when accessing the Internet?
8   What is an e-mail attachment?
9   How do you send e-mail messages to more than one person at the same time?
10 What is an e-mail signature? Why would you use one?
11 In e-mail, what is an Address Book and why is it useful?
12 How do you save a copy of an e-mail for yourself?
13 What is a group address list?

Practical tasks

1   Find out what is on at the London theatres. Send two sentences about two events via e-mail to your supervisor/tutor.
2   Find two different airline sites. What are the differences between them and which one do you prefer? Send an e-mail to your supervisor/tutor containing the names of the sites and three points in favour of your preferred site.
3   Find two organisations specialising in distance learning. Do either of them offer qualifications in languages? Send a short e-mail to your supervisor/tutor reporting what you have found.

Note: This is only a practice test. Successful completion does not imply certification of the module by the ECDL Foundation.

Answers to Exercises

Module 3, Section 1.8, Exercise 5

LANDMARKS IN LONDON

St Paul's Cathedral

St Paul's Cathedral is one of London's landmarks and is renowned throughout the world. It is the largest church in the city and was built on the same site and to replace a Norman church that was destroyed by the Great Fire of 1666.

The Whispering Gallery

This famous Renaissance building was designed by Sir Christopher Wren and has many interesting features. One of its most intriguing is the Whispering Gallery which runs round the inside of the great dome. If you speak in this gallery the sound waves of your voice are carried round the entire circumference of the gallery because the waves are prevented from going outwards by the stones lining the circular wall. These acoustic properties enable someone sitting far away on the opposite side of the gallery to hear your voice, even if you are whispering.

Famous people

Many famous people are buried at St Paul's and their tombs can be found either in the church or in the crypt beneath. They include Nelson, Wellington, Turner and Sir Christopher Wren.

Module 3, Section 2.13, Exercise 12

LANDMARKS IN LONDON

St Paul's Cathedral

St Paul's Cathedral is one of London's landmarks and is renowned throughout the world. It is the largest cathedral in the city and was built to replace a Norman cathedral that was destroyed by the Great Fire of 1666.

Sir Christopher Wren

Over the north door, Wren's epitaph is inscribed in Latin. It is - Si monumentum requiris, circumspice. This translated into English means - If you seek his memorial, look around you.

The Whispering Gallery

This famous Renaissance building was designed by Sir Christopher Wren and has many interesting features. One of its most intriguing is the Whispering Gallery which runs round the inside of the great dome. If you speak in this gallery the sound waves of your voice are carried round the entire circumference of the gallery because the waves are prevented from going outwards by the stones lining the circular wall. These acoustic properties enable someone sitting far away on the opposite side of the gallery to hear your voice, even if you are whispering.

Famous people

Many famous people are buried at St Paul's and their tombs can be found either in the cathedral or in the crypt beneath. They include Roberts, Jellicoe, Beatty, Nelson, Wellington, Turner and Sir Christopher Wren.

LANDMARKS IN LONDON

Module 3, Section 2.14, Exercise 15(A)

Picnics can be enjoyed in the summer when the weather is usually warm and dry.

St Paul's Cathedral is one of London's landmarks and is renowned throughout the world. It is the largest cathedral in the city and was built to replace a Norman cathedral that was destroyed by the Great Fire of 1666.

Module 3, Exercise 15(B)

St Paul's Cathedral is one of London's landmarks and is renowned throughout the world. It is the largest cathedral in the city and was built to replace a Norman cathedral that was destroyed by the Great Fire of 1666.

Famous people

Many famous people are buried at St Paul's and their tombs can be found either in the cathedral or in the crypt beneath. They include Roberts, Jellicoe, Beatty, Nelson, Wellington, Turner and Sir Christopher Wren.

LANDMARKS IN LONDON Walkabouts Company ©

Module 3, Section 2, Practice 3, Step 4

THE WORLD WIDE WEB

Many commercial services are now offered on the WWW. You can order books, arrange a car rental anywhere in the world, and even purchase and download new software direct to your computer. If you live in the right area, you can even order a pizza via the WWW!

It was developed to help scientists share information and has rapidly become a general service for everyone. Using a suitably configured computer, users can access information on the WWW (known as web pages) from anywhere in the world. These pages can be created by anyone, from schoolchildren right up to the world s largest companies.

The ability to combine text, pictures, videos and sound makes the WWW ideal for entertainment pages. Most bands, films and computer games have their own official pages, and there are often many more set up by fans.

Be wary of what you find on the WWW. Always check the source of any information given. Remember that anyone can set up a website and the content authenticity will not always have been scrutinized.

Many commercial services are now offered on the web. If you live in the right area, you can even order a pizza via the web! You can order books, arrange a car rental anywhere in the world, and even purchase and download new software direct to your computer.

The possibilities are endless. User groups are growing daily. Who would have thought that people would be doing their weekly grocery shopping using the web?

It was developed to help scientists share information and has rapidly become a general service for everyone. Using a suitably configured computer, users can access information on the web (known as web pages) from anywhere in the world.

The ability to combine text, pictures, videos and sound makes the web ideal for entertainment pages. Most bands, films and computer games have their own official pages, and there are often many more set up by fans.

Be wary of what you find on the web. Always check the source of any information given. Remember that anyone can set up a website and the content authenticity will not always have been scrutinized.

The ability to combine text, pictures, videos and sound makes the web ideal for entertainment pages. Most bands, films and computer games have their own official pages, and there are often many more set up by fans.

Be wary of what you find on the web. Always check the source of any information given. Remember that anyone can set up a website and the content authenticity will not always have been scrutinized.

Module 3, Section 2, Practice 4, Step 4

Thank you for filling in our recent Holiday questionnaire.

We are constantly striving to improve our services for you and to offer the kind of holidays that you will enjoy. Your comments have been noted and we will do our best to exceed your expectations.

Our new brochure features more than 1,100 idyllic cottages, 160 luxury villas with pools (usually available in the summer months only), more than 2,000 hotels and over 40 apartments at holiday villages, with superb on-site facilities. We also offer deluxe camping and mobile homes at 20 wonderful 4-star sites and theme parks including Disneyland, Paris, Parc Asterix and Futuroscope.

We would like to reward you for helping us with our survey. We are delighted to offer you a 10% saving on your next holiday. If you would like to benefit from this offer, please quote code Q2000 when you call.

We look forward to hearing from you soon.

Module 3, Section 2, Practice 4, Step 11

Thank you for filling in our recent Holiday questionnaire.

We are continually striving to improve our services for you and to offer the kind of holidays that you will enjoy.

We would like to reward you for helping us with our survey. We are delighted to offer you a 10% saving on your next holiday. However, you must act within 28 days. If you would like to benefit from this offer, please quote code Q2000 when you call.

Our new brochure features more than 1,100 idyllic cottages, 160 luxury villas with pools (usually available in the summer months only), more than 2,000 hotels and over 40 apartments at holiday villages, with superb on-site facilities. We also offer deluxe camping and mobile homes at 20 wonderful 4-star sites and theme parks including Disneyland, Paris, Parc Astérix and Futuroscope.

We look forward to hearing from you soon.

LANDMARKS IN LONDON

St Paul's Cathedral

St Paul's Cathedral is one of London's landmarks and is renowned throughout the world. It is the largest cathedral in the city and was built to replace a Norman cathedral that was destroyed by the Great Fire of 1666.

Sir Christopher Wren

Over the north door, Wren's epitaph is inscribed in Latin. It is - *Si monumentum requiris, circumspice.* This translated into English means - If you seek his memorial, look around you.

The Whispering Gallery

This famous Renaissance building was designed by Sir Christopher Wren and has many interesting features. One of its most intriguing is the Whispering Gallery which runs round the inside of the great dome. If you speak in this gallery the sound waves of your voice are carried round the entire circumference of the gallery because the waves are prevented from going outwards by the stones lining the circular wall.

These acoustic properties enable someone sitting far away on the opposite side of the gallery to hear your voice, even if you are whispering.

Famous people

Many famous people are buried at St Paul's and their tombs can be found either in the cathedral or in the crypt beneath. They include Roberts, Jellicoe, Beatty, Nelson, Wellington, Turner and Sir Christopher Wren.

LANDMARKS IN LONDON <u>Walkabouts Company</u> ©

LANDMARKS IN LONDON

St Paul's Cathedral

St Paul's Cathedral is one of London's landmarks and is renowned throughout the world. It is the largest cathedral in the city and was built to replace a Norman cathedral that was destroyed by the Great Fire of 1666.

Sir Christopher Wren

Over the north door, Wren's epitaph is inscribed in Latin. It is

- *Si monumentum requiris, circumspice.* This translated into English means - If you seek his memorial, look around you.

The Whispering Gallery

This famous Renaissance building was designed by Sir Christopher Wren and has many interesting features. One of its most intriguing is the Whispering Gallery which runs round the inside of the great dome. If you speak in this gallery the sound waves of your voice are carried round the entire circumference of the gallery because the waves are prevented from going outwards by the stones lining the circular wall. These acoustic properties enable someone sitting far away on the opposite side of the gallery to hear your voice, even if you are whispering.

Famous people

Many famous people are buried at St Paul's and their tombs can be found either in the cathedral or in the crypt beneath. They include Roberts, Jellicoe, Beatty, Nelson, Wellington, Turner and Sir Christopher Wren.

LANDMARKS IN LONDON Walkabouts Company ©

London Information   11 July 2000   Angela Bessant

London Information   11 July 2000   Angela Bessant

World Wide Web

Angela Bessant

THE WORLD WIDE WEB

Many commercial services are now offered on the web. If you live in the right area, you can even order a pizza via the web! You can order books, arrange a car rental anywhere in the world, and even purchase and download new software direct to your computer.

The possibilities are endless. User groups are growing daily. Who would have thought that people would be doing their weekly grocery shopping using the web?

3

World Wide Web

Angela Bessant

It was developed to help scientists share information and has rapidly become a general service for everyone. Using a suitably configured computer, users can access information on the web (known as web pages) from anywhere in the world.

The ability to combine text, pictures, videos and sound makes the web ideal for entertainment pages. Most bands, films and computer games have their own official pages, and there are often many more set up by fans.

Be wary of what you find on the web. Always check the source of any information given. Remember that anyone can set up a website and the content authenticity will not always have been scrutinized.

4

Details of your reward

Thank you for filling in our recent Holiday questionnaire.

We are continually striving to improve our services for you
and to offer the kind of holidays that you will enjoy.

We would like to reward you for helping us with our survey.
We are delighted to offer you a 10% saving on your next
holiday. However, you must act within 28 days. If you
would like to benefit from this offer, please quote code
Q2000 when you call.

Our new brochure features more than 1,100 idyllic
cottages, 160 luxury villas with pools (usually
available in the summer months only), more
than 2,000 hotels and over 40 apartments at
holiday villages, with superb on-site facilities.
We also offer deluxe camping and mobile
homes at 20 wonderful 4-star sites and theme
parks including Disneyland, Paris, Parc Astérix
and Futuroscope.

We look forward to hearing from you soon.

VOLUNTEERS REQUIRED

Do you meet the following criteria?

- Age range 16 to 40
- Computer literate
- Available during the hours of 16.00 and 18.00

We are looking for volunteers to take part in a survey on computer usage. We are able to offer you a small payment and a cup of tea or coffee! If you think that you may be able to help us, we would like to hear from YOU.

Please contact one of the following:

Mike	ext 4448
Chris	ext 4462
Jane	ext 4463
Felicity	ext 6884

We look forward to your call.

Park Hose, London SW6 3JT Tel: 020 8223 3555 Fax 020 8223 3566

Get Noticed

Fax

To:	Anthony Bailey	**From:**	Angela Bessant
Fax:	01234 734999	**Pages:**	1
Phone:	01234 734820	**Date:**	22/11/2000
Re:	Appointment date	**CC:**	Ben Liar

☐ **Urgent**   ☐ **For Review**   ☐ **Please Comment**   ✓ **Please Reply**   ✓ **Please Recycle**

● **Comments:**

We are sorry that you are unable to make the appointment this week. Is it possible for you to visit next Tuesday 18 July at 10.30 am?

GRAND OPENING
THE COMPUTER SHOP
SATURDAY 25 MARCH 2000

Many opening bargains including

- ◆ **Computers**
- ◆ **Printers**
- ◆ **Scanners**
- ◆ **Modems**
- ◆ **Software**

Come and see for yourself

Our prices are keen:
Internal Zip drives from.. £102.95
Hard drives 20Gb from... £129.99
Scanners from £79.99

The first 10 customers will each receive boxed software of their choice up to the value of £50

We look forward to welcoming you!

THE COMPUTER SHOP

Memo

To: Andrea Whitely

From: Paul Hunter

CC: Gita Meehan

Date: 22/11/2000

Re: Delivery of laptops

Thank you for the delivery that I received this morning. As you know we are opening next Saturday and you would be most welcome to come and join us then. Please let me know if you can make it.

Best Regards

● Page 1

Module 3, Section 5.5

Largest Continents	Largest Countries	Largest Oceans and Seas	Largest Islands
Asia	Russian Federation	Pacific	Greenland
North America	China	Indian	Borneo
South America	USA	Arctic	Madagascar
Antarctica	Brazil	South China	Baffin

Module 3, Section 5, Practice 9, Step 9

Mercalli	Richter	Characteristics
1	Less than 3.5	Only detected by seismograph
2	3.5	Only detected by people at rest
3	4.2	Similar to vibrations from HGV
4	4.5	Felt indoors; rocks parked cars
5	4.8	Generally felt; awakens sleepers
6	6.1	Causes general alarm; building walls crack
12	Greater than 8.1	Total destruction of area

Module 3, Practice 10, Step 7

Earthquake Measurements

The magnitude of earthquakes is measured in units on the Richter Scale and their intensity on the Mercalli Scale.

Richter	Characteristics
Less than 3.5	Only detected by seismograph
3.5	Only detected by people at rest
4.2	Similar to vibrations from HGV
4.5	Felt indoors; rocks parked cars
4.8	Generally felt; awakens sleepers
6.1	Causes general alarm; building walls crack
Greater than 8.1	Total destruction of area

10 February 2000

Mr Murray Dixon
63 Harpur Street
Luton
LU6 1AS

Dear Murray

Box Office Film Club

I am pleased to enclose details of our forthcoming film season.

All films will be shown in the Lecture Room on the Hemsley Hall Campus. Ample free parking spaces are available at both sides of the hall. If you are travelling by public transport, the nearest bus stop is in Regent Avenue. May I remind you that guest tickets will be on sale in the Hemsley Bar 20 minutes before each performance.

I look forward to welcoming you this season.

Yours sincerely

Club Secretary

Enc

Letters also to: Miss Lynne Carter,
Mr Jack Hobson, Mrs Susi Malucci

---

11 July 2000

Miss King
8 Wendover Place
Kempston
Bedford
MK32 9TG

Dear Miss King

Town and Country Enterprise AGM

Please note that the AGM will take place on Tuesday 20 June at 7.30 pm in the
Coleridge Meeting Room. I am enclosing the agenda. Please let me know if you have
any further items to add.

Coffee and light snacks will be provided. I look forward to seeing as many of our
members as possible.

Yours sincerely

Jenny Jinx
Secretary

Enc

| Letters also to: Mr Gregory and |
| Dr Walpole |

Module 3, Section 6, Practice 12, Step 2

Miss King
8 Wendover Place
Kempston
Bedford
MK32 9TG

Mr Gregory
10 George Gardens
Silsoe
Bedford
BD27 9JU

Dr Walpole
118 Exeter Way
Harrold
Bedford
MK55 2AS

Module 3, Section 7.4

Shakespeare Season

ROMEO AND JULIET

All this week at 7 pm in the Drama Studio

Tickets available at the door

Angela Bessant

Sample extract

The people of Europe speak many different languages. English is termed a 'Germanic' language. This is because it is related to languages such as Dutch as well as German. The links are not as easily noticed in modern day English but the relationship is much clearer in **Old** English.

Old English is the name given to the English language up to *c.*1150. It was spoken from the fifth century. It has different vocabulary, word meanings and spellings to modern English. It even has letters, such as *þ* that are not found in modern English. Its pronunciation and grammar and the ways it was used are also different. So much so in fact that it would be most unlikely that **Old** English would be understood by the average English speaker today. Although anyone speaking or writing English at the beginning of the 21st century is using a language that dates back to Anglo Saxon times.

There is also the subject of accents and dialects to consider. Accents can be defined as the same language but differing in terms of pronunciation. Dialects differ in terms of grammar and vocabulary as well.

Nearly one billion people speak different varieties of modern-day English. There are mother tongue speakers, second language speakers and those for whom it is a foreign language. The spread of English to different parts of the world and it being used as an international language has caused much debate.

This is just a taster of course content. We have many others and are confident that you will find something interesting and worthwhile. Please ring for details of courses in:

- **French**
- **German**
- **Spanish**
- **Welsh**
- **Italian**

The people of Europe speak many different languages. English is termed a Germanic language. This is because it is related to languages such as Dutch as well as German. The links are not as easily noticed in modern day English but the relationship is much clearer in **Old** English.

5

Module 3, Advanced Practice Task 2, Step 7

Languages Course Details   11 July 2000

Angela Bessant
Ref 9054

Dear

Sample extract

The people of Europe speak many different languages. English is termed a 'Germanic' language. This is because it is related to languages such as Dutch as well as German. The links are not as easily noticed in modern day English but the relationship is much clearer in **Old** English.

1	Early Old English	450 - 850
2	Later Old English	850 - 1100
3	Middle English	1100 - 1450
4	Early Modern English	1450 - 1750

There is also the subject of accents and dialects to consider. Accents can be defined as the same language but differing in terms of pronunciation. Dialects differ in terms of grammar and vocabulary as well.

Nearly one billion people speak different varieties of modern-day English. There are mother tongue speakers, second language speakers and those for whom it is a foreign language. The spread of English to different parts of the world and it being used as an 'international' language has caused much debate.

This is just a taster of course content. We have many others and are confident that you will find something interesting and worthwhile. Please ring for details of courses in:

- **French**
- **German**
- **Spanish**
- **Welsh**
- **Italian**

> The people of Europe speak many different languages. English is termed a 'Germanic' language. This is because it is related to languages such as Dutch as well as German. The links are not as easily noticed in modern day English but the relationship is much clearer in **Old** English.

Yours sincerely

Module 3, Advanced Practice Tasks 2, Step 10

Languages Course Details   11 July 2000

Angela Bessant
Ref 9054

Miss Smith
29 Hobsons Way
Bristol
BS6 5ER

Dear Miss Smith

Sample extract

The people of Europe speak many different languages. English is termed a 'Germanic' language. This is because it is related to languages such as Dutch as well as German. The links are not as easily noticed in modern day English but the relationship is much clearer in **Old** English.

1	Early Old English	450 - 850
2	Later Old English	850 - 1100
3	Middle English	1100 - 1450
4	Early Modern English	1450 - 1750

There is also the subject of accents and dialects to consider. Accents can be defined as the same language but differing in terms of pronunciation. Dialects differ in terms of grammar and vocabulary as well.

Nearly one billion people speak different varieties of modern-day English. There are mother tongue speakers, second language speakers and those for whom it is a foreign language. The spread of English to different parts of the world and it being used as an 'international' language has caused much debate.

This is just a taster of course content. We have many others and are confident that you will find something interesting and worthwhile. Please ring for details of courses in:

- **French**
- **German**
- **Spanish**
- **Welsh**
- **Italian**

> The people of Europe speak many different languages. English is termed a 'Germanic' language. This is because it is related to languages such as Dutch as well as German. The links are not as easily noticed in modern day English but the relationship is much clearer in **Old** English.

Yours sincerely

Letters also to Mr Ahmed; Mrs Zwetsloot; Dr O'Byrne; Ms Jones

facsimile transmittal

To:	Lycée la Rochelle	**Fax:**	00 33 23 44 76 98 11
From:	Angela Bessant	**Date**:	22/11/2000
Re:	Exchange Visits	**Pages:**	1
CC:	[Click here and type name]		

☐ Urgent   ☐ For Review   ✓ Please Comment   ☐ Please Reply   ☐ Please Recycle

Thank you for your interest. I will send details as soon as possible.

Module 4, Section 1.7, Exercise 5

Month	Casualco	Smartco	Partyco	Sales
May	990	830	770	2590
June	550	880	220	1650
July	330	660	700	1690
August	400	550	820	1770
Total	2270	2920	2510	

Module 4, Section 1.8, Exercise 6

Month	Casualco	Smartco	Partyco	Sales
May	990	830	770	=SUM(B2:D2)
June	550	880	220	=SUM(B3:D3)
July	330	660	700	=SUM(B4:D4)
August	400	550	820	=SUM(B5:D5)
Total	=SUM(B2:B5)	=SUM(C2:C5)	=SUM(D2:D5)	

Module 4, Section 1, Practice 1, Step 5(A)

EXPENSES

	AUG	OCT	NOV
RENT	350	350	350
ELEC	45	50	60
GAS	18	25	40
LOAN	55	55	55
PETROL	75	60	60
INS	20	20	20
TOTALS	563		

Module 4, Section 1, Practice 1, Step 5(B)

EXPENSES

	AUG	OCT	NOV
RENT	350	350	350
ELEC	45	50	60
GAS	18	25	40
LOAN	55	55	55
PETROL	75	60	60
INS	20	20	20
TOTALS	=SUM(B3:B8)		

Module 4, Section 1, Practice 2, Step 4(A)

Sales

	Tue	Wed	Thu	Fri	Sat	Total
Food	550	660	500	900	1120	3730
Menswear	200	190	300	100	780	
Fashions	300	625	740	800	1500	
Baby	200	450	380	590	213	
Cosmetics	77	90	65	105	280	
Home	500	1800	1200	954	3080	

Sales	Tue	Wed	Thu	Fri	Sat	Total
Food	550	660	500	900	1120	=SUM(B3:F3)
Menswear	200	190	300	100	780	
Fashions	300	625	740	800	1500	
Baby	200	450	380	590	213	
Cosmetics	77	90	65	105	280	
Home	500	1800	1200	954	3080	

Module 4, Section 2.7

Month	Casualco	Jeansco	Partyco	Shoesco	Sales
May	850	600	770	621	2841
June	550	700	220	890	2360
July	470	850	700	700	2720
August	400	650	820	440	2310
Total	2270	2800	2510	2651	10231

Module 4, Section 2.9, Exercise 10

Month	Casualco
May	850
June	550
July	470
August	400
Total	2270

Module 4, Section 2, Practice 3, Step 12

EXPENSES

	AUG	SEPT	OCT	NOV	TOTAL
RENT	350	350	350	350	1400
ELEC	35	50	50	60	195
GAS	18	20	25	54	117
LOAN	55	55	55	55	220
INS	20	20	20	20	80
TOTALS	478	495	500	539	2012

Module 4, Section 2, Practice 3, Step 13

```
TOTAL
=SUM(B3:E3)
=SUM(B4:E4)
=SUM(B5:E5)
=SUM(B6:E6)
=SUM(B7:E7)
=SUM(B8:E8)
```

Module 4, Section 2, Practice 4, Step 11

Sales

	Mon	Tue	Wed	Thu	Fri	Sat	Total	Profit
Food	25	550	660	500	900	1120	3755	751
Menswear	180	200	190	350	100	780	1800	360
Fashions	270	300	625	740	800	1500	4235	847
Baby	52	200	450	380	610	213	1905	381
Home	25	500	1800	1200	954	3080	7559	1511.8

Module 4, Section 3.6

CLOTHING COMPANY SALES

Month	Casualco	Jeansco	Partyco	Shoesco	Monthly Sales	Average Sales
May	850	600	770	621	2841	710.25
June	550	700	220	890	2360	590.00
July	470	850	700	700	2720	680.00
August	400	650	820	440	2310	577.50
Total	**2270**	**2800**	**2510**	**2651**	**10231**	**2557.75**

Module 4, Section 3.10

CLOTHING COMPANY SALES

Month	Casualco	Jeansco	Partyco	Shoesco	Monthly Sales	Average Sales
May	850	600	770	621	2841	710.25
June	550	700	220	890	2360	590.00
July	470	850	700	700	2720	680.00
August	400	650	820	440	2310	577.50
Total	**2270**	**2800**	**2510**	**2651**	**10231**	**£ 2,557.75**

CLOTHING COMPANY SALES

Month	Shoesco	Commission rates
May	621	5%
June	890	8%
July	700	10%
August	440	3%
Total	**2651**	

Module 4, Section 3.18

Produced by Angela Bessant   22/11/2000

CLOTHING COMPANY SALES

Month	Casualco	Jeansco	Partyco	Shoesco	Monthly Sales	Average Sales
May	850	600	770	621	2841	710.25
June	550	700	220	890	2360	590.00
July	470	850	700	700	2720	680.00
August	400	650	820	440	2310	577.50
Total	*2270*	*2800*	*2510*	*2651*	*10231*	*£ 2,557.75*

CLOTHING COMPANY SALES

Month	Shoesco	Commission rates
May	621	5%
June	890	8%
July	700	10%
August	440	3%
Total	*2651*	

Module 4, Section 3.18

Produced by Angela Bessant   22/11/2000

CLOTHING COMPANY SALES

Surname	First Name	Start Date
Gill	Sanjit	10-Oct-99
Jones	Bronwen	2-May-00
Jones	Julia	14-Feb-96
Wright	Dominic	29-Sep-98

Module 4, Section 3.18

Produced by Angela Bessant   22/11/2000

Surname	First Name	Start Date	Tel	Week1	Week2	Week3	Week4
Gill	Sanjit	10-Oct-99	01234 752999				
Jones	Bronwen	2-May-00	01234 621900				
Jones	Julia	14-Feb-96	01908 554211				
Wright	Dominic	29-Sep-98	01908 338554				

EXPENSES	AUG	SEPT	OCT	NOV	TOTAL	AVERAGE
RENT	350.0	350.0	350.0	350.0	£1,400.00	350
ELEC	35.0	50.0	50.0	60.0	£195.00	49
GAS	18.0	20.0	25.0	54.0	£117.00	29
LOAN	55.0	55.0	55.0	55.0	£220.00	55
INS	20.0	20.0	20.0	20.0	£80.00	20
TOTALS	478.0	495.0	500.0	539.0	£2,012.00	503

22/11/2000

ECDL 2000

YEARLY EXPENSES

	Jan-99	Feb-99	Mar-99	Apr-99	May-99	Jun-99	Jul-99	Aug-99	Sep-99	Oct-99	Nov-99	Dec-99
RENT								350.0	350.0	350.0	350.0	
ELEC								35.0	50.0	50.0	60.0	
GAS								18.0	20.0	25.0	54.0	
LOAN								55.0	55.0	55.0	55.0	
INS								20.0	20.0	20.0	20.0	
TOTALS								478.0	495.0	500.0	539.0	

Module 4, Section 3, Practice 6, Step 15(A)

			HOUSEHOLD SALES						
	Mon	Tue	Wed	Thu	Fri	Sat	Total	Predicted Increased Sales	Profit
Food	25.00	550.00	660.00	500.00	900.00	1120.00	3755.00	1%	751.00
Home	25.00	500.00	1800.00	1200.00	954.00	3080.00	7559.00	4%	1511.80

Sales	Mon	Tue	Wed	Thu	Fri	Sat	Total	Profit
Food	25.00	550.00	660.00	500.00	900.00	1120.00	3755.00	751.00
Menswear	180.00	200.00	190.00	350.00	100.00	780.00	1800.00	360.00
Ladies Fashions	270.00	300.00	625.00	740.00	800.00	1500.00	4235.00	847.00
Baby	52.00	200.00	450.00	380.00	610.00	213.00	1905.00	381.00
Home	25.00	500.00	1800.00	1200.00	954.00	3080.00	7559.00	1511.80
Average Store Sales	110.40	350.00	745.00	634.00	672.80	1338.60		

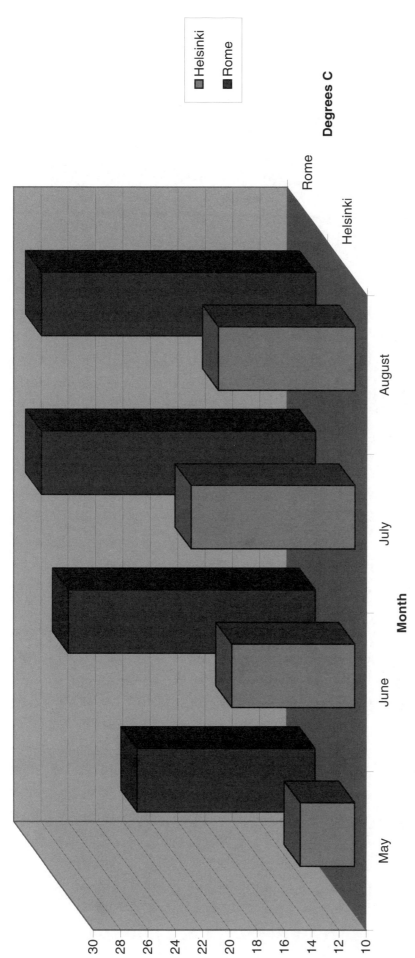

Temperature Comparison (Helsinki, Rome)

Module 4, Section 4, Practice 7, Step 10

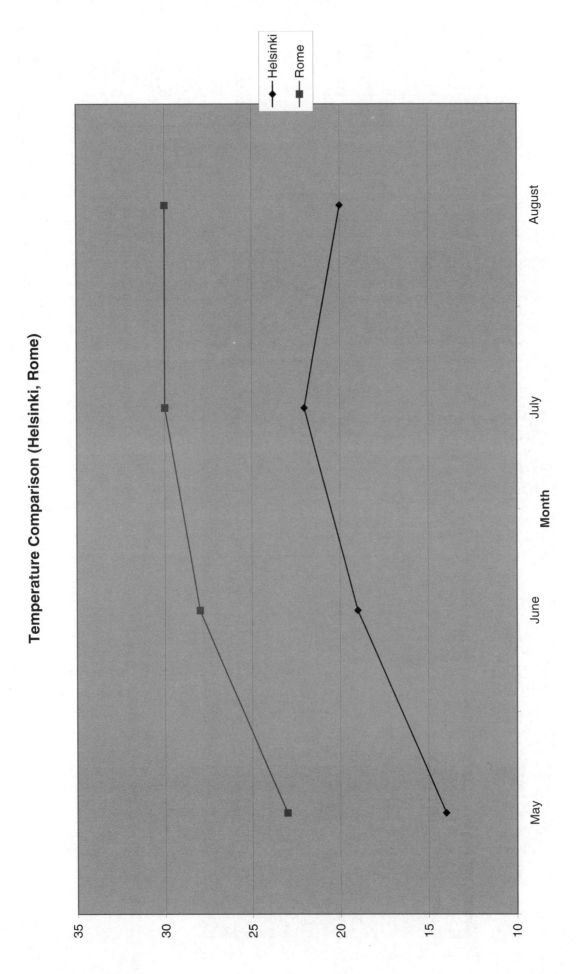

Module 4, Section 4, Practice 8, Step 6

Temperature Chart						Degrees F
Degrees C						
	May	June	July	August	4-Month Average	May
Amsterdam	18	21	22	22	20.75	64.4
Athens	25	30	33	33	30.25	77
Berlin	19	22	24	23	22	66.2
Budapest	22	26	28	27	25.75	71.6
Copenhagen	16	19	22	21	19.5	60.8
Dublin	15	18	20	19	18	59
Helsinki	14	19	22	20	18.75	57.2
London	17	20	22	22	20.25	62.6
Madrid	21	27	31	30	27.25	69.8
Oslo	16	20	22	21	19.75	60.8
Paris	20	23	25	24	23	68
Rome	23	28	30	30	27.75	73.4
Stockholm	14	19	22	20	18.75	57.2
Vienna	19	23	25	24	22.75	66.2
Zurich	19	23	25	24	22.75	66.2

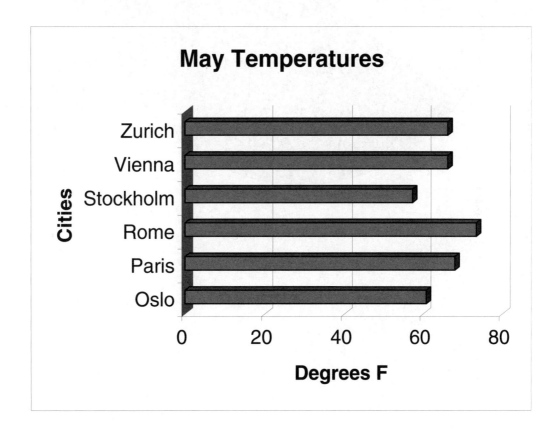

Attendance Figures

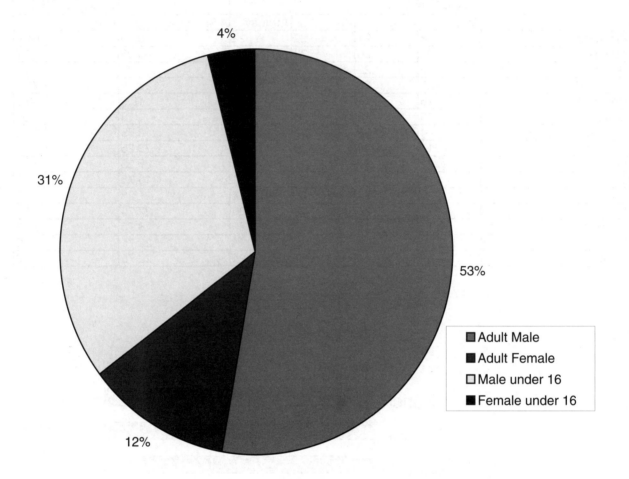

Attendance Figures

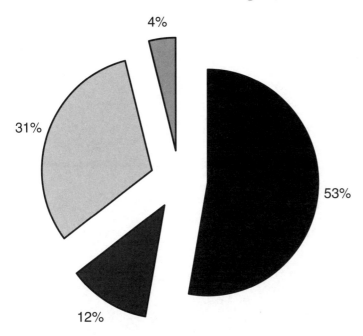

4%

31%

53%

12%

■ Adult Male
■ Adult Female
□ Male under 16
■ Female under 16

Angela Bessant

Spreadsheet produced by Angela Bessant

Temporary register payments

Name	Hourly rate	Weekend rate	Weekly hours	Weekend hours	Hourly rate total	Weekend total	Total pay
Rachel Simms	£ 6.80	£ 8.16	18	12	£ 122.40	£ 97.92	£ 220.32
Gareth Philips	£ 10.50	£ 12.60	22.5	8	£ 236.25	£ 100.80	£ 337.05
Jeanna Larouse	£ 6.80	£ 8.16	30	2	£ 204.00	£ 16.32	£ 220.32
Mark Anthony	£ 7.80	£ 9.36	21	2	£ 163.80	£ 18.72	£ 182.52
Philip Smith	£ 5.80	£ 6.96	10	7	£ 58.00	£ 48.72	£ 106.72
Greg Moore	£ 6.80	£ 8.16	17	5	£ 115.60	£ 40.80	£ 156.40
Jayne Temple	£ 7.80	£ 9.36	30	0	£ 234.00	£ -	£ 234.00
Sara Janes	£ 10.50	£ 12.60	30	0	£ 315.00	£ -	£ 315.00
Tom Batco	£ 10.50	£ 12.60	25	3	£ 262.50	£ 37.80	£ 300.30
Total Temp pay							£ 2,072.63

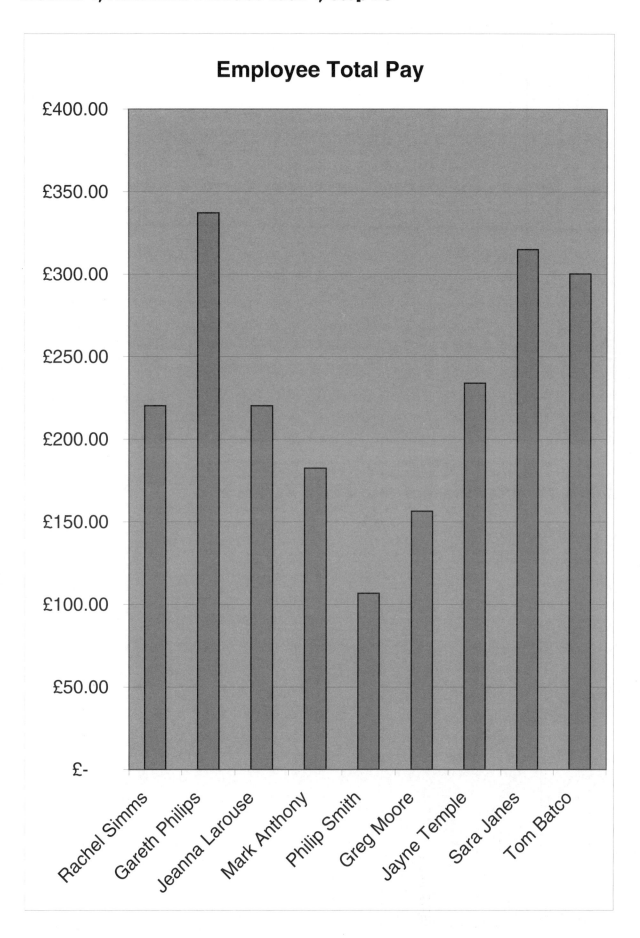

Employee Total Pay

Module 4, Basic Practice Task 2, Step 11

No of pounds for exchange	Your £ buys 10,190		
Country	Currency	Exchange rate	Exchange result
Belgium (Franc)	BEF	64.26	BEF 654,809.40
France (Franc)	FRF	10.47	FRF 106,689.30
Germany (Deutsche Mark)	DEM	3.11	DEM 31,690.90
Italy (Lira)	ITL	3086	ITL 31,446,340.00
Spain (Peseta)	ESP	276	ESP 2,812,440.00

Module 4, Advanced Practice Task 2 Step 21, 1 of 2

No of pounds for exchange	Your £ buys 10,190		
Country	Currency	Exchange rate	Exchange result
Belgium (Franc)	BEF	64.26	BEF 654,809.40
France (Franc)	FRF	10.47	FRF 106,689.30
Germany (Deutsche Mark)	DEM	3.11	DEM 31,690.90
Spain (Peseta)	ESP	276	ESP 2,812,440.00

Exchange result on 10,190GBP

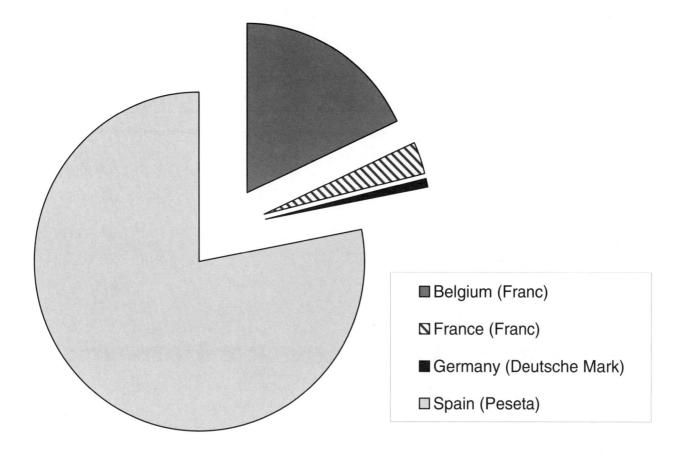

■ Belgium (Franc)

◪ France (Franc)

■ Germany (Deutsche Mark)

☐ Spain (Peseta)

Module 5, Section 2.2, Exercise 2

CLASSES   24/02/00

CLASS	DAY	ROOM	INSTRUCTOR	NUMBER OF WEEKS
AEROBICS	MONDAY	HALL	KENNY	10
AEROBIKING	WEDNESDAY	GYM	SALLY	10
FIT AND FUNKY	THURSDAY	DANCE STUDIO	LYNNE	15
SYNC AND SWIM	WEDNESDAY	POOL	DUNCAN	5
POWER HOUR	FRIDAY	HALL	LARRY	10
BODY BLITZ	TUESDAY	DANCE STUDIO	LYNNE	20

Module 5, Section 2.8

CLASSES

CLASS	ROOM	DAY	MEMBER	INSTRUCTOR	NUMBER OF WEEKS
AEROBICS	GYM	MONDAY	☐	KENNY	10
AEROBIKING	GYM	WEDNESDAY	☑	SALLY	10
FIT AND FUNKY	DANCE STUDIO	THURSDAY	☐	LYNNE	15
SYNC AND SWIM	POOL	WEDNESDAY	☐	DUNCAN	6
BODY BLITZ	DANCE STUDIO	TUESDAY	☐	LYNNE	20
TONE AND TRIM	GYM	FRIDAY	☑	LYNNE	20

Module 5, Section 2, Practice 3, Step 2

Clients   29/03/00

SOLICITOR	CLIENT NAME	REF NO	DAY	TIME	PREVIOUS VISITS
PATEL	JONES L	J120	WED	09:30	6
PATEL	SMITH C	J561	TUE	12:00	10
PATEL	CLARKSON J	M124	SAT	16:00	4
PATEL	GRIGGS S	N6570	FRI	13:45	10
COLLINS	DENT J	C780	SAT	09:00	12
COLLINS	JENKINS Z	E120	WED	10:30	0
COLLINS	DENNIS M	L833	SAT	10:00	8
COLLINS	MOWHILL S	H777	FRI	17:45	12
McBRIDE	HARMAN D	G652	THU	11:00	12
McBRIDE	PETERS H	Y444	FRI	18:30	6
McBRIDE	CLARKE F	R567	SAT	09:30	0
McBRIDE	PAUL G	H800	SAT	11:00	6
McBRIDE	MULERO M	D437	WED	15:00	2
SIMPSON	ANDREWS C	G123	WED	10:00	6
SIMPSON	GOODYEAR K	H321	WED	11:00	6
SIMPSON	STEWART J	L909	SAT	12:00	10
SIMPSON	GREGORY A	F549	THU	16:00	10

Module 5, Section 2, Practice 3, Step 9

Clients   29/03/00

SOLICITOR	REF NO	CLIENT NAME	DAY	TIME	PREVIOUS VISITS	TITLE
PATEL	J120	JONES L	WED	09:30	6	MISS
PATEL	J561	SMITH C	TUE	12:00	10	MRS
PATEL	M124	CLARKSON J	SAT	16:00	4	MS
PATEL	N6570	GRIGGS S	SAT	13:45	10	MISS
COLLINS	C780	DENT J	SAT	09:00	12	MR
COLLINS	E120	JENKINS Z	WED	10:30	0	MR
COLLINS	H777	MOWHILL S	FRI	17:45	12	DR
McBRIDE	G652	HARMAN D	THU	11:00	12	MISS
McBRIDE	Y444	PETERS H	FRI	18:30	6	MS
McBRIDE	R567	CLARKE F	SAT	09:30	0	MR
McBRIDE	H800	PAUL G	SAT	11:00	6	MR
McBRIDE	D437	MULERO M	WED	16:00	2	DR
SIMPSON	G123	ANDREWS C	WED	10:00	6	MR
SIMPSON	H321	GOODYEAR K	WED	11:00	6	MS
SIMPSON	L909	STEWART J	SAT	12:00	10	MR
SIMPSON	F549	GREGORY A	THU	16:00	10	MISS
PATEL	D321	SAMUEL S	SAT	10:00	0	MR

Stock   29/03/00

STORE	TYPE	MODEL	COLOUR	PRICE	NO IN STOCK
MILTON KEYNES	RACER	SPIRIT20	BLUE	359.99	10
MILTON KEYNES	RACER	SPEEDY18	GREEN	359.99	2
MILTON KEYNES	TRICYCLE	PIXIE5	YELLOW	60.50	6
MILTON KEYNES	RACER	SPIRIT18	RED	279.99	10
OLNEY	TANDEM	TWIN20	RED	399.00	1
OLNEY	MOUNTAIN	ROUGHTRACK1	BLUE	89.99	5
OLNEY	MOUNTAIN	ROUGHTRACK6	SILVER	129.99	6
OLNEY	TRICYCLE	PIXIE5	YELLOW	60.50	8
OLNEY	TRICYCLE	PIXIE10	RED	65.99	6
NEWPORT PAGNELL	RACER	SPEEDY18	SILVER	339.99	4
NEWPORT PAGNELL	TRICYCLE	PIXIE5	YELLOW	60.50	2
NEWPORT PAGNELL	MOUNTAIN	ROUGHTRACK1	BLUE	89.99	14
NEWPORT PAGNELL	RACER	SPIRIT18	BRONZE	279.99	2
CRANFIELD	RACER	SPIRIT20	BLACK	359.99	5
CRANFIELD	MOUNTAIN	ROUGHTRACK6	GREEN	129.99	6

29/03/00

Stock

STORE	COLOUR	TYPE	MODEL	PRICE	NO IN STOCK	SALE PRICE
MILTON KEYNES	BLUE	RACER	SPIRIT20	359.99	10	329.99
MILTON KEYNES	GREEN	RACER	SPEEDY18	359.99	2	329.99
MILTON KEYNES	YELLOW	TRICYCLE	PIXIE5	60.50	6	50.50
MILTON KEYNES	RED	RACER	SPIRIT18	279.99	10	259.99
OLNEY	BLUE	MOUNTAIN	ROUGHTRACK1	89.99	5	79.99
OLNEY	SILVER	MOUNTAIN	ROUGHTRACK6	129.99	6	119.99
OLNEY	YELLOW	TRICYCLE	PIXIE5	60.50	8	50.50
OLNEY	RED	TRICYCLE	PIXIE10	65.99	6	55.99
NEWPORT PAGNELL	BLUE	RACER	SPEEDY18	339.99	4	300.99
NEWPORT PAGNELL	YELLOW	TRICYCLE	PIXIE5	60.50	2	50.50
NEWPORT PAGNELL	BLUE	MOUNTAIN	ROUGHTRACK1	89.99	10	79.99
NEWPORT PAGNELL	BRONZE	RACER	SPIRIT18	279.99	2	259.99
CRANFIELD	BLACK	RACER	SPIRIT20	359.99	5	329.99
CRANFIELD	GREEN	MOUNTAIN	ROUGHTRACK6	129.99	6	119.99
CRANFIELD	BRONZE	MOUNTAIN	ROUGHTRACK3	99.99	2	89.99

Page 1

30/03/00

Weeks des and Instructor asc

CLASS	ROOM	DAY	MEMBER	INSTRUCTOR	NUMBER OF WEEKS
TONE AND TRIM	GYM	FRIDAY	☑	LYNNE	20
BODY BLITZ	DANCE STUDIO	TUESDAY	☐	LYNNE	20
FIT AND FUNKY	DANCE STUDIO	THURSDAY	☐	LYNNE	15
AEROBICS	GYM	MONDAY	☐	KENNY	10
AEROBIKING	GYM	WEDNESDAY	☑	SALLY	10
SYNC AND SWIM	POOL	WEDNESDAY	☐	DUNCAN	6

Page 1

24/02/00

Day ascending

CLASS	ROOM	DAY	MEMBER	INSTRUCTOR	NUMBER OF WEEKS
TONE AND TRIM	GYM	FRIDAY	☑	LYNNE	20
AEROBICS	GYM	MONDAY	☐	KENNY	10
FIT AND FUNKY	DANCE STUDIO	THURSDAY	☐	LYNNE	15
BODY BLITZ	DANCE STUDIO	TUESDAY	☐	LYNNE	20
SYNC AND SWIM	POOL	WEDNESDAY	☐	DUNCAN	6
AEROBIKING	GYM	WEDNESDAY	☑	SALLY	10

Page 1

24/02/00

Classes GYM

CLASS	ROOM	DAY	MEMBER	INSTRUCTOR	NUMBER OF WEEKS
AEROBICS	GYM	MONDAY	☐	KENNY	10
AEROBIKING	GYM	WEDNESDAY	☑	SALLY	10
TONE AND TRIM	GYM	FRIDAY	☑	LYNNE	20

Page 1

Module 5, Section 3.10, Exercise 6

24/02/00

Gym less than 15 weeks

CLASS	ROOM	DAY	MEMBER	INSTRUCTOR	NUMBER OF WEEKS
AEROBICS	GYM	MONDAY	☐	KENNY	10
AEROBIKING	GYM	WEDNESDAY	☑	SALLY	10

Page 1

Module 5, Section 3.11, Exercise 7

Lynne more than 15 weeks   24/02/00

CLASS	DAY	NUMBER OF WEEKS
BODY BLITZ	TUESDAY	20
TONE AND TRIM	FRIDAY	20

Module 5, Section 3, Practice 5, Step 2

Clients   30/03/00

SOLICITOR	REF NO	CLIENT NAME	DAY	TIME	PREVIOUS VISITS	TITLE
SIMPSON	G123	ANDREWS C	WED	10:00	6	MR
McBRIDE	R567	CLARKE F	SAT	09:30	0	MR
PATEL	M124	CLARKSON J	SAT	16:00	4	MS
COLLINS	C780	DENT J	SAT	09:00	12	MR
SIMPSON	H321	GOODYEAR K	WED	11:00	6	MS
SIMPSON	F549	GREGORY A	THU	16:00	10	MISS
PATEL	N6570	GRIGGS S	SAT	13:45	10	MISS
McBRIDE	G652	HARMAN D	THU	11:00	12	MISS
COLLINS	E120	JENKINS Z	WED	10:30	0	MR
PATEL	J120	JONES L	WED	09:30	6	MISS
COLLINS	H777	MOWHILL S	FRI	17:45	12	DR
McBRIDE	D437	MULERO M	WED	16:00	2	DR
McBRIDE	H800	PAUL G	SAT	11:00	6	MR
McBRIDE	Y444	PETERS H	FRI	18:30	6	MS
PATEL	D321	SAMUEL S	SAT	10:00	0	MR
PATEL	J561	SMITH C	TUE	12:00	10	MRS
SIMPSON	L909	STEWART J	SAT	12:00	10	MR

Module 5, Section 3, Practice 5, Step 3

Clients   30/03/00

SOLICITOR	REF NO	CLIENT NAME	DAY	TIME	PREVIOUS VISITS	TITLE
McBRIDE	R567	CLARKE F	SAT	09:30	0	MR
COLLINS	E120	JENKINS Z	WED	10:30	0	MR
PATEL	D321	SAMUEL S	SAT	10:00	0	MR
McBRIDE	D437	MULERO M	WED	16:00	2	DR
PATEL	M124	CLARKSON J	SAT	16:00	4	MS
PATEL	J120	JONES L	WED	09:30	6	MISS
McBRIDE	Y444	PETERS H	FRI	18:30	6	MS
McBRIDE	H800	PAUL G	SAT	11:00	6	MR
SIMPSON	G123	ANDREWS C	WED	10:00	6	MR
SIMPSON	H321	GOODYEAR K	WED	11:00	6	MS
SIMPSON	L909	STEWART J	SAT	12:00	10	MR
PATEL	N6570	GRIGGS S	SAT	13:45	10	MISS
SIMPSON	F549	GREGORY A	THU	16:00	10	MISS
PATEL	J561	SMITH C	TUE	12:00	10	MRS
COLLINS	H777	MOWHILL S	FRI	17:45	12	DR
COLLINS	C780	DENT J	SAT	09:00	12	MR
McBRIDE	G652	HARMAN D	THU	11:00	12	MISS

Module 5, Section 3, Practice 5, Step 4

SOLICITOR	REF NO	CLIENT NAME	DAY	TIME	PREVIOUS VISITS	TITLE
COLLINS	E120	JENKINS Z	WED	10:30	0	MR
McBRIDE	D437	MULERO M	WED	16:00	2	DR
SIMPSON	H321	GOODYEAR K	WED	11:00	6	MS
SIMPSON	G123	ANDREWS C	WED	10:00	6	MR
PATEL	J120	JONES L	WED	09:30	6	MISS

Module 5, Section 3, Practice 5, Step 5

CLIENT NAME	TIME
JONES L	09:30
JENKINS Z	10:30
CLARKE F	09:30
PAUL G	11:00
ANDREWS C	10:00
GOODYEAR K	11:00
SAMUEL S	10:00

Module 5, Section 3, Practice 6, Step 2

30/03/00

Stock

STORE	COLOUR	TYPE	MODEL	PRICE	NO IN STOCK	SALE PRICE
OLNEY	RED	TRICYCLE	PIXIE10	65.99	6	55.99
NEWPORT PAGNELL	YELLOW	TRICYCLE	PIXIE5	60.50	2	50.50
OLNEY	YELLOW	TRICYCLE	PIXIE5	60.50	8	50.50
MILTON KEYNES	YELLOW	TRICYCLE	PIXIE5	60.50	6	50.50
NEWPORT PAGNELL	BLUE	MOUNTAIN	ROUGHTRACK1	89.99	10	79.99
OLNEY	BLUE	MOUNTAIN	ROUGHTRACK1	89.99	5	79.99
CRANFIELD	BRONZE	MOUNTAIN	ROUGHTRACK3	99.99	2	89.99
CRANFIELD	GREEN	MOUNTAIN	ROUGHTRACK6	129.99	6	119.99
OLNEY	SILVER	MOUNTAIN	ROUGHTRACK6	129.99	6	119.99
NEWPORT PAGNELL	BLUE	RACER	SPEEDY18	339.99	4	300.99
MILTON KEYNES	GREEN	RACER	SPEEDY18	359.99	2	329.99
NEWPORT PAGNELL	BRONZE	RACER	SPIRIT18	279.99	2	259.99
MILTON KEYNES	RED	RACER	SPIRIT18	279.99	10	259.99
CRANFIELD	BLACK	RACER	SPIRIT20	359.99	5	329.99
MILTON KEYNES	BLUE	RACER	SPIRIT20	359.99	10	329.99

Page 1

Module 5, Section 3, Practice 6, Step 3

Stock

STORE	COLOUR	TYPE	MODEL	PRICE	NO IN STOCK	SALE PRICE
CRANFIELD	BLACK	RACER	SPIRIT20	359.99	5	329.99
MILTON KEYNES	GREEN	RACER	SPEEDY18	359.99	2	329.99
MILTON KEYNES	BLUE	RACER	SPIRIT20	359.99	10	329.99
NEWPORT PAGNELL	BLUE	RACER	SPEEDY18	339.99	4	300.99
NEWPORT PAGNELL	BRONZE	RACER	SPIRIT18	279.99	2	259.99
MILTON KEYNES	RED	RACER	SPIRIT18	279.99	10	259.99
CRANFIELD	GREEN	MOUNTAIN	ROUGHTRACK6	129.99	6	119.99
OLNEY	SILVER	MOUNTAIN	ROUGHTRACK6	129.99	6	119.99
CRANFIELD	BRONZE	MOUNTAIN	ROUGHTRACK3	99.99	2	89.99
NEWPORT PAGNELL	BLUE	MOUNTAIN	ROUGHTRACK1	89.99	10	79.99
OLNEY	BLUE	MOUNTAIN	ROUGHTRACK1	89.99	5	79.99
OLNEY	RED	TRICYCLE	PIXIE10	65.99	6	55.99
NEWPORT PAGNELL	YELLOW	TRICYCLE	PIXIE5	60.50	2	50.50
OLNEY	YELLOW	TRICYCLE	PIXIE5	60.50	8	50.50
MILTON KEYNES	YELLOW	TRICYCLE	PIXIE5	60.50	6	50.50

Page 1

30/03/00

Stock

STORE	COLOUR	TYPE	MODEL	PRICE	NO IN STOCK	SALE PRICE
NEWPORT PAGNELL	YELLOW	TRICYCLE	PIXIE5	60.50	2	50.50
OLNEY	YELLOW	TRICYCLE	PIXIE5	60.50	8	50.50
MILTON KEYNES	YELLOW	TRICYCLE	PIXIE5	60.50	6	50.50

Page 1

Module 5, Section 3, Practice 6, Step 5

STORE	COLOUR	TYPE	MODEL
OLNEY	SILVER	MOUNTAIN	ROUGHTRACK6
CRANFIELD	GREEN	MOUNTAIN	ROUGHTRACK6

Module 5, Section 4.1, Exercise 1

CLASSES

CLASS	ROOM	DAY	MEMBER	INSTRUCTOR	NUMBER OF WEEKS
AEROBICS	GYM	MONDAY	☐	KENNY	10
AEROBIKING	GYM	WEDNESDAY	☑	SALLY	10
BODY BLITZ	DANCE STUDIO	TUESDAY	☐	LYNNE	20
FIT AND FUNKY	DANCE STUDIO	THURSDAY	☐	LYNNE	15
SYNC AND SWIM	POOL	WEDNESDAY	☐	DUNCAN	6
TONE AND TRIM	GYM	FRIDAY	☑	LYNNE	20

24 February 2000

Module 5, Section 4.2, Exercise 2

Fitness Centre Events

INSTRUCTOR	CLASS	ROOM	DAY	MEMBER	NUMBER OF WEEKS
DUNCAN					
	SYNC AND SWIM	POOL	WEDNESDAY	☐	6
					6
KENNY					
	AEROBICS	GYM	MONDAY	☐	10
					10
LYNNE					
	BODY BLITZ	DANCE STUDIO	TUESDAY	☐	20
	FIT AND FUNKY	DANCE STUDIO	THURSDAY	☐	15
	TONE AND TRIM	GYM	FRIDAY	☑	20
					55
SALLY					
	AEROBIKING	GYM	WEDNESDAY	☑	10
					10
Grand Total					81

24 April 2001

Page 1 of 1

Module 5, Section 4.2, Exercise 2　373

Module 5, Section 4.3, Exercise 3

Fitness Centre Events

INSTRUCTOR	CLASS	ROOM	DAY	MEMBER	NUMBER OF WEEKS
DUNCAN					
	SYNCHRONISED SWIMMING (BEGINNERS)	POOL	WEDNESDAY	☐	6
					6
KENNY					
	AEROBICS	GYM	MONDAY	☐	10
					10
LYNNE					
	BODY BLITZ	DANCE STUDIO	TUESDAY	☐	20
	FIT AND FUNKY	DANCE STUDIO	THURSDAY	☐	15
	TONE AND TRIM	GYM	FRIDAY	☑	20
					55
SALLY					
	AEROBIKING	GYM	WEDNESDAY	☑	10
					10
Grand Total					81

24 April 2001

Fitness Centre Events — *Report produced by Angela Bessant*

INSTRUCTOR	CLASS	ROOM	DAY	MEMBER	NUMBER OF WEEKS
DUNCAN	SYNCHRONISED SWIMMING (BEGINNERS)	POOL	WEDNESDAY	☐	6
					6
KENNY	AEROBICS	GYM	MONDAY	☐	10
					10
LYNNE	BODY BLITZ	DANCE STUDIO	TUESDAY	☐	20
	FIT AND FUNKY	DANCE STUDIO	THURSDAY	☐	15
	TONE AND TRIM	GYM	FRIDAY	☑	20
					55
SALLY	AEROBIKING	GYM	WEDNESDAY	☑	10
					10
Grand Total					81

Report designed to show total hours for each instructor

24 April 2001

Clients grouped by solicitor   Angela Bessant 10.00 am

SOLICITOR	CLIENT NAME	REF NO	DAY	TIME	PREVIOUS VISITS	TITLE
COLLINS						
	MOWHILL S	H777	FRI	17:45	12	DR
	JENKINS Z	E120	WED	10:30	0	MR
	DENT J	C780	SAT	09:00	12	MR
McBRIDE						
	PETERS H	Y444	FRI	18:30	6	MS
	PAUL G	H800	SAT	11:00	6	MR
	MULERO M	D437	WED	16:00	2	DR
	HARMAN D	G652	THU	11:00	12	MISS
	CLARKE F	R567	SAT	09:30	0	MR
PATEL						
	SMITH C	J561	TUE	12:00	10	MRS
	SAMUEL S	D321	SAT	10:00	0	MR
	JONES L	J120	WED	09:30	6	MISS
	GRIGGS S	N6570	SAT	13:45	10	MISS
	CLARKSON J	M124	SAT	16:00	4	MS
SIMPSON						
	STEWART J	L909	SAT	12:00	10	MR
	GREGORY A	F549	THU	16:00	10	MISS
	GOODYEAR K	H321	WED	11:00	6	MS
	ANDREWS C	G123	WED	10:00	6	MR

31 March 2000

Client appointments this week, grouped by solicitor   Angela Bessant 10.00 am

SOLICITOR	CLIENT NAME	REF NO	DAY	TIME	PREVIOUS VISITS	TITLE
COLLINS						
	MOWHILL S	H777	FRI	17:45	12	DR
	JENKINS Z	E120	WED	10:30	0	MR
	DENT J	C780	SAT	09:00	12	MR
McBRIDE						
	PETERS H	Y444	FRI	18:30	6	MS
	PAUL G	H800	SAT	11:00	6	MR
	MULERO M	D437	WED	16:00	2	DR
	HARMAN D	G652	THU	11:00	12	MISS
	CLARKE F	R567	SAT	09:30	0	MR
PATEL						
	SMITH C	J561	TUE	12:00	10	MRS
	SAMUEL S	D321	SAT	10:00	0	MR
	JONES L	J120	WED	09:30	6	MISS
	GRIGGS S	N6570	SAT	13:45	10	MISS
	CLARKSON J	M124	SAT	16:00	4	MS
SIMPSON						
	STEWART J	L909	SAT	12:00	10	MR
	GREGORY A	F549	THU	16:00	10	MISS
	GOODYEAR K	H321	WED	11:00	6	MS
	ANDREWS C	G123	WED	10:00	6	MR

31 March 2000

Store Stock 31 March 2000

STORE	TYPE	MODEL	PRICE	NO IN STOCK	SALE PRICE
CRANFIELD					
	MOUNTAIN	ROUGHTRACK3	99.99	2	89.99
	MOUNTAIN	ROUGHTRACK6	129.99	6	119.99
	RACER	SPIRIT20	359.99	5	329.99
			589.97	13	539.97
MILTON KEYNES					
	TRICYCLE	PIXIE5	60.50	6	50.50
	RACER	SPIRIT18	279.99	10	259.99
	RACER	SPEEDY18	359.99	2	329.99
	RACER	SPIRIT20	359.99	10	329.99
			1060.47	28	970.47
NEWPORT PAGNELL					
	TRICYCLE	PIXIE5	60.50	2	50.50
	MOUNTAIN	ROUGHTRACK1	89.99	10	79.99
	RACER	SPIRIT18	279.99	2	259.99
	RACER	SPEEDY18	339.99	4	300.99
			770.47	18	691.47

31 March 2000

Report produced by Angela Bessant

Page 1 of 2

STORE	TYPE	MODEL	PRICE	NO IN STOCK	SALE PRICE
OLNEY					
	TRICYCLE	PIXIE5	60.50	8	50.50
	TRICYCLE	PIXIE10	65.99	6	55.99
	MOUNTAIN	ROUGHTRACK1	89.99	5	79.99
	MOUNTAIN	ROUGHTRACK6	129.99	6	119.99
			346.47	25	306.47
Grand Total			2767.38	84	2508.38

Report produced by Angela Bessant

31 March 2000

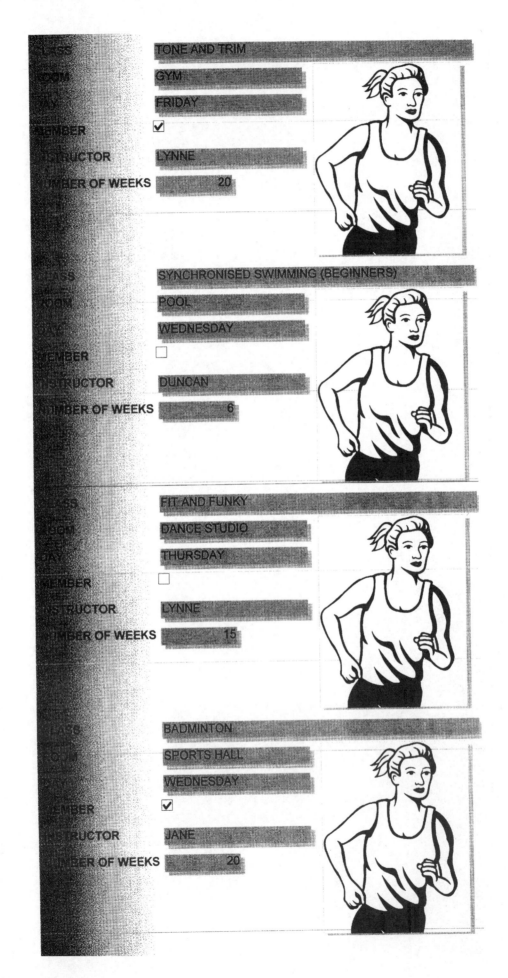

CLASS	TONE AND TRIM
ROOM	GYM
DAY	FRIDAY
MEMBER	✓
INSTRUCTOR	LYNNE
NUMBER OF WEEKS	20

CLASS	SYNCHRONISED SWIMMING (BEGINNERS)
ROOM	POOL
DAY	WEDNESDAY
MEMBER	☐
INSTRUCTOR	DUNCAN
NUMBER OF WEEKS	6

CLASS	FIT AND FUNKY
ROOM	DANCE STUDIO
DAY	THURSDAY
MEMBER	☐
INSTRUCTOR	LYNNE
NUMBER OF WEEKS	15

CLASS	BADMINTON
ROOM	SPORTS HALL
DAY	WEDNESDAY
MEMBER	✓
INSTRUCTOR	JANE
NUMBER OF WEEKS	20

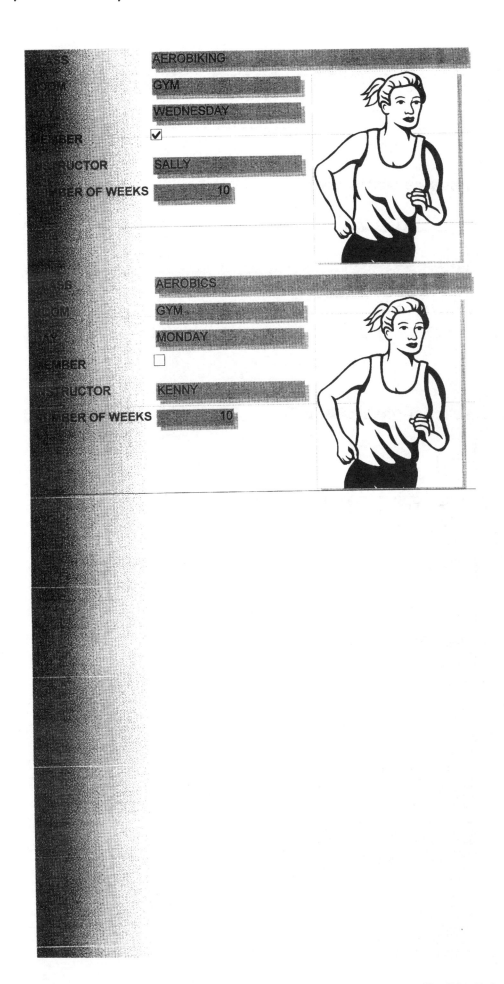

Module 5, Practice Task 1, Step 1

3 bedrooms

09/11/00

Location	Postcode	Type	Beds	Garage	Garden	Rent £	Available
Elstow	BD41 5RW	House	3	✔	☐	600	June
Carlton	MK44 9AS	House	3	✔	✔	1100	June

Module 5, Practice Task 1, Step 2

Location (B)

09/11/00

Location	Postcode	Type	Beds	Garage	Garden	Rent £	Available
Bedford	BD23 1AS	Flat	1	☐	☐	400	July
Brickhill	MK54 3LP	House	2	✔	✔	550	June
Bodington	NN12 5RP	Flat	1	☐	☐	300	May

Module 5, Practice Task 1, Step 3

No Garage

09/11/00

Location	Rent £	Available
Bedford	400	July
Devonlly	420	May
Bodington	300	May

Module 5, Practice Task 1, Step 9

Count

09/11/00

Location	Postcode	Type	Beds	Garage	Garden	Rent £	Available
Glasgow	GL4 6RP	Flat	1	☐	☐	400.00	June
Bodington	NN12 5RP	Flat	1	☐	☐	300.00	May
Bedford	BD23 1AS	Flat	1	☐	☐	400.00	July
Harrold	MK49 4HX	Flat	2	✔	☐	600.00	July
Devonlly	MK29 7TD	Flat	2	☐	✔	420.00	May
Rushden	NN14 8PT	House	2	✔	✔	500.00	June
Brickhill	MK54 3LP	House	2	✔	✔	550.00	June
Carlton	MK44 9AS	House	3	✔	✔	1100.00	June
Elstow	BD41 5RW	House	3	✔	☐	600.00	June
Oakley	OS2 6RW	House	4	✔	✔	850.00	May
Goldington	BG31 8QT	House	5	✔	✔	875.00	August

Types of Rental Property   *Angela Bessant*

Type	Location	Rent £	Available
Flat			
	Glasgow	400.00	June
	Harrold	600.00	July
	Bodington	300.00	May
	Devonlly	420.00	May
	Bedford	400.00	July
House			
	Carlton	1100.00	June
	Rushden	500.00	June
	Oakley	850.00	May
	Goldington	875.00	August
	Brickhill	550.00	June
	Elstow	600.00	June

Multimedia on the web

Multimedia Workshop 2000

The Grand Hotel Conference Centre

Bristol BS8 2TS

Tel 0117 21021102

E-mail: mow@multicon.ac.uk

The following topics will form the basis of the multimedia workshop:

☐ Text
☐ Graphics
☐ Video
☐ Sound

Video and Sound Workshops

Video

This will concentrate on accessing two websites with video content. The content will be compared and contrasted with a view to finding out what works and what falls flat. Website addresses will be specifically selected for this workshop.

Sound

For this workshop there will be four websites to focus on. Some have streaming audio. The quality and accessibility of the sound will be judged and rated out of ten for each of the two categories.

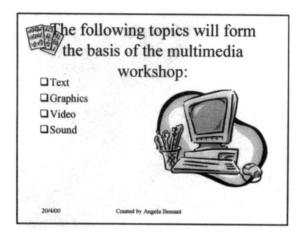

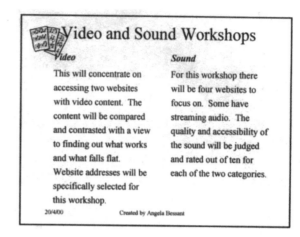

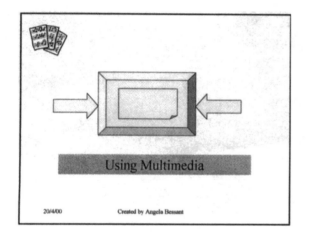

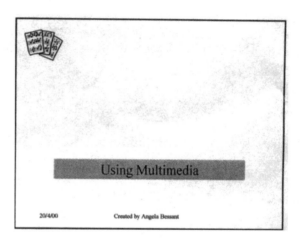

Multimedia is fun!

Using Multimedia

Opening slide for uses of multimedia in web designs.

1

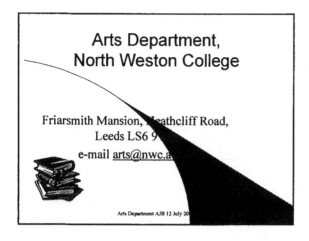

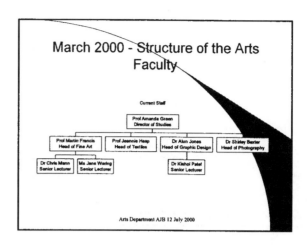

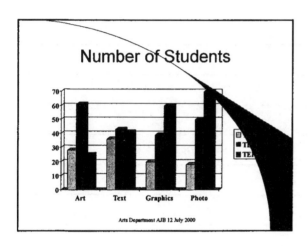

Summer Madness 2000

Angela Bessant 20/4/00

Many models on offer

✓ Vauxhalls
✓ Fords
✓ Toyotas
✓ Volkswagens

Angela Bessant 20/4/00

Meet the Team

Jean Moneypenny
Managing Director

Jack Quincy
Sales Manager

Jill Bailey
Sales Manager

Paul Jones

Kiki Young

Angela Bessant 20/4/00

1

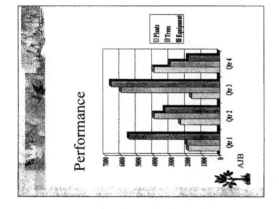

Figures do not include bedding plant sales.

3

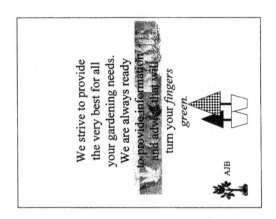

We strive to provide the very best for all your gardening needs. We are always ready to provide information and advice that will turn your *fingers green.*

AJB

Glossary

This glossary gives a short description of commonly used computing terms used throughout the book.

Alignment	Positioning of text or graphics on a page in relation to other elements.
Application	Another word for 'program' or 'application program'. An application enables you to do something specific (eg word processing, payroll).
Aspect ratio	The ratio of width to height of an object. Maintaining the aspect ration means not making the object taller or wider.
Backup	A second, safe copy of data on a different storage media made for security reasons.
Browser	A program that enables you to view web pages on the Internet.
Bullets	A small graphic eg ● or ■ used to emphasise and separate items in a list.
Buttons	Using the mouse, you click on buttons to select actions. There are toolbar buttons, dialogue box buttons and so on.
Character formatting	Changing a character's look by altering font, size, style and so on.
Chart	Graphical display of information (eg bar chart, organisational chart).
Clicking	Pressing and releasing the left mouse button
Clip Art	Artwork available for you to insert into documents.
Clipboard	The Clipboard is where the computer stores items you have copied or cut, ready to paste somewhere else.
Cursor	A symbol (which changes shape depending on what you are doing) displayed on the screen showing where the next character will be displayed.
Dialogue box	A window that is displayed asking you for information.
Document	A file containing text or pictures.
Double-clicking	Quickly pressing and releasing the left mouse button twice.
Dragging	Moving things around using the mouse.
Drive	The device that reads and writes on to disks.
E-mail	Short for 'electronic mail'. Mail sent via a network or the Internet.
File	A unit of information stored on the computer (eg a Word file, an Excel file).
File name + extensions	The name given to a file. The extension is the letters after the filename that allow the computer to identify its type.
Floppy disk	A portable storage medium that is floppy but protected by having a plastic case.
Folder	A storage location to keep related files together. Sometimes known as a 'directory'.
Font	A character set with predefined styles and sizes (eg Times New Roman, Courier).
Form letter	The main document used in a mail merge.
Header and footer	Special areas at the top and bottom of pages for information that can appear on all pages of a document.
Help	Press **F1** to access information on topics you are unsure of.
Hover	Place the mouse pointer over an object for a few seconds.
Icon	Small pictures that represent objects in a graphical user interface (GUI).

Margin	The distance of text and graphics from the edges of printed pages.
Menu (*drop-down and pop-up*)	A *menu* is a list of commands grouped into related tasks from which you can choose. A *drop-down* (or pull-down) menu is displayed from the top of the screen downward when it is selected. A *pop-up* menu (usually activated using the right mouse button) pops up on screen.
Menu bar	A row of menu options.
Multitasking	The ability of a computer to run two or more programs at the same time.
Non-printing characters	Symbols that can be displayed on screen using the Show/Hide facility but which are not printed out.
Panes	When a window is split into several parts, each part is called a pane.
Pointer	The symbol on the screen that moves when you move the mouse or another pointing device.
Print queue	When more than one document has been sent to the printer, a print queue forms so documents are stored and printed in turn. Print queues are common on networks.
Recycle Bin	Deleted files are sent to the Recycle Bin. They can be recovered from here if necessary depending on the setup. Files deleted from floppy disks are not sent to the **Recycle Bin**.
Right-click	Click the right mouse button. Usually this reveals a context-sensitive menu.
Scroll bar	A horizontal or vertical strip that appears on the right or bottom of the window and lets you move through a document using the mouse to reveal previously hidden parts that couldn't fit in the window.
Select	To highlight a portion of text or an object on the screen so you can manipulate it.
Spellcheck	A command that compares the spelling in a document with that in the program's dictionary.
Style	A collection of formatting choices applied to text that can be saved and used again.
Subfolder	A folder within a folder.
Tab (in text)	A preset position for aligning text.
Taskbar	A strip (usually) along the bottom of the Windows desktop containing the Start button, icons for all active tasks, quick launch icons and the system tray.
Template	Templates have styles and page layout settings preset you can use to create a document.
Text editor	A very basic word processing program for editing plain text.
Toolbar	A line of buttons containing clickable short-cut icons.
Undo	A command that reverses your most recent action(s).
Wildcard	A character (eg *, ?), used to represent unknown characters when searching for information/files.
Window	A rectangular screen area in which applications and documents are displayed.
Word wrap	A word processing feature that automatically starts a new line when the text reaches the end of the current line.
World Wide Web	The visible part of the Internet containing linked HTML documents accessed through browsers. Often abbreviated to 'the web'.

Appendix

Changing defaults in Word

Office Assistant

To hide the Office Assistant
Right-click: over the Office assistant, select: **Options** and set them to your preferences. Click on **OK**.

To turn the Office Assistant on
Click on the ❓ **Office Assistant** toolbar button. Click on **Options** and set preferences. Click on **OK**.

Checking spelling and grammar

There are many options available. Throughout the book, I have chosen not to check on an ongoing basis but after keying in entire documents. Should you wish to choose other options:

From the **Tools** menu, select: **Options**. Click on the **Spelling & Grammar** tab. Select your preferences and click on: **OK**.

Changing the unit of measure

To change the unit of measure from inches to cms or vice versa:
1   From the **Tools** menu, select: **Options**, and then click on the **General** tab.
2   In the **Measurement units** box, click on the down arrow and then on the option you want.
3   Click on: **OK**.

File maintenance within programs

In addition to using Windows Explorer and My Computer, you can carry out file maintenance within programs. When opening or saving a file, you are able to gain access to your files within the window (shown below). This is common to most Office programs. This window was opened in Word and displays Word documents only (by default). If you want to see other documents, click on: the down arrow next to **Files of Type** and make your selection.

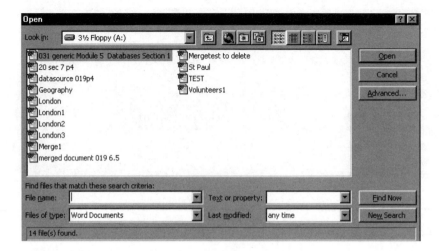

The main shortcut buttons you will find useful are shown below. Using these will enable you to create folders and to find out details of your files. In **Save As** dialogue boxes the ⌐ **Create New Folder** button is useful.

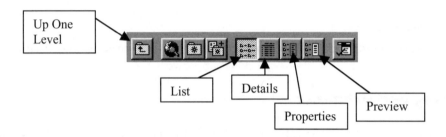

Right-clicking on a file/folder will bring up the pop-up menu shown. This allows you to carry out any of the tasks on the menu.

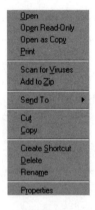

A quicker way to delete a file or folder is by selecting it and pressing: **Delete**.

Note: You cannot carry out file maintenance when a file is open.

A guide to document layout

When you have edited text or moved text within an exercise, remember that adjustment of line spacing is often necessary. When proofreading, pay particular attention to line spacing between paragraphs.

When inserting a sentence within a paragraph, make sure the spacing after any punctuation marks remains consistent. Make the necessary adjustments if required.

Use the Spellchecker but do realise its limitations.

Line spacing between paragraphs

Press: the return key twice to leave one clear line space between paragraphs.

Underlining/underscoring

Underlining should not extend beyond the word. For example:
<u>word</u> is correct   <u>word </u>is incorrect

Punctuation

Be consistent with your spacing after punctuation marks. Use the following as a guide:

Punctuation	Mark	Number of spaces before/after
Comma	,	No space before – 1 space after
Semicolon	;	No space before – 1 space after
Colon	:	No space before – 1 or 2 spaces after
Full stop	.	No space before – 1 or 2 spaces after
Exclamation mark	!	No space before – 1 or 2 spaces after
Question mark	?	No space before – 1 or 2 spaces after

Hyphen

No space is left before or after a hyphen (eg dry-clean).

Dash

One space precedes and follows a dash – never place a dash at the left-hand margin when it is in the middle of a word or a sentence, always place it at the end of the previous line.

Brackets

No spaces are left between brackets and the word enclosed within them For example (solely for the purposes of assignments).

Keyboard shortcuts that work (almost) everywhere

Keyboard	Menu
F1	Help
F7	Tools, Spelling and Grammar
Ctrl + N	File, New
Ctrl + O	File, Open
Ctrl + S	File, Save
F12	File, Save As
Ctrl + W	File, Close
Ctrl + P	File, Print
Alt + F4	File, Exit
Ctrl + X	Edit, Cut
Ctrl + C	Edit, Copy
Ctrl + V	Edit, Paste
Ctrl + Z	Edit, Undo
Ctrl + A	Edit, Select All
Esc	Cancels items

Don't forget

Right-clicking over objects displays pop-up menus in Office 97.